DISCARD

W9-CAE-212

The Women's
Passover
Companion

The Women's Passover Companion

Women's Reflections
on the Festival of Freedom

Edited by Sharon Cohen Anisfeld,
Tara Mohr & Catherine Spector

Foreword by Paula E. Hyman

JEWISH LIGHTS Publishing
Woodstock, Vermont

The Women's Passover Companion:
Women's Reflections on the Festival of Freedom

Grateful acknowledgment is given for permission to use material from the following sources:

"Their Lives a Page Plucked from a Holy Book," by Margaret Moers Wenig, © Margaret Moers Wenig, is adapted from *Birthing the Sermon: Women Preachers on the Creative Process,* edited by Jana Childers. Copyright © 2001 Chalice Press. Reprinted by permission of Chalice Press. All rights reserved.

"The Secret of Redemption: A Tale of Mirrors," by Avivah Gottlieb Zornberg, was previously published in *The Particulars of Rapture: Reflections on Exodus* (New York: Doubleday, 2001). It appears by permission of the publisher.

"To be of use," by Marge Piercy, previously appeared in *Circles on the Water,* by Marge Piercy (New York: Random House, 1982). Used here with permission.

Library of Congress Cataloging-in-Publication Data
The women's Passover companion : women's reflections on the festival of freedom / edited by Sharon Cohen Anisfeld, Tara Mohr, and Catherine Spector.
    p.   cm.
Includes bibliographical references and index.
ISBN 1-58023-128-4 (HC)
1. Passover. 2. Jewish women—Religious life. 3. Seder. 4. Haggadah—Adaptations. 5. Feminism—Religious aspects—Judaism. 6. Women in Judaism. I. Anisfeld, Sharon Cohen, 1960– II. Mohr, Tara, 1978– III. Spector, Catherine, 1978–
BM675.P3 Z85 2003
296.4'5371'082—dc21

2002151098

10 9 8 7 6 5 4 3 2 1

Manufactured in the United States of America

Published by Jewish Lights Publishing
A Division of LongHill Partners, Inc.
Sunset Farm Offices, Route 4, P.O. Box 237
Woodstock, VT 05091
Tel: (802) 457-4000   Fax: (802) 457-4004
www.jewishlights.com

Thanks to Miriam the rock gave water.*

In honor of Miriam Botwinik Horowitz
(APRIL 7, 1912–APRIL 7, 1999)

who continues to be a source of sustenance in the wilderness

** Carved in Jerusalem stone
inside Joseph Slifka Center for Jewish Life at Yale.*

Contents

≋ **Part 2: Reclaiming and Re-creating Passover Rituals for Women**

≋ **Part 3: Women of Exodus**

Foreword

When a Jewish women's movement emerged in America some thirty years ago, its primary goal was to alert the Jewish community to the discrimination suffered by women as Jews. Issues ranging from the disabilities imposed on women by Jewish law to our relative invisibility in Jewish culture to our absence from positions of spiritual and communal leadership were highlighted in public statements. Jewish feminists were preoccupied above all with issues of equal access. Women should be counted in the *minyan* (the quorum necessary for public prayer), taught all types of Jewish learning, and accepted as rabbis, cantors, and communal professionals. Women's experiences should be recovered and rescued from the ignorance and lack of interest of male scholars who defined history as what men did. When women looked into the mirror of Judaism, we wanted to see our own faces.

These issues of equal access were not too difficult to resolve in the institutions of non-Orthodox Judaism, although positions of power in communal organizations remain largely in the hands of men, even today. The language of equality resonates strongly with American Jews, and non-Orthodox synagogues were already used to accommodating both tradition and change. But "equal access" did not satisfy the desire of Jewish women to wrestle with Jewish texts and to contribute our own understanding of Judaism to a culture that was constantly in the process of becoming. Jewish women came together to create rituals that reflected our own experience as female Jews and that incorporated women's traditions as well. The first feminist ritual was for us, as young women, an obvious necessity: a baby-naming ceremony for newborn girls. It would compensate for the lack of attention paid to females in the community, literally from their birth. By 1973, Ezrat Nashim, one of the first American Jewish feminist groups, had privately published and disseminated a collection of baby-naming ceremonies that feminist parents had developed. Some women also embraced Rosh Chodesh, the New Month, traditionally a mini-holiday for women, as a time to celebrate and learn together. As Esther Broner notes in her reflection, the first feminist seder was held as early as 1976. With the baby-naming ceremonies for daughters leading the way, some feminist rituals became so widely accepted within the Jewish community that it was hard to remember that they had not always existed.

Most importantly, women asserted our right and ability to learn as well as our authority to interpret Jewish texts and experience. By the early 1980s, feminists were calling for a "women's midrash," a commitment of women to read themselves into Jewish texts from which they had been absent. Dazzled by the wealth of Jewish sources and experience, women eagerly inserted themselves into the process of creating Jewish culture, following traditional patterns of interpretation but also, as newcomers less constrained by traditional modes, creating novel approaches. Recognizing that women were full partners in the task of finding meaning in Jewish symbols and language, feminists challenged the limitations of a God language created only by men and dominated by masculine metaphors. And feminist historians assiduously set about discovering "lost" Jewish women and exploring both the attitudes toward women in Jewish tradition and the roles of Jewish women in various Jewish societies.

In response to the feminist challenge, Jewish institutions expanded the educational resources available to girls and women and muted the gender distinctions that had characterized traditional Jewish learning. While denying that feminism had anything to do with it, modern Orthodox schools and synagogues, too, encouraged women to learn texts that had once been denied them. By the 1990s, a powerful international feminist movement had emerged in the modern Orthodox world. Enhanced educational opportunities and the feminist affirmation of women's abilities within the Reform, Reconstructionist, and Conservative movements stimulated a younger generation of women to confidently approach the challenge of finding meaning in Judaism. And, as this collection demonstrates, the wisdom of the first generation of women rabbis is the most powerful affirmation of the truth of feminist assertions about the importance of listening to women's voices.

The Women's Passover Companion is a splendid fulfillment of the vision of the Jewish women's movement. Like the traditional haggadah itself, this book is an anthology of questions and insights, a tapestry of reflections on the meanings of liberation as well as on the text of the haggadah. It also demonstrates the breadth and depth of the women's midrash that has come into being in the past several decades. It is a resource not only for those seeking to organize a women's seder but also for all Jews who wish to incorporate new reflections into a family or communal seder and to engage others, both living and dead, in a discussion of the meaning of the Exodus from Egypt.

The participants in this endeavor represent the spectrum of diversity of Jewish life. Most of the contributors are North American, but Israeli feminists such as Leah Shakdiel and Avivah Zornberg share their midrashic talents in this volume.

In the contemporary Jewish community in America, diversity is often subsumed in the terms "Conservative," "Orthodox," "Reconstructionist," "Reform," and occasionally "unaffiliated." As this collection demonstrates, however, such a definition of American Jewry limits us and omits large numbers of American Jews. The women speaking in *The Women's Passover Companion* do, of course, derive from various denominations of Judaism, but their denominational affiliations do not account for their differences or necessarily predict their attitudes. Their rationales for taking part in women's seders differ, as do their definitions of feminism. Yet, whatever their self-definitions, they are all participants in a vibrant Jewish women's movement. Reading

their contributions, we enter into conversation with women unlike ourselves, women who may challenge our view of the Pesach seder and of
the place of women's experience in it.

More important than the denominational representation, however,
is the inclusion of women of different generations, all of whom are
deemed authentic voices and interpreters of women's experience.
Reflections by veteran Jewish feminist leaders like Letty Cottin Pogrebin and Martha Ackelsberg, by feminist theologians such as Judith
Plaskow, by women rabbis like Sandy Eisenberg Sasso and Sharon
Cohen Anisfeld, and by scholars of women and Judaism like Judith
Baskin and Norma Joseph stand side by side with the articulate assertions of a younger generation of Jewish women. Jewish feminists of this
second generation are shaping, and questioning, their place in the contemporary American Jewish community. Leora Eisenstadt, for example,
provides a feminist reading of the Four Sons of the traditional haggadah, while Ophira Edut questions the relevance of traditional texts to
her sense of Jewishness, opting to find a place for rebellious Jewish
women such as Bette Midler and Emma Goldman at women's seder
tables.

The hegemony of heterosexuality is challenged by the forceful writing of Tamara Cohen and Sharon Kleinbaum. They give voice to the
specific alienation of lesbians both within Jewish tradition and in the
contemporary Jewish community, and they bring to our reading of
the Exodus story yet another dimension of liberation.

The variety of the contributors to this volume is matched by the
diversity of subjects they address and the genres they have chosen for
their reflections. Some analyze the traditional themes and characters
of the Pesach story but with a new twist; others draw directly on their
personal experience. Some assume the formerly male mantle of Torah
interpretation; others reflect on women's traditional work during the
Passover season, such as housecleaning and food preparation.

In *The Women's Seder Sourcebook,* the companion volume to this
anthology, the editors have given us a collection of women's writings
that can be incorporated into the Pesach seder. The *Sourcebook* offers

a stunning assortment of poetry and liturgical readings, as well as personal reflections and creative midrash. Its open-ended structure gives us the opportunity to shape our own conversations within and around the structure of the Pesach seder, and to determine our own seder (literally "order" in Hebrew), much as the rabbis did when they compiled the original haggadah.

Together, these two books teach us that we must take responsibility for creating our own Judaism, in conversation with the generations of Jews who have preceded us, so that we may transmit the legacies of the past and of the present to the next generation, who will continue the process of living, and renewing, Judaism.

Paula E. Hyman,
Lucy G. Moses Professor
of Modern Jewish History,
Yale University

Preface

Playwright Lillian Hellman once wrote, "Nothing, of course, begins at the time you think it did."[1] Reflecting on the origins and development of *The Women's Passover Companion* and *The Women's Seder Sourcebook*, we appreciate the wisdom of her words. For while we began formal work on the then-titled *Yale Women's Haggadah Project* in the spring of 2000, our efforts stood upon a foundation laid by many other women throughout the 1990s.

The seeds of this project lie in Jewish Women at Yale, a student group whose members have been creating superior women's programming on the Yale University campus for many years. With the leadership of Rabbi Sharon Cohen Anisfeld, then associate rabbi of Joseph Slifka Center for Jewish Life at Yale, the group held the first Yale Women's Seder in 1993. This event quickly became a beloved annual tradition that provided a unique forum for students, professors, and community members to come together. For the first seder, students wrote the *Yale Women's Haggadah,* which included commentaries, alternative texts, and creative writing on the traditional haggadah and themes of the holiday. Over the course of eight years, undergraduates revised and enhanced this unique piece of liturgy.

The *Yale Women's Haggadah* was but one manifestation of what became a vibrant Jewish feminist community at the university. In 1996, a student proposed hosting the first national Jewish women's conference for young women. During the next several months, a diverse group of students and faculty shaped what evolved into a groundbreaking, three-day event that attracted hundreds of college students from around the country. Inspired by its success, a new group of students began work two years later on a second conference, this time centered on the theme of Jewish women and freedom.

A provocative and powerful conversation—across religious denominations, generations, and national boundaries—emerged among presenters and participants. Jewish Women at Yale wanted, and indeed felt they had an obligation, to capture this dialogue and share it with a wider audience. At the same time, some students began talking about the possibility of expanding and potentially publishing the *Yale Women's Haggadah*.

In the fall of 1999, these two projects converged. A group of undergraduate women led by Rabbi Cohen Anisfeld began work on a feminist haggadah that would include student writings as well as commentaries from the authors, activists, artists, and scholars who had been part of the conferences. The small committee soon realized, however, that creating this haggadah would be more than a part-time, extracurricular activity. In order to complete the project, Tara Mohr and Catherine Spector decided to spend a postgraduate year in New Haven working on the haggadah with Sharon Cohen Anisfeld. The three of us began serious work on the project together in the fall of 2000. With the help of many supporting individuals and institutions, Tara and Catherine were able to work full-time on what became a two-year endeavor.

From its earliest stages, the project aimed to use the framework of the haggadah to create a comprehensive, pluralistic resource that would further Jewish women's explorations of significant questions about freedom, oppression, spirituality, feminism, and tradition and change. As time went on, however, we confronted the challenges of creating pluralistic liturgy. In addition, we struggled with how to achieve our goal of creating a feminist haggadah that could easily be used at family seders. As we spoke with dozens of women's seder organizers around the country, we learned that many communities had chosen to create their own women's haggadahs not simply because of the dearth of available resources but also because they felt that the process of putting together the haggadahs had great inherent value. As seder organizers who had experienced the impact of this process ourselves, we shared this feeling. Furthermore, as the project developed, we decided that our circle of contributing authors should extend beyond those who had been part of the conferences, the Yale Women's Seder, or Jewish Women at Yale. These concerns gradually led us to conceive a new vision for the book that would better meet our goals: Rather than producing another women's haggadah, we would create a women's sourcebook for Passover.

As we further refined this vision, we considered what kind of materials we ourselves desired, both as seder organizers and as individuals celebrating the holiday. We felt it was important that the anthology address all aspects of women's relationships to the Passover holiday, from cleaning for the holiday to sitting at the family seder table to organizing a women's seder. Thus, we decided to feature readings and rituals to be included in the seder as well as reflections to be read in advance or during the week of Passover. It soon became clear that there was enough important material to merit expanding the book into two volumes. One volume would include longer writings, and the other would consist of material for the actual seder; the two could be used separately or in conjunction with each other. In this way, we would be able to fulfill the many needs of the different women and men who we hoped would find these anthologies meaningful.

These are some of the central considerations and influences that have guided the development of *The Women's Passover Companion* and *The Women's Seder Sourcebook*. The result is a collection featuring diverse voices writing in a myriad of forms: poetry, prose, memoirs, commentaries, and creative and traditional exegesis. These writings discuss biblical texts, seder rituals, and passages from the haggadah, as well as Jewish women's history, personal experiences, and relevant political issues. The writers are scholars, activists, rabbis, authors, artists, political leaders, and students.

Over the past two years, we have had the extraordinary privilege of working inside a fascinating dialogue currently occurring among these Jewish women. And we have had the extraordinary blessing of sharing an intensely collaborative process and a true labor of love. Our hope is that these volumes will help the Jewish community hear, respect, and include women's voices. And we hope that they inspire you for many Passovers to come.

Acknowledgments

We are deeply grateful to the many supporters who have made it possible for us to see this project through to completion. We wish to thank the women whose advice steered us in the right direction at so many crucial points in the project: Paula Hyman, Claire Sufrin, Hilary Kaplan, Laura Wexler, Sydney Perry, Carol Diament, Karyn Kedar, Linda Altshuler, Peri Smilow, Merle Feld, Shulamit Reinharz, Naomi Danis, and the staff of the Jewish Women's Resource Center. Your counsel and encouragement were invaluable to us.

Those who took the time to read our manuscript offered insightful and important feedback: Judith Plaskow, Eve Landau, Rachel Cymrot, Sarah Anne Minkin, and, in particular, Ruth Kaplan. Your questions, concerns, and editorial suggestions improved the manuscript and helped us to include the full breadth of voices represented in the anthology.

The Joseph Slifka Center for Jewish Life at Yale was instrumental in both the genesis and the development of this project. Slifka Center's support of student-initiated women's programming at Yale and its continued involvement with these books over the past two years have been remarkable. It was a great blessing to work at the Slifka Center during the initial year of the project, and we wish to thank the staff who enriched our year through conversation and friendship: Amy Aaland, David Cavill, Leah and Ilan Haber, Robbie Hobson, Susan Jeanette,

Karen Medin, Dennis Panasci, James and Elana Ponet, Catherine Sat-
ula, Jordana Schuster, and Jeanette Vega.

In addition to those with whom we worked directly at the Slifka
Center, we thank each of the women who wrote the *Yale Women's
Haggadah*, as well as the women who created Yale's two conferences
on Jewish women in 1997 and 1999. Your work—courageous, innovative, and inspiring—is the foundation of this project. We owe a particular debt of gratitude to Sara Meirowitz, whose vision was the
inspiration for the first conference and whose guidance and support
have been vital to us during the project.

We were overwhelmed and heartened by the thorough, impassioned responses we received to our survey of women's seder organizers. The ideas, advice, and memories, as well as the original women's
haggadahs that these women shared with us, shaped our research
throughout this project. We are especially appreciative of Hadassah and
the National Council for Jewish Women, which helped the surveys
reach seder organizers.

In an independent project such as this one, specific needs for help
and resources often arise. Ilana Kurshan, Doreen Semel, and Yossi
Abromowitz and Susan Berrin at Jewish Family and Life! each gave
generously to this project, offering help with kindness and enthusiasm.

The staff at Jewish Lights has been attentive, considerate, and
thoughtful throughout this project. We are grateful for the experience
of a richly collaborative and enjoyable editorial process. Thank you to
Emily Wichland, managing editor at Jewish Lights, for her guidance,
and to Alys Yablon, for her perceptive and helpful editing, which greatly improved these volumes. Our thanks also to Stuart M. Matlins, publisher of Jewish Lights, for understanding the need for this anthology
and valuing the material enough to feel it merited two volumes.

We want to express our deepest gratitude to those individuals and
foundations whose support made this project possible; without it, a
book of this scope and size could never have been created. Even more
significantly, their support demonstrated a faith in this project that has
sustained and inspired us in our work. We wish to thank The Dobkin

Family Foundation, Judy Katz and the Miriam Horowitz Fund, Diane Troderman and the Harold Grinspoon Charitable Trust, Brenda and Al Curtis, Sarah and Will Richmond, The Eugene Lang Foundation, The Hadassah Foundation, The Shefa Fund, and The Bronfman Youth Fellowships in Israel. We want to express a particular thank-you to the Charles and Lynn Schusterman Family Foundation, which offered funding to the project in its earliest stages. To David and Goldie Blanksteen: We have been moved by your ongoing involvement in this project, and we are enormously thankful for your interest in its subject and in each of us. It has been a joy to share this work with you. Finally, we extend a profound personal thank-you to Barbara Dobkin, who not only made these books possible but, through her faith, guidance, and generosity, also made the experience all the more meaningful for us.

And to our friends and family: Your encouragement, support, and optimism were there when we most needed them. At times, you provided more than counsel, and we were touched by your offers to contribute so much of your time and talent to this endeavor. Thanks to Laura Crescimano for her extensive help with graphic and web design and to Andrew Krause for his wise editorial advice.

In addition, we would each like to offer some personal words of gratitude. From Tara: Thank you to Eric Ries for the hundreds of ways you have supported the project and enriched my life as I have been working on these books; William and Harriet Mohr for your help and encouragement over the past two—and indeed twenty-four—years; and my teachers Judith Komoroske, Melissa Wilson, and Katherine Rowe, to whom more than a small share of this accomplishment is due.

From Catherine: Thank you to Nancy, Ken, David, and Rebecca Spector, my family, for their unwavering support and advice through the many struggles and successes of this project; and the friends who have played the roles of cheerleader, commiserator, and counselor, Laura Chen, Caitrin Moran, Liz Schroeder, and Rasika Jayasekera.

From Sharon: Thank you to my first and most important teachers, my parents, Jules and Doris Cohen, who have always encouraged me to search for the right questions; to my husband, Shimon Anisfeld, whose companionship, wisdom, and sense of humor have sustained me throughout this project; to my children, Daniel and Tali Anisfeld, whose sweet exuberance and love inspire me every day; to my friends, Susan Fendrick, Sharon Kleinbaum, and Dianne Cohler-Esses, who have deeply influenced my understanding of Torah and who have given generously of themselves to make these volumes a reality.

We would also like to thank one another. Two years ago, we encountered one another's very different ways of thinking, reading, and writing. Over the course of working together, we have not only developed the deepest appreciation for one another but also learned from one another in countless ways.

And the deep collaboration of this project extends far beyond the three of us, to the more than one hundred and fifty generous, enthusiastic, and talented women who have given the entire Jewish community words that will inspire and teach for years to come. We are in awe of your accomplishment, and we give you our deepest thanks.

Introduction

Passover is likely the most widely celebrated of all Jewish holidays, and the Passover seder has become one of the most significant rituals of the Jewish year. The seder ritual requires not only that we learn about our Jewish history but also that we bring our own experiences, perspectives, and questions to the table. We are each encouraged and even instructed to take an active role in this holiday celebration. The commemoration of our Exodus from Egypt has a special resonance for contemporary Jewish women. Through this holiday, women forge a powerful connection to the Jewish people, including biblical foremothers as well as female ancestors, and to their own oppression, liberation, and journeys to the Promised Land.

Just as importantly, women's celebrations of Passover are linked to their families. Many women have learned how to make the seder through sharing the task with their mothers, grandmothers, and other female relatives since they were children. For hundreds of years, Jewish women have undertaken the extensive work of preparing for Passover, spending days or even weeks attending to the exhaustive cooking, cleaning, organizing, and shopping that precede the holiday. Indeed, for many women, readying the home for the holiday has been one of the most important—and difficult—obligations of the Jewish year.

Yet, despite women's central role in the domestic holiday preparations, we have often played a marginal role in the seder itself, unable to lead—or even participate fully in—telling the Exodus story. The Jewish feminist movement has reclaimed women's place at the seder table, in large part through the creation of a new ritual: the women's seder. At women's seders, women shape and lead the celebration, performing the rituals and contributing to the discussion. The introduction to one women's haggadah captures the power of this new Passover seder:

> Always, in times past, it was men who told the story: men who passed it down from father to son. And for centuries women did the actual physical work of the seder—the cleaning, the cooking, the washing up—while the men reclined and told the story. Tonight, as free Jews, women and men, we tell the story from father to daughter and son, from mother to son and daughter, and from friend to friend. Tonight we affirm that just as we are all here together now, so we were all together in *Mitzrayim,* and together we will journey forth from the narrow places.[1]

Women's seders are an extraordinary phenomenon in contemporary Jewish life. Thousands of women take part in women's seders each year, and the experience often draws them into a deeper relationship with Jewish tradition as well as with one another. At these seders, we dedicate one night of the year to celebrating together as women, enjoying the rituals and stories of the Passover seder without being exhausted from the preparations or distracted by the need to serve the meal. Notably, in recent decades these seders have begun to attract an increasingly diverse group of women: observant and secular, young and old, liberal and conservative. As Maida E. Solomon points out: "What began as a movement for change by those on the margins is now becoming the practice of those much closer to the mainstream of Judaism."[2]

Significantly, many women also incorporate the readings and rituals from these seders into their family and community seders. Indeed, it was not long after the first women's haggadahs were written in the 1970s that "women's haggadot moved out of women's centers and into women's homes."[3] The ritual innovations popularized by women's seders, particularly that of Miriam's Cup and the inclusion of an orange on the seder plate, are now accepted customs at many family and community seders.

Women's seders have not only popularized new Passover rituals but also generated important alternative interpretations of the traditional seder rituals and liturgy. These innovations have grown from the hundreds of local seders occurring in communities around the United States—and, increasingly, around the world—as well as from the Jewish feminist scholarship produced in recent decades.

With *The Women's Passover Companion* and *The Women's Seder Sourcebook*, we hope not only to document this exciting and vibrant tradition but also to enhance it. *The Women's Seder Sourcebook* provides the tools to bring women's voices to the Passover seder, offering hundreds of readings and rituals that can be incorporated into a women's or a family seder. These sources offer women and men the opportunity to enrich their Passover celebration with the fresh perspectives that have risen out of women's traditional Passover experiences as well as the more recent creation of the women's seder.

The Women's Passover Companion offers an in-depth examination of women's relationships to Passover. The reflections in this volume address three principal subjects: the Passover holiday, the Book of Exodus, and women's Passover seders. Yet, because of the nature of their topics and the scope of their insights, they also shed light on the wider subjects of contemporary Jewish feminist thought and practice. In the five parts of *The Women's Passover Companion,* the authors use the lessons and stories of the Passover holiday as an important starting point for contemplating key questions and issues central to Jewish feminism and to Judaism itself.

Part 1, "Why Women's Seders?," explores the goals and history of the women's seder, a ritual initiated less than thirty years ago. Recounting the earliest women's seder as well as the evolution of women's seders in recent decades, these chapters offer a collection of impassioned voices discussing—in diverse ways—the ritual's value, uniqueness, and important function in contemporary Jewish communities.

Part 2, "Reclaiming and Re-creating Passover Rituals for Women," illustrates how women are transforming the Passover ritual not only at women's seders but also in their own homes. These reflections, which focus on several specific aspects of the Passover seder and holiday, capture some of the most fascinating and important feminist ritual and liturgical innovations being created by contemporary Jewish women.

Moving from the seder ritual to the biblical narrative of the Exodus, part 3, "Women of Exodus," examines the remarkable group of women in this text, investigating their stories and the legacy they have passed on to us. In addition to shedding new light on our biblical foremothers, the diverse modes of textual interpretation in these chapters provide models of contemporary feminist approaches to biblical exegesis.

Uncovering and reinterpreting the stories of our foremothers has been one of the most powerful achievements of the Jewish feminist movement. It has allowed contemporary women to see their own stories as linked to a rich history of women's strength and courage. Sharing personal stories has also been central to feminist spirituality and to women's seders.

Part 4, "Telling Our Stories," collects a variety of personal reflections focusing on the holiday's themes of the Exodus and exile, oppression and liberation, history and memory, as they relate to contemporary women's lives.

To conclude the book, part 5, "Visions and Challenges for the Future," articulates key issues facing women's seders, Jewish feminism, and the Jewish community as a whole. These provocative reflections and calls to action speak with foresight and courage about urgent matters we are all obligated to confront.

The reflections in *The Women's Passover Companion* offer compelling and unique perspectives, and are most illuminating when read as voices in the midst of a dialogue. These reflections are here to place our questions in a larger context, to challenge and uplift us as we go through the process of planning a women's seder or preparing for Passover.

The individual reader will find material to savor while preparing for the Passover holiday as well as resources to enrich the seder itself. For those learning about the seder for the first time, this collection offers a vibrant and welcoming introduction to the holiday and to a community of female Jewish leaders.

This anthology will also be extremely useful for those individuals and groups creating women's seders in their communities. The writings in this book, whether focused specifically on women's seders or more broadly on Passover and Jewish feminist issues, provide a variety of materials that can enrich and inform the seder planning process.

As women bring their questions and insights to the texts, rituals, and ideas of this foundational part of Jewish life, they bring us to new understandings of our history and our future, as Jews and as women. In their voices we hear the solemn echo of centuries of oppression—suffered by Jews, by slaves, by women, by "the stranger." And we hear the fierce compassion and righteousness that was in Egypt, and is today, the heart of redemption. May their words sustain you on your journey.

1

Why Women's Seders?

The model of the feminist seder has provided women both with a window into the tradition through their experience as women and with a window into themselves through an encounter with the tradition. It is a communal ritual model that draws its strength from the coming together of people with a shared history and destiny.

—RABBI JOY D. LEVITT, *VOICES FOR CHANGE*

E ach year, thousands of Jewish women come together in celebration at women's seders, which have become one of the most vibrant and popular communal gatherings in contemporary Jewish life. In communities around the world—from Kansas City to Manhattan, New Orleans to Berlin—women create haggadahs and plan seders with creativity, energy, and dedication. The largest of these gatherings attracts more than two thousand participants, and hundreds of smaller seders are held in living rooms, synagogues, and campus Hillels around the world.

As Karen Smith of Knoxville, Tennessee, notes, these seders are of deep personal and religious significance for participants: "The women's seder has become for me and for other women a very spiritual event. We pause in our busy lives for an evening of thought and reflection, sharing a common tradition.... We are given a further sense of identification with our people, with our Jewishness, and with our God." Many participants agree that a women's seder is a unique opportunity to create a women's community, deepen the spirituality of their Passover celebration, and explore their Jewish identity in a new context.

The writings in part 1 explore this extraordinary phenomenon and ask some fundamental questions about the origin, meaning, and purpose of women's seders. Why were the earliest women's seders created? How have women's seders evolved over the past thirty years? What exactly *is* a women's seder? Is it an event for women only or about women only? Is it an inherently feminist ritual, and should it be? What does a women's seder mean to the different women who participate in it? And how should a women's seder approach traditional Passover liturgy, texts, and rituals?

In part 1, the authors address these questions from a wide range of experiences and perspectives. Some have been seder organizers for years—writing haggadahs, creating rituals, and shaping the event for hundreds, even thousands of other women around the world. Other contributors bring their academic and activist perspectives to the discussion, exploring women's seders from a more theoretical perspective. Each author links her discussion of women's seders with an examination of broader feminist concerns or larger questions about the history and meaning of the Passover holiday.

In "For Women Only," Esther Broner, creator of the first women's seder, reflects on the origins and goals of the women's seder she has organized each Passover for nearly thirty years. Describing the exceptional intimacy, honesty, and trust among attendants, Broner contends that this atmosphere would not have been possible in a group including men.

Broner's personal account of the need for these seders in her own life and in the lives of the women who attend them is complemented by "The Continuing Value of Separatism." In this reflection, scholar and activist Judith Plaskow argues that all-women's gatherings are significant because they provide not simply a women's space but a feminist space in which women have the opportunity to "critique normative texts and to create alternative rituals and liturgies that place women at the center."

"Creating the Ma'yan Women's Seder: Balancing Comfort, Challenge, and Community" further explores the ways in which women's seders enable women to challenge traditional texts and experiment with new rituals and liturgy. It features companion pieces by Tamara Cohen and Erika Katske, former staff members at Ma'yan: The Jewish Women's Project of the Jewish Community Center of the Upper West Side. Ma'yan organizes the largest women's seder in the world, and its published haggadah is used in dozens of smaller seders each year. Cohen, the primary author of the Ma'yan haggadah, focuses her attention on the process of writing liturgy for a women's seder, while Katske, a veteran seder organizer and former program coordinator at Ma'yan, analyzes the meaning and implications of the decision to include—or exclude—men at feminist seders.

The next piece follows the Ma'yan haggadah to a remarkable women's seder where it is used. In "Miriam and Our Dance of Freedom: Seder in Prison," Bedford Hills inmate Judith Clark reflects on the significance of celebrating freedom at the Passover seder while serving a life sentence in prison. Clark describes how participating in a women's seder allowed her to find a "new way into the meaning of Passover," rekindling her "quest for holiness, freedom, and community."

The range of women's seders described in the opening pieces reveals the stunning diversity of individuals and communities celebrating this ritual. Catherine Spector's "Every Voice Matters: Community and Dialogue at a Women's Seder" contends that we must highlight, explore, and celebrate this diversity. Discussing numerous strategies for doing so, Spector suggests that pluralism requires us to do more than simply invite all women to join us at the table; it demands that we find ways to make every woman feel that her voice and contributions are a central, treasured part of the event.

In "God's Redemption: Memory and Gender on Passover," Norma Baumel Joseph focuses not only on women's seders but on Passover, more broadly, as a holiday that engages women in meaningful religious celebration. Looking at Passover as a holiday of redemption, Joseph discusses the divine model presented in the Book of Exodus. Joseph invites us to reflect on the ways that Jewish women can—and must—act in the image of the redeeming God of the Exodus narrative.

Tara Mohr's "An Embrace of Tradition" examines the factors contributing to the popularity and appeal of women's seders. In this reflection, Mohr explores the ways in which women's seders create a unique space for Jewish women, asking us to understand women's seders as a space for authentic engagement with Jewish ritual and tradition.

Together, these voices explore the myriad ways in which women's seders encourage such engagement, connecting Jewish women to their tradition, and bringing forth contributions that will enrich, renew, and transform Jewish life for generations to come.

For Women Only

ESTHER BRONER

In the beginning—and we were the beginning, this curious group of New Yorkers who gathered for the first women's seder in 1976—we did not know that the seder would become part of our lexicon of holidays and that it would continue to be a women's ritual and religious event.

The original company included Gloria Steinem, Letty Cottin Pogrebin, myself, and others, summoned to the West End Avenue apartment of Phyllis Chesler. The following year, Bea Kreloff and Lilly Rivlin were added, and, as we went along, Bella Abzug, Michele Landsberg, and Edith Isaac-Rose. These were the matriarchs.

Dr. Esther Broner is the author of ten books, including *A Weave of Women* and *The Telling,* and coauthor of the original *The Women's Haggadah.* She is a scholar, playwright, fiction writer, and professor emerita.

That first night was prophetic of what was to come. The small group present introduced ourselves by our maternal lineage, which would never have occurred to us before this time. When I asked, "Who are your mothers?" some knew, but others hesitated. "Martha Graham," said one dancer, whose own mother had been at best disinterested in her daughter's daily trip to the city for dance lessons, and, at worst, abusive to her for her ambitions. Some thoughtfully talked about being mothers to themselves.

So there we were, daughters, with the shadows of our mothers, learning a new way. Some of what we heard was new to us then, like a lesbian couple speaking in both pain and love about being lesbians at that early time, not yet recognized by the women's movement. A Miss USA, passing by, and never part of the group again, spoke of the humiliation—not of the contest, but of being ignorant of the economics involved and being cheated out of the award money.

The women spoke of suddenly feeling the need for ritual. Letty was beside herself. She had abandoned Jewish ritual, enraged at being excluded from her mother's kaddish (mourners' prayer). She thought she would never forgive, and now she did not need to. She would remember and honor her mother, and continue to be a Jew, but in her own way.

None of this would have been possible if men had been present. The men might have commented, contradicted, corrected. We never found out. We were not about to take a chance on sharing our sacred time and space, when so much of this sacred space had already been taken over in our lives.

At our seders, we spoke so intimately, intensely; why would we have wanted a judgmental voyeur sitting in our circle? The women's movement and the consciousness-raising groups taught us, and still teach us, that our words are documents, our memories historical. We honored ourselves and one another with our dress, our lovingly prepared food, and the honesty of our tales.

Going down the elevator of our apartment building, my sons have met seder sisters coming up. My husband calls his brother and says,

"It's that time of year again. What are you doing tonight?" Should I feel guilty? Never. I make the family seder and celebrate with them the march of holidays throughout the year.

Recently, at a television interview, the distinguished provost of a graduate school asked, "But isn't it natural for men and women to be together? Isn't that the ideal, the longed for?" Only if the man respects the words of the women, does not display revulsion or morbid curiosity, speaks to the remarks at hand, is not competitive, never interrupts. It's hard to think of such a man sitting alongside us and not getting up, bored, pouring himself a glass of water, wending his way through the women seated on the floor to find something in the kitchen to munch on during the long hours of our holiday.

At our twenty-fifth seder, overlooking the sparkling lights and reservoir of Central Park West, our host spoke of her cancer and what it felt like to have a mastectomy. She had read this memoir of illness and healing to a group of friends, and the men objected to its being made public. But for us, sharing our experiences at the seder was not merely making them public. It was part of becoming speakers, full participants in the seder telling, commentators on our own Torah. Another young woman wept as she remembered being raped when she was a child in the neighborhood where we were gathered. This confession could only have been made within the arms and on the laps of the motherly women present.

Others have told of being hidden or of being brought up in labor camps in Siberia. Where was safety? They still needed to be reminded that they had, if not family, the family in this circle. One woman grieved at the loss of a son from AIDS. This mother, reading the words she had written so she could have the courage to get through them, knew that her love for her son was instructive to us, as were her grief and her work with other families who had experienced the loss of a child.

We have a chance to be noble on this night. The young may sing; a child asks the four questions and then discourses on what she wants to have happen in *Ha'olam Ha Ba,* the world to come. "No war," she always says.

We proclaimed and heeded our prophets. Bella Abzug spoke to us of her vision of the future and her fear of what was happening in the present. She had spoken to many, many crowds, but, she once told me, "It is in the women's seder that I feel my soul."

"Soul," "sole": both separated from our usual context and inclusive in a new one, we find our way in the sand. No one else cared about Miriam—the rabbinic literature slights and blames her, depriving her of her place on the prophet's throne, punishing her simply for wanting to be near God on the Mount. We cared. She was our prophet, our mystery. We have given new voice to many of the figures in the haggadah and the Exodus story. We have discussed with thoughtfulness all the aspects of the four daughters. We discovered just last year that the simple child was simple only when not treated respectfully, when not heeded. When the simple child was listened to, the simplicity dissolved, and we could hear the wisdom in her words.

At the silver anniversary, the twenty-fifth women's seder, we had silver plastic dishes on our floor/table, a Bella cup alongside a Miriam Cup in memory of our prophet Bella who had recently passed away. We had potted plants strewn so that we were in the Garden of Eden. We often feel that way.

I consult with the seder-goers each year about a relevant theme. As a supplement to the Broner/Nimrod *The Women's Haggadah*, we read words written about the theme of the year, discussing it in relation to political issues, biblical texts, and personal experiences. The topic for the twenty-sixth women's seder was "Living Under Pharaoh." A psychoanalyst wrote of "The Pharaoh of the Unconscious"; a historian wrote of the Pharaoh in the "Golden Land" (the United States); an activist read her words about the Pharaoh in the "Promised Land" of Israel today; a political prisoner read "The Pharaoh of the Slave System of Prisons"; and a health care expert discussed "The Pharaoh of Breast Cancer." A human rights activist and the executive director of the United Nations spoke on "World Wide Pharaohs." Each year we make a wall poster, "Women's Plagues," and a scribe writes down the plagues we call out—plagues that have beset us.

When I arrange for a topic and give out assignments, women sometimes call back for clarification or to talk about their wish to take another assignment. I'm not sure men would say, "Oh, yes, that is our topic for this year. How can I fit in and enrich it?" Would they be the rebellious sons, the ones who say "you" and not "we"?

In the early years, when the seder began to receive some coverage, mothers and daughters thought of it as a way of coming together at holiday time. Why was it that Passover seemed like such an ideal time for us to come together as women? There are Rosh Chodesh groups that usually meet in the early morning, and the women speak, sing, and meditate on the meaning of the particular Hebrew month. Except for the Women of the Wall in Israel, whose Rosh Chodesh celebration is a moving political statement of women's right to participate in religion, women's Rosh Chodesh gatherings consist largely of study groups.

As for Purim, another natural candidate for women's religious celebrations, it has only recently become enlarged from the coarse beauty parade of yore. In New York, in 2001, there was an "After the Beauty Parade" program, with women rabbis deconstructing the Book of Esther and comedians making Esther into a kind of *Clueless* innocent who gradually learns. But Purim has a past of such rowdiness and masquerade that we can hardly shake off its unruliness—all we can do is applaud Vashti and try to re-create Esther.

Pesach, however, is the heart of the Jewish people, and our Exodus speaks loudly, especially to women who have been impeded in crossing the Reed Sea or surviving on land.[1] As for the rituals of Pesach, women have traditionally been the preparers and not the performers. Perhaps because Passover is such a domestic holiday, and because we women talk and plan around the table, it has become our war room, so to speak—our declaration of rights for women, and now a universal feminist holiday. Miriam is now invited to drink from her cup at tables everywhere.

It was a family holiday I rewrote, with my coauthor Nomi Nimrod. We showed the way, but, since then, women have created roomfuls of women's haggadahs. One sees them, published or laptop printed, illustrated with beautiful artwork or simple cartoons. One can imagine hundreds of women taking these pamphlets or booklets in hand and singing their history.

What happens when there is a chorus of women's voices that climbs from alto to soprano? In such a chorus, we are not drowned out by deeper voices; we are not intimidated by the basso profundo. There is a purity to our song, our range, and our words are heard, not blurred in a general choir.

So, we must continue these songs of celebration and lamentation, mothers and daughters and granddaughters, together in a holy lineage. And then God will say, "Come to the top of the mountain," and we will not be left behind.

≋

The Continuing Value of Separatism
JUDITH PLASKOW

For the increasing number of American Jewish women who live and/or grew up in egalitarian Jewish communities, the need for separate women's spaces is less self-evident than it was in the early days of Jewish feminism. Thirty years ago, when even liberal synagogues offered few opportunities for women to take leadership roles or participate as equals in public worship, women-only groups provided rare opportunities for women to begin to examine barriers to equality, articulate critiques of Jewish ritual and God language, ask daring new questions about women's history, and acquire skills long denied them. At the beginning of the twenty-first century, as women's full access to public roles is the norm in more and more congregations, separatism often feels like reneging on a bargain that, while rarely made explicit, is still morally and psychologically compelling. If the synagogue, and particularly

---

Dr. Judith Plaskow is professor of religious studies at Manhattan College and author of *Standing Again at Sinai: Judaism from a Feminist Perspective*.

the *bimah,* are no longer clubs marked "for men only," then why should women create women-only spaces that seem as exclusive as the men's spaces of previous generations? Doesn't a commitment to egalitarianism involve a commitment on the part of both women and men to make integrated spaces work for everyone?

This general skepticism about the continuing value of separatism might apply with special force to women's seders, currently proliferating in communities and on college campuses around the country. Because the Passover seder celebrates a founding moment in the history of the Jewish people, it is a ritual that seems to cry for inclusive community. As part of the throng brought forth from Egypt "with a mighty hand and an outstretched arm"—and, indeed, as crucial actors in the events leading up to and surrounding the Exodus—women have a rightful and important place at the communal Passover table. The fact that most seders are celebrated in the home, moreover, rather than in public institutions, means that any particular seder is likely to include a substantial proportion of women. Some of these women may find that small communities of families and friends provide more comfortable contexts for experimenting with leadership, participation, and the content of the seder than do synagogue-based rituals.

Yet, at the same time that Passover seems like an especially inopportune moment for separatism, the Festival of Freedom also crystallizes the contradictions surrounding women's inclusion and exclusion that continue to characterize even liberal Judaism, and that point to the great unfinished agenda of Jewish feminism. I leave aside the massive preparation that the holiday requires and that continues to fall in women's domain, so that all too many women are unable to join fully either in the seder itself or in the leisurely enjoyment of the festive meal that they have prepared. Beyond the important point that Jewish feminists need to challenge the gendered division of labor and not simply women's exclusion from public religious roles, there is another dimension of women's marginalization at the Passover table that women's seders address. Just as women's often invisible work and energy are the essential "background" of the seder celebration, so women's work and contributions are relegated to the background of the haggadah. Although the biblical account of the Exodus makes clear that women participated in the liberation of the Jewish people as midwives, rescuers, and cultic leaders, not a single woman is mentioned by name in the haggadah itself. And while, to be sure, the haggadah focuses on *God's* role in the Exodus, so that even Moses is referred to only briefly, a parade of rabbis and patriarchs flows in and out of the text—a text that repeatedly adjures *men* to teach their *sons* the story of the going out from Egypt. Inclusive translations that change "son" to "child" do not thereby make women visible or give substance to the shadowy forms of Mrs. Rabbi Eliezer, Joshua, and Akiba. These women hover outside the boundaries of the text, just as they obviously were excluded from their husbands' paradigmatic seder.

It is this crucial contradiction between the increased participation of women in all aspects of Jewish life and the *content* of the tradition that, in my view, provides the warrant and necessity for women-only spaces, including women's seders. Such seders function on several levels. First, they furnish occasions for women to *sit* and/or to serve themselves, rather than always caring for others. Second, they are contexts in which women have special opportunities to teach and preside—a dimension of women's seders that may be especially important to those from traditional backgrounds. Third, in a knowledge-based tradition in which those without extensive Jewish educations—educations traditionally unavailable to women—often feel inadequate and silenced, women's seders allow those present to claim ownership of their Judaism and begin to take power to shape and transmit it. Fourth, and most important, women's seders allow participants to redefine their relationship to tradition by raising questions and exploring perspectives that would most likely be regarded as distractions in the framework of an ordinary seder. Whether a particular women's seder uses the haggadah as a starting point for talking about the incomplete liberation of women or attempts to highlight women's roles in the story of Jewish liberation from Egypt, it is still almost entirely in separate spaces that women have the opportunity to critique normative texts and to create alternative rituals and liturgies that place women at the center.

Women's space is important, as I see it, precisely insofar as it becomes feminist space: space for questioning the received tradition and for pioneering new forms of Jewish expression that have the potential to transform the self-understanding of the whole Jewish community. Not all women's spaces are feminist spaces in this sense. Feminism entails a personal and political commitment to religious and social change, a commitment that is neither a natural outgrowth of being a woman nor necessarily limited to women alone. Feminism involves adopting a set of critical lenses for viewing Judaism and the world—lenses that must be turned on women's seders themselves whenever they fall into speaking about "the feminine" instead of women, or whenever they define women or feminism in monolithic terms. Separatism is important not because women as women have some unique and shared vision that the Jewish community needs, but because women have been excluded from the formulation of Jewish texts and traditions, and because men's comments, questions, and agendas tend to be taken more seriously in integrated contexts, while feminist questions and perspectives are often trivialized and treated with impatience.

If it is the critical and transformative perspective of women's seders that constitutes their rationale and main contribution, then the presence of men at such seders is by no means an oxymoron. I have learned over many years of teaching Jewish feminism and participating in feminist liturgies in a variety of contexts that men who are willing to take part in such events on women's terms can enter fully into their spirit and make powerful and important contributions to the proceedings. On the other hand, given the ways in which gender role socialization can lead even assertive and feisty women to defer or fall silent in the face of certain kinds of male posturing, given the many forces still aligned against women claiming the right to shape and transform Jewish tradition, and given the ways in which women's leadership continues to be feared and undermined, it must be up to the women planning any particular seder to decide whether it makes sense to invite men to the event.

Whether women's seders will be a temporary means to a more inclusive tradition or a permanent feature of Jewish life, it is much too soon to judge. For now, there is no conflict between the continuation of women-only spaces and their contribution to a richer Judaism for all. The wonderful new ritual innovations, poems, songs, and pieces of liturgy that have been created for women's seders provide invaluable resources for incorporation into family and community seders. At our family seder, we always put the cup of Miriam next to the cup of Elijah, read some poems about the importance of women's history, and celebrate the midwives' civil disobedience. There is no reason why, as families mention the Holocaust, contemporary poverty and homelessness, or peace in the Middle East at their seder tables, they should not also make the role of women in the Exodus and in Judaism a theme for the seder. But the experimentation that is generating this new material and making it available for wider use takes place at women's seders, where the restoration of women's rightful place in the reenactment of the central event of Jewish history is not *a* theme but *the* theme.

It may be that some day, all haggadahs and all seders will reflect the idea that the whole Jewish people went forth from Egypt. Until that day arrives, women's seders remain necessary—both for individuals trying to claim a history from which they and their foremothers have been erased, and for the future of a Jewish community that has yet to fully realize the liberating vision of Passover.

≋

Creating the Ma'yan Women's Seder: Balancing Comfort, Challenge, and Community

TAMARA COHEN AND ERIKA KATSKE

Writing Towards Liberation: Thoughts on Composing a Feminist Haggadah

Tamara Cohen

I still feel a sense of awe when I think about the day I wrote my first piece of liturgy for the Ma'yan haggadah. A recent college graduate, I had, through good fortune, ended up in the tiny office of a new organization with a big vision about changing the Jewish community for women. One of the ways we were going to make change was by bringing hundreds of women together for a different kind of Passover seder, and I was to share the sacred responsibility of shaping that seder. I had no idea at the time that the document we would ultimately create would make its way to thousands of seder tables at synagogues, Rosh Chodesh groups, and family gatherings across North America and Israel.

Like every committee that creates a feminist or women's haggadah, the staff and volunteers who worked on the Ma'yan haggadah faced many questions about our audience, our liturgy, and the broader goals of the seder itself. Sometimes we were able to answer these questions

---

Tamara Cohen was the program director at Ma'yan: The Jewish Women's Project of the Jewish Community Center of the Upper West Side in Manhattan for seven years. She edited *The Journey Continues: The Ma'yan Passover Haggadah* and led numerous Ma'yan seders in New York and around the country. She is currently living in Gainesville, Florida, with her partner. She continues to consult with Ma'yan, write poetry, and serve as the spiritual leader of the Greater Washington Coalition for Jewish Life.

Erika Katske works with Citizen Action of New York, a coalition of labor, senior citizen, women's, student, tenant, and community organizations working toward social and economic change. After graduating from Smith College, she worked as the program coordinator at Ma'yan: The Jewish Women's Project.

through conversations and negotiations. At other times, we were unable to fully resolve our differences. Yet, our disagreements—even when they were difficult—were instructive. They illuminated the challenges involved in creating community ritual and provided a creative tension that ultimately enriched our final product.

Early in our planning process, we decided that the haggadah would be written primarily for use at feminist and women's seders. However, we strove to write it in such a way that it could also be used, as a whole or in parts, at family seders. Although we reached a consensus on this principle, translating it into actual text was never simple.

One of the most important questions we faced was how to handle God language. Ma'yan opted to include each blessing in the haggadah three times: twice in Hebrew (and transliteration) and once in English:[1]

בְּרוּכָה אַתְּ יָהּ
אֱלֹהֵינוּ רוּחַ הָעוֹלָם
אֲשֶׁר קִדְּשַׁתְנוּ בְּמִצְוֹתֶיהָ וְצִוַּתְנוּ
לְהַדְלִיק נֵר שֶׁל (שַׁבָּת וְשֶׁל) יוֹם טוֹב.

בָּרוּךְ אַתָּה יְיָ
אֱלֹהֵינוּ מֶלֶךְ הָעוֹלָם
אֲשֶׁר קִדְּשָׁנוּ בְּמִצְוֹתָיו וְצִוָּנוּ
לְהַדְלִיק נֵר שֶׁל (שַׁבָּת וְשֶׁל) יוֹם טוֹב.

You are Blessed, Our God, Spirit of the World,
who makes us holy with *mitzvot* and
commands us to kindle the light of
(Shabbat and of) the festival day.

The first Hebrew version is a grammatically feminine rendering of the *bracha,* which uses alternative, nonhierarchical God language. The second is the traditional blessing. The English translation avoids gendered language altogether and unites the two Hebrew versions by recognizing that both choices can be understood to express the same sentiment.

We chose to include all the *brachot* because we wanted to offer a choice, to make both options as accessible as possible. We believed in the simple power of having these alternatives together on a single page. Whichever *bracha* people would choose to read aloud, they would have to consider the other version as a possibility, reflecting on their relationship to both versions. The planning committee agreed that one of the most important functions of the haggadah was exposing women's seder participants throughout the country to the full range of feminist thinking and creativity—including new approaches to God language. In this way, the haggadah would gently challenge seder participants to deepen and expand their own thinking about the range of approaches to Jewish feminism.

Although we reached a consensus on the issue of God language, when it came to other editorial decisions, we found ourselves enmeshed in conflicting opinions on our most fundamental political and religious beliefs about what Jewish feminism is and should be. For some, a feminist or women's seder is primarily an opportunity to explore their spirituality and to cultivate a sense of personal empowerment. For others, the seder is a time to reaffirm and strengthen their commitment to a set of political goals and to speak out against oppression in contemporary society. As a result, our haggadah includes readings that reflect both these approaches. It also invokes Jewish women's history and attempts to honor the experiences of both religious and secular Jewish women. These are delicate balancing acts. What one woman finds deeply relevant, another finds limited in scope and dispensable.

The decision to add "Do Something" sidebars to the 2000 edition grew out of discussions about the goals of the Ma'yan seders, one of which was creating change for women in the Jewish community. It was important to us that the seders not merely discuss redemption in the abstract but also offer readers ways to get involved with organizations doing the daily work of *tikkun olam*. For example, alongside the reading for *maror*, the bitter herb, we included the following sidebar:

Do Something! Help end the bitterness of domestic violence in Jewish women's lives by supporting the Association of Rape Crisis Centers in Israel and the Center for the Prevention of Sexual and Domestic Violence in Seattle. Call the Jewish Orthodox Feminist Alliance to find out how you can support *agunot*, Jewish women whose husbands have refused to give them a *get*, a Jewish bill of divorce.

At the end of the haggadah, we listed contact information for these organizations. In this way, we balanced the elevated language of our liturgy with simple, achievable ideas.

In addition, by including these "Do Something" boxes, we aimed to link our commitment to Jewish women with a larger commitment to social justice. Although members of the Ma'yan staff often debated the definition of feminism, we chose to embrace a broad understanding of the term, discussing issues such as gay and lesbian rights, Arab-Israeli girls, and environmental activism in the haggadah.

One of my pieces in the haggadah links the Israelites' slavery in Egypt to the conflict between Sarah and Hagar through the use of a classical midrashic technique.[2] Sometimes, when I am leading a Ma'yan seder and I get to this page, I pause for a moment before going forward. I do not assume that every woman who feels comfortable at a women's seder agrees that the Israeli-Palestinian conflict is a feminist issue. I take a breath and begin the responsive reading:

Go forth and learn. All who have been oppressed can also oppress. Sarah our Mother oppressed her Egyptian maidservant Hagar....

Have I lost anyone? Do they understand that I am not just talking about the past when I say that even our foremother Sarah had some Pharaoh in her? I like the fear that I feel when I lead this reading because it reminds me that a feminist seder is not just about celebration; it is also about taking risks. I want everyone to be comfortable at the seder most of the time, but a good seder also pushes everyone to feel a little uncomfortable some of the time and to learn from that discomfort. I want us to use the opportunity of women's seders to confront our differences as Jewish women as well as to celebrate our bonds.

Sarah and Hagar were never able to reconcile their differences or find a way to live together. Their conflict birthed a cycle of hatred and oppression that still haunts our people and our world today. Even if we understand their story as myth, we can recognize in it a truth about the great difficulty of forming alliances between women. That truth needs to be spoken of at women's seders, because it is as real as the sisterhood we feel when we dance hand in hand. The women's movement was greatly weakened and limited in its impact on American society by its refusal to acknowledge and honor the differences among women. Women's and feminist seders can be part of a new women's movement built on the strength of celebrating our differences rather than ignoring them.

An hour into a seder, I always start to relax. The music is good; the wine and matzah provide the comfort of the familiar; the women are enjoying the company of other women. But what about the liturgy? *Karpas* and the blossoming of our bodies go well; *Ha lachma anya* and the statistics about the feminization of poverty quiet everyone for a few moments; the *mi shebeirach* (prayer for an individual's health and well-being) elicits tears. Still, a part of me is apprehensive, waiting for Miriam's song and, after it, *Dayeinu*—because at that moment something remarkable happens. A room full of Jewish women—grandmothers, single women, twelve-year-old girls and their mothers, executives in suits and full makeup—will sit back down after dancing hand in hand and join together to recite, among other more poetic verses, a line particularly close to my heart: "If we fight economic injustice, racism, sexism, homophobia, *Dayeinu* (it is enough)."

It is just one sentence, and yet each time I hear that line, something is healed within me and my hope for the future is lifted a little. I never would have expected to find affirmation as a lesbian from the members of a suburban synagogue sisterhood who join us at the seder. I never imagined I could share the feminist theory I learned in women's study class with Jewish day school teachers just like the ones who first taught me the traditional haggadah. But somehow, this seder can bring us together. Somehow, with all our differences, we still join together in speaking new truths aloud and expressing bold visions for the future. Certainly, speech is different from action. And the seder is just one night. But articulating the words, learning the language, is a beginning—a beginning that could, with the right effort, help lead us to a better world. Isn't that what remembering the Exodus is all about?

The Men Question

Erika Katske

"The men question" inevitably arises in planning a women's seder. "What do we do about the men? Do we want them to attend? Do we want them to feel welcome? Will women feel uncomfortable if men are there?"

In asking the seemingly pragmatic question of whether or not to include men, seder organizers brush the surface of issues central not only to women's seders but also to all of Jewish feminism: What do we hope to create through feminist ritual? What kind of power does our separation and re-creation of a Jewish ritual hold? How will it change us? How will it change Judaism?

I encountered the power of those questions when I began working for Ma'yan after I graduated from college. By the time I came to the organization, the Ma'yan feminist seders, the most well-known and well-attended women's seders in the United States, were in their fifth year. Like every women's seder, the Ma'yan seder has a complex history with the men question, which arose during the organizers' very first seder planning meeting in 1993. Would the ritual include men and women and therefore be a glimpse of the kind of egalitarian Judaism they hoped the community would someday achieve? Or was it intended solely to feed Jewish women hungry for a feminist spiritual experience?

The women on the committee were aware of the substantial responsibility of creating new ritual, as well as the fact that it would force them to choose between conflicting values. How, the committee members wondered, can we—who know what it feels like to be excluded from traditional seders—not share this empowering experience with the men in our lives: our partners, fathers, and sons? Then again, how can we give women the opportunity to reclaim the Passover holiday without creating an all-women's space? How can we challenge the status quo of tradition without creating a radically new environment?

The planning committee ultimately decided that this seder would address Jewish women and highlight their experiences. It would not attempt to be egalitarian. Men would not be prevented from attending, but they would not be explicitly invited, either. The women who attended the seder did not object to this decision. Rather, they appreciated having a women's space that allowed them to explore the meaning of the ritual for themselves.

While the planning committee decided to create a seder intended for women, they also wanted to be sure to separate themselves lovingly. They did not want to exclude men out of anger. In early conversations about the tone of the event, they looked for ways to avoid being stereotyped as "man-hating feminists." In addition, many women wanted to acknowledge the role that men played in their lives and recognize their potential role as partners in making feminist change. Thus, the committee decided that although the haggadah's liturgy would not explicitly address men, they would be allowed to attend the seder.

In the end, only a few men have attended the seders, which attract over two thousand women each year. This group is affectionately known in the Ma'yan office as our "smattering" of men. They clearly constitute less than a third of the participants—the magic number, according to sociologists, at which a subgroup begins to noticeably affect the dynamics of the larger group.[3] A smattering, for most, does not affect the distinct sound of women's voices when participants sing or read aloud from the haggadah. For many, the power created by the sound of five hundred women's voices in unison is essential to the seder experience. It reminds women to listen for the voices of women. It reminds women to listen for their own voices. And yet, the smattering of men is significant in another sense. Many participants are disappointed that even a few men attend the seder; they have looked forward to being in a group of women exclusively. How can Jewish women truly redefine Jewish ritual for themselves if men attend their rituals?

But the presence of men at the Ma'yan seder can be illuminating for both the men and the women in the room. The experience gives these few men insight into the nature of gendered experiences in Judaism. They say they feel overwhelmed and "out of their element" at the seder. Impressed with the size of the event and with the spirit and energy in the room, they are aware that they cannot claim the experience as their own.

One man attended the Ma'yan seder with his wife. As Debbie Friedman's "Miriam's Song" roused the group, his wife asked him to join the dancing. He replied, simply, that he couldn't. The verse stated that "all the women followed Miriam with timbrels"—not the men. In that moment, he admitted, he understood the power of language. As a male, he had always been addressed by the text; he had never experienced feeling excluded from the liturgy. With hundreds of Jewish women dancing around him, he understood that this moment was not his. The experience sparked an interest in Jewish feminism, and he began studying with the Ma'yan staff regularly.

I have often wondered why the men question is so challenging to those of us creating a women's ritual. Why are we so concerned with how men will figure (or not figure) into our seder? I have come to believe that the men question helps us articulate our struggle with power. The questions and decisions involved in planning a women's seder are closely tied to questions about the ways in which women-defined spaces and all-women's spaces challenge the gender status quo. In her essay "Some Reflections on Separatism and Power," feminist theorist Marilyn Frye explains that all-women's spaces are "seen as a device whose use needs much elaborate justification. I think this is because conscious and deliberate exclusion of men by women, from anything, is blatant insubordination...." In the language of the Exodus, Frye points out, "the slave who decides to exclude the master from her hut is declaring herself not a slave."[4]

And this is the essence of women's seders: the opportunity for women to leave *mitzrayim,* the narrowness of patriarchal definitions, a chance for women to reclaim and redefine our experience in our own words. As we rethink these events and liturgies we do the work of feminist change; we experiment with new definitions of ourselves, test the boundaries of old patriarchal definitions, and gradually shed the language that our culture and tradition have used to define us. If our goal is to ensure women a whole, equal place within Jewish tradition and the Jewish community, we need to become comfortable with asking and answering the men question—with our power and with the process of exercising it.

≈≈≈

Miriam and Our Dance of Freedom: Seder in Prison
JUDITH CLARK

Since 1983, when I first arrived at Bedford Hills Correctional Facility, I have participated in our annual seders.[1] The very effort to contemplate and celebrate the meaning of freedom in prison is an act of faith. The ritual of the seder provokes us to focus on our most important journey: to seek freedom from our internal prisons and find freedom through community.

At the prison, our seders are precious. They are the one time of the year when our families are allowed into the prison to celebrate with us. Year after year, my parents and daughter as well as other family members and friends come to celebrate Passover at Bedford. We sit with other women and their families, our rabbi, and volunteers from

---

In prison since 1981, **Judith Clark** facilitates prenatal classes and parenting groups for nursing mothers. Her writing on mothers in prison has been published in *The Prison Journal* and *Zero to Three;* her poetry and prose appear in *The New Yorker, Doing Time, Aliens at the Border,* and *Red Diapers: Growing Up in the Communist Left.* She is coauthor of *Breaking the Walls of Silence,* about the building of AIDS Counseling and Education (ACE).

the synagogue at a beautiful, long table laden with traditional Passover foods generously provided by the Sisterhood of Bet Torah, our rabbi's synagogue. Rabbi Fine leads us through the traditional prayers, ritual telling, questions, and answers, so that my daughter, over time, has learned to answer the rabbi's questions (and finish his jokes) before he even asks them.

How can I express the meaning of our seders in here? Prison is exile. But on this night, we are one with our families and community. Like Jews everywhere, we draw on ritual, prayer, and repetition to look past our own circumstances in order to reexperience our forbears' and others' slavery, exodus, and spiritual awakening. Prison is shame, but on this night I can teach my daughter the traditions I grew up with and participate as an equal at the table. Prison is deprivation, rigidity, and rules, but on this night we recline into the sumptuous comfort of generosity and caring. On this night, we transcend the walls and razor-wire fences to contemplate and celebrate deeper meanings of freedom-in-community.

How can I share our experiences at the seders? There was our joy and our sadness. There was the dynamic tension between our commitment to the slow unfolding of ritual and our desire to enjoy the rare relaxed intimacy with our families and friends. There was that moment when we could not throw open the door for Elijah and would not wish on anyone that they might have to enter the prison doors.

Over the years, however, I had felt a growing restlessness as Passover approached. My parents had died and my child was away in college. Though friends continued to join me, the seder became a reminder of my bound state rather than a spiritual celebration of freedom. Faced with the weight of decades of imprisonment, I needed a new way into the meaning of Passover, to rekindle my quest for holiness and freedom; I needed a seder that challenged me to deepen my reparative efforts. The answer to my prayers came from the women's community, which had created new rituals and traditions and incorporated them into *The Journey Continues,* the Ma'yan haggadah.

Several miracles helped to extend the reach of the local Jewish women's community to us. First was the miracle of a fifth question: "Why don't we have Miriam's Cup at this seder?" and the miracle of friendly debate (what seder is complete without it?) over the appropriateness of adding new elements to the traditional seder. Then there was the miracle of sisterhood: friends who had shared our Passover celebration committed themselves to making this women's seder. Then there was the miracle of a woman rabbi joining Bet Torah, a woman who had herself taken part in women's seders and offered to conduct our seder. And there was the miracle of the determined sister who donated copies of the Ma'yan haggadah and who arrived on the night of our seder with tambourines, taped music, and—of course—Miriam's Cup.

Why is this night different from all other nights? We felt it in the air: the energy and excitement of something new, of honoring tradition through change, of finding new meaning in familiar words spoken in a new voice and sharing new rituals that strengthen our sense of participation in the seder. Strangers introduced themselves to each other: "I am Judith, *bat* (daughter of) Ruth *bat*...." Laughter and talk rippled softly around the table. A tape of Debbie Friedman's clear, beautiful voice in song lifted the room with holy joy. I felt a heady sense of liberation as a woman rabbi took the seat at the head of the table and led the seder.

Why was this night different from all other nights? We began by filling Miriam's Cup. Serious. Joyful. Finally, we were giving Miriam her rightful place in sacred history. In honoring Miriam, we brought ourselves—broken women rebuilding ourselves, imprisoned women in search of freedom, isolated women in search of family and community, skeptical women in search of faith—to the table. As we each poured water into Miriam's Cup we brought to our table the power of giving life and the responsibility of holding life sacred. Through using water—so simple and so plentiful—as a key element of sacred ritual, we celebrated the sacredness in the ordinary.

Let us sing a new song. Let us sing a song of liberation. Miriam's spirit moved through us. We read in union and shared questions and insights into the meanings of each new and old tradition. We dipped and washed and wondered, recited prayers, broke matzah and ate bitter herbs and sweet *charoset*. We sang, passing around our tambourine and welcoming each individual's joyful rhythms. We solemnly recited the Ten Plagues, knowing so well the price of freedom. And then, Miriam's spirit of feisty celebration raised us out of our seats, and we danced in a long rhythmic line, winding around the table, beating the tambourine—laughing at our outrageous wildness, our sacred disorderliness breaking through the numbing familiarity of prison routine. We were for that moment the first astounded, unruly band of desert wanderers gathering at the water's edge, joining in Miriam's new song. Who knew where the journey would take them; who among them could say they were prepared? Like them, we are ill prepared yet yearning for freedom. Like them, we need faith and community.

Miriam, Miriam: we too dance to miracles. This too is a miracle: this exhilarating joy, this wild abandonment of decorum, our clasped hands and awkward dancing feet, our laughter with which we shed self-consciousness, beckoning toward strangers to join our uncommon dance. With this moment of miracle, we replenish our faith and our energy to keep on through the desert of days that await us. The spirit in our clasped hands and dancing bodies reminds us of the holy connection between freedom and the responsibility of the bonds between us.

Completing our circle, we took our seats and continued toward the conclusion of our seder. But the spirit that we created together that night has stayed with me. Once again, this night affirmed the power of ritual and the potential of women dipping into our own spiritual sources. I wanted to find a way to bring its sacred message of hope to my life work as co-facilitator of prenatal classes available to all pregnant women coming into Bedford prison. Each group meets every day for six weeks, sharing information and experiences and support for the difficult challenges of having a baby while in prison. Our graduation is a baby shower, with beautiful gifts for each baby. The most important gift is that the mother herself shares a poem, a letter, or a song—an expression from her heart to her baby.

Now I have added a new ritual. Throughout the weeks of class, we serve the women water. I wish I could give them fruit and other healthy treats. But we have none, and I am not allowed to. So we give them water. At the beginning of the baby shower, I pour a cup of water for each person and say:

"Every day we gave each other water because water was all we had to give. So today, we honor the spirit of nurturing each other through this cup of water. And we think about how fitting it is. Water means life. We need it to survive. We are made of it. All life began in water; each life begins in water. You carry your babies for these months in a warm sea, and they will be born into this life in a flood of breaking waters. Now to bless this circle of life, this gathering of mothers, full of the promise of new life and new lives, fearful and faithful, we lift our cups to each other and exclaim, *'L'chaim!'* 'To life!'"

≋

Every Voice Matters: Community and Dialogue at a Women's Seder

CATHERINE SPECTOR

Each year at our seder tables we recite the questions of the four sons: one wise, one wicked, one simple, and one who does not know how to ask. Traditionally, we respond to three of these children with an understanding of their individual strengths and needs. Yet, our reply to the wicked son differs in tone. He asks, "What does this service mean to you?" We answer, "It is because of this, that the Lord did for *me* when I went free from Egypt." With this answer, we emphasize that the Exodus was for us and not for him; we exclude the wicked son from

Catherine Spector attends the University of Chicago Law School. She graduated from Yale University in 2000 with a B.A. in political science. As an undergraduate, she was the coordinator of Jewish Women at Yale and part of the steering committee for Yale's two national conferences on women and Judaism. She is coeditor of *The Women's Passover Companion* and *The Women's Seder Sourcebook* (both Jewish Lights Publishing).

Jewish history and from our community. We even warn him that, if he had been enslaved in Egypt, he would not have been redeemed.

At women's seders, many participants find it difficult to respond so harshly to the child's question and have undertaken the task of transforming our understanding of the wicked son. In women's haggadahs, where the four sons are often recast as four daughters, the wicked daughter is frequently imagined in new ways: the irreverent daughter, the uninvolved daughter, the angry daughter, the bitter daughter, or the daughter who wants to erase her difference.[1]

Even in women's haggadahs that continue to label this child wicked, new answers to her question have been crafted, responding to her with empathy and encouragement. They urge us not to cast the wicked daughter out of our seder but instead to bridge the distance that she feels from the Jewish community and religious practice. The *Yale Women's Haggadah,* for example, suggests responding to the "scornful" daughter "with patience because her pain is familiar.... At our seder, we cannot afford to cast out this daughter; her scorn is too much a part of us. Tell her that her rage is our pain, and that the only way to make meaning of her rage is to seek answers for her questions. She too is worthy of redemption."[2]

As the *Yale Women's Haggadah* reveals, the authors of women's haggadahs include the wicked daughter in their Passover celebration in part because they identify with her pain and confusion. They refuse to reject this daughter because they, too, have at times felt excluded from important Jewish rituals and celebrations. They understand the wicked daughter's question and reinterpret it as an important message, challenging us to reflect on what it is that has alienated this child from Judaism. Rather than dismiss her question as wicked, women's haggadahs allow it to initiate a dialogue about the aspects of our tradition that exclude women.

A second reason why the authors of women's haggadahs respond to this daughter in untraditional ways is their commitment to pluralism—a commitment informed by their own experience of exclusion. Women's seders are an opportunity for the entire spectrum of Jewish women to come together in celebration. In many communities, seder organizers work very hard to ensure that women of different ages, religious affiliations, backgrounds, and nationalities are part of the seder. Furthermore, many women's seder organizers find it painful to exclude men, non-Jewish women, or young children from the seder, even if they believe that a seder for Jewish women only would be more meaningful and beautiful. They question the need to turn anyone away from the event, to make anyone feel left out.

Yet, a commitment to pluralism requires more than offering everyone a seat at the seder table. The seder is focused on a discussion of slavery and liberation, of Jewish history and memory. At a women's seder, Jewish women with vastly different perspectives on these issues are able to explore them together rather than in isolation. Pluralism asks us to listen to women whose experiences, questions, and challenges are different from our own. And, ultimately, pluralism requires even more than this, asking us to open not only our ears but our hearts and minds. It demands that we allow ourselves to learn from one another, and, potentially, to be transformed by each other. The central challenge of creating a pluralistic women's seder, therefore, is not merely to gather a group of diverse women together but to create a dynamic conversation among everyone in the room.

I encountered the difficulty—and value—of this challenge when I was on the planning committees for two national conferences on women and Judaism held at Yale University in 1997 and 1999. We quickly realized that in order to create a conference that would represent the diversity of young Jewish women in this country, one that could make all these women feel that their interests and concerns were addressed in the conference, we ought to have a planning committee that represented their experiences and perspectives. We were proud to be a group of Ashkenazi, Sephardi, lesbian, straight, Orthodox, Conservative, Reconstructionist, Reform, unaffiliated, political, apolitical, secular, and spiritual women.

With our many different backgrounds, we brought an array of values, priorities, and beliefs to each meeting. Although at first it was difficult for us to bridge the differences among us in order to work together, in the end we were able to find solutions to what seemed like insurmountable challenges. Importantly, our diverse perspectives forced us to confront issues of inclusion from the beginning of the planning process: How could we ensure that an observant woman would feel comfortable with our prayer service? Did our programming include the lesbian community? Would a political activist agree that we had raised the most important issues facing Jewish women?

Because we had such a diverse committee, and because we had these questions in mind throughout our planning process, we were able to address each of them. As we came to understand one another's perspectives, we all became increasingly aware of the issues of inclusion at stake in each planning decision. The planning process became a genuine learning experience, whose lessons we could bring with us to other communities.

Similarly, women's expectations and goals for a women's seder often conflict, and it is difficult to shape the event to reflect everyone's concerns. This makes it particularly important to include on your planning committee a cross-section of the women you would like to welcome to your seder. Having a diverse planning committee will help you find readings and rituals to fill the needs of all the women at your seder. However, what some women find powerful and inspirational may be startling, or even offensive, for other women in the room.

It is not necessary for every moment in the seder to be in harmony with each participant's everyday Jewish practice. Our coming together as women for these seders offers a rare and precious chance to reflect on our identity as Jewish women with others who are engaged in the same exploration. We open ourselves to new aspects of contemporary Judaism and feminism by being willing to push the limits of our personal practices, whether by experimenting with feminine God language or by learning about the harsh political realities facing women around the world.

Some women may find the most important expression of their Jewish identity to be fulfilling their obligation of *tikkun olam* through social action. Others may believe that passing on a Jewish identity to their children is their most important religious duty. At a women's seder, we learn about all the ways to be a Jewish woman. Women take home the memories of moments that were particularly moving, both for themselves and for others. Having been exposed to these moments stretches their consciousness and perhaps even alters their beliefs. They may choose to bring these new perspectives and rituals home to their own seders in order to share them with friends and family.

However, beyond the ideological issues that divide Jewish women, there are the halakhic concerns that must be addressed within the planning process. For example, in Wilmington, Delaware, the Orthodox women on the seder planning committee thought that the *shehecheyanu* prayer (the blessing for a special, long-awaited occasion) should not be said at the annual women's seder.[3] For these women, the women's seder did not technically qualify as a holy event warranting the *shehecheyanu* blessing. But, because the *shehecheyanu* marks an event as holy, the non-Orthodox women on the planning committee—who felt more comfortable reinterpreting the halakhah—believed that it was important to be able recite the prayer together. In a compromise, the Orthodox women wore new clothing to the seder, which gave them a halakhic reason to say the *shehecheyanu* with the other women. This solution was successful because the planning committee listened to everyone's perspectives and came to decisions that respected everyone's beliefs. Because both Orthodox and non-Orthodox women were part of the planning process, the committee had an opportunity to work out this reasonable—if unusual—solution to the problem that arose.

Sometimes, during our planning of the Yale conferences, we found that instead of seeking solutions that could speak for the entire spectrum of Jewish women, it was more appropriate to offer the women several options from which to choose—workshops, affinity groups, or prayer services. In the same way, women's seder organizers may have a difficult time finding rituals or liturgy that represent all the women at the seder. Offering multiple options at particular moments in the seder—blessings or dinner table discussions—validates the choices, and therefore the beliefs, of each woman present. In addition, this solution is a powerful way to affirm that Jewish women can celebrate together without having to obscure the differences among us.

Another way to embrace diversity is to encourage the women in the room to tell their own stories. Many women's seders supplement their haggadahs with personal reflections from participants on the wide array of political, spiritual, and cultural themes addressed by the seder. During the *maggid* section of the seder, individual women may be asked to tell their own stories of exile and liberation. Or perhaps, at a particular moment in the seder, such as the Four Questions, each woman in the room will be able to recite the text in her native language. It is extremely powerful for women to know that all backgrounds and beliefs are relevant to the seder.

During the seder we read, "Let all who are hungry come and eat. Let all who are in need come and celebrate Pesach." Just as we welcome guests into our homes at the family seder, the women's seder asks us to welcome other women into our hearts. And what does it mean to make a person feel welcome? We must not only include each voice but respect it. Pluralism does not simply demand that we permit the "wicked" daughter to join us at the table. Rather, it asks us to embrace her question and whatever challenge or discomfort it may bring. Our goal at a women's seder is by no means to obscure or evade the differences among women but rather to highlight and celebrate the range of perspectives among us. This is the truest definition of community, and it can only be achieved when everyone in the room understands that her voice and perspectives are treasured as a central part of the event.

≋

God's Redemption:
Memory and Gender on Passover

NORMA BAUMEL JOSEPH

I love Passover. I work like a slave, yet, I feel exalted, emancipated, and just plain great. I love the sights, sounds, and tastes of it, the idea and ideas of it. My memories of growing up, establishing my own home, and being Jewish are all entwined with this holiday.

My earliest memories of Pesach are in my bubbe's *home. My zayde was long since dead, but* bubbe's *household remained the place for our family's observances. While my memory did not retain a picture of the seder with its male physiognomy, I do recall the women as they bustled about the kitchen, their central meeting place, sharing, directing, controlling, and laughing.*

Today, I begin planning for the seder early in January. (Any woman who "makes" a seder certainly can claim management expertise and status.) Since I married thirty-six years ago, the seder has been my responsibility. Nonnegotiable. For I won't give up the feeling that comes each year as I watch my parents, in-laws, children, and grandchildren joined together in my home, singing, eating (my food), talking, telling stories, and celebrating together because I successfully managed to make Pesach again! It represents one of my central roles in a Judaism that is not synagogue bound.

Passover is filled with contradictions and consolations. It resonates with ambiguity and lucidity. It represents our collective consciousness and molds our personal identity. It forces us to remember that which we did not experience. It expresses complex theological truths in the most mundane activities. It is at once absurd and sublime. And the place of women at the table is both established and problematic.

Passover forces us to focus on the home, on the ritual centrality of

---

Dr. Norma Baumel Joseph is an associate professor in the Department of Religion at Concordia University. She is director of the women and religion specialization and graduate program director. She is also an associate of the Concordia Institute for Canadian Jewish Studies.

this sacred domestic site. Its ritual experts are not trained, paid clergy but members of the household. Everyone has a role to play, even—especially—the youngest child. In this crucial family celebration of the birth of a nation, women are the architects. Although the text and order of the ritual have been designed by a male elite, the actual texture and taste, the full sensual experience, depend on female religious management.

Given women's central role in making the holiday, in cleaning and cooking and crafting the seder, how is it that so many women today feel passed over? Why do women feel so left out? And why create separate women's seders?

American Judaism has developed an attachment to institutional formats for ritual involvement. Many Jews think that they "do Jewish" only in public venues such as the synagogue or the cemetery.[1] Yet, the classical tradition of rabbinic Judaism did not depend so heavily on the synagogue. Nor was there so sharp a division between domestic and public. The home was often the locus of ritual participation and public celebration.[2] In that environment, even given the segregation of the sexes, women had a recognized—and appreciated—role to play. When all ritual depends on public spaces and professions that exclude women, their loss of position and esteem comes to the fore.

The efforts of feminist Jews to create women's seders and haggadahs are, of course, directly related to the search for a feminist Judaism that recognizes women's equality and independence. Celebrating women's roles is a necessary and sufficient response to modern living, to modernity's challenge of equality and individualism. And it is a religious, even redemptive, response. Judaism teaches that all humans are equal, created in the image of God. As God's covenantal partners, our task is to redeem Judaism for women and women for Judaism.

The contemporary search for a female presence and representation[3] is not an attempt to deny memories such as mine of my grandmother's house, nor it is an attempt to deny the religiously fulfilled women such recollections recall. Notably, it neither wishes to limit women to a form of kitchen Judaism nor to declare that only when women participate in or imitate male ritual activities is there any value. Rather, it springs out of a yearning for religious vehicles of expression that authentically represent Jewish values, especially those celebrated by Passover. It is struggling to find a voice, a way to dance and sing with Miriam as she leads the women in praise of God's liberating hand.

The story of the Exodus is referred to in our liturgy throughout the year, but at Passover it assumes a sublime status. Through bizarre ritual enactment, Jews attempt to re-create facets of that emancipating experience. During the seder, the claim is made that each of us personally went out of Egypt. I am supposed to experience this ritual as if I had been there—me, not my ancestors. In this ritual storytelling, the space-time continuum ceases to exist. The key events that formed the nation are remembered not as some long-ago happening. The matzah and bitter herbs are present to stimulate the individual's personal memory of oppression and slavery. Discussing freedom as a philosophical idea or political commitment is not sufficient; the ritualized commemoration insists on an immediate, embodied experience and celebration.

In that moment of personalizing history, of making it my own story, it becomes the source of a profound pledge to respond and be responsible. Jewish tradition builds on this personal sense of involvement to make the claim that Jews must eradicate the memory of slavery for ourselves and for others. We must liberate the world, as we once experienced bondage and freedom. Our ancestors lived through these experiences, and so must we. In the language of the Bible, the covenant is made with those who stood at Sinai "and also with those who are not here this day."[4] The redemptive responsibility is—for men and for women—both personal and political.

More than liberation, Passover stands for redemption. Liberation is about freedom, suggesting a civil status. Redemption occurs in a covenantal context as a response to a commitment. In the story of the Exodus, God saves the People of Israel from slavery, with many signs and speeches, with a strong and mighty hand. The significance of this central myth is not to be found in the simple liberation of a people. Surely, much of the holiday focuses on our national existence. Passover is the Jewish "Independence Day." Moreover, the daily liturgical emphasis on remembering that God took *us* out of Egypt connotes a nationalism of pride and chosenness.

Nonetheless, the significance of the remembered experience far exceeds such narrow chauvinism. Rather, it is to be found in the theological model set forth: God redeems. And because of that, we humans must learn how to continue that process. We are left with the mandate: Because you were slaves in Egypt, you must eradicate oppression. Because God chose to liberate you, you must liberate others. Because we have a covenant with God, we must redeem. The charge to be Godly brings with it a great responsibility.

What sort of model does God's liberating hand offer or impose on us?

In the Exodus story, frequently retold in the Bible,[5] we are taught, in distinct permutations: "God heard our voice and saw our oppression and took us out of Egypt. God freed us with awesome power, brought us to this place, and gave us this land." Such recitations are replayed on many ritual occasions. Strikingly, the discernible sequence of God's actions becomes the standard for redemptive action, a guide for human behavior.

Israel cried out, and God responded. The first lesson that this model of redemption offers is that the persecuted or aggrieved must first ask for help or voice their distress. God's redemption is a response to Israel's cries, rather than a preemptive action, which can often be paternalistic or imperialistic.

Significantly, the story notes that God hears and sees. In a sincere endeavor to understand the task given to us by God, we cannot ignore this sensory metaphor. First we are told that God hears.[6] The verb form used *(va'yishma)* connotes more than mere aurality; it indicates understanding. Then we are told that God also sees *(va'yar)*. Once comprehension prevails, there is no looking away. Painful as it may sometimes be, we are instructed to look, to see, and to hear oppression wherever it occurs. The second lesson we learn about redemption from the

model of the Exodus is not to turn away from the distasteful realities
that surround us. When the oppressed are ready to cry out, we must listen and try to understand. We are obligated to hear what victims of
oppression—or our neighbors—are crying out for or telling us.

God's motivations are also clearly explored and expressed in the
story. The people are given two predominant reasons for God's action:
God's love and God's commitment to our ancestors. So the Bible commands that we too remember, and this is the third lesson we must take
from the model of redemption offered us. Our memory of our own
redemption from slavery in Egypt imposes on us a commitment to
redeem—just as God remembered our ancestors and redeemed us.
But love? That next step in the model is most difficult. God loves all
of creation. Are we capable of such committed, affective action? Is that
not an ideal to strive for?

Yet, when we attempt to accept this responsibility to act in the
image of our redeeming God, we may doubt that we are equal to the
task. Surely we cannot replicate God's redemptive actions. Who can
claim such powers? When Moses tries to prepare the Israelites for their
entrance into the Land of Israel, he warns them that they might feel
fearful of the neighbors, unsure of their ability to conquer the land, and
hesitant to assume their full responsibilities.[7] So he reminds them of
God's saving action and commitment to them. And what does it all
mean for us? Like our ancestors of yore, or in our most humble
moments, we might shy away from the immense task of redemption.
How can *we* possibly be responsible for ending oppression?

Anticipating our doubt and indecision, the story is told and retold
in many formats to impress on us the verity of our liberation. We were
slaves and God saved us, and because of that we must save others. That
is our destiny. But Moses wisely goes further. He tells them—and us—
that God will help. By showing us the way and giving us the means,
God will help. Moreover, Moses warns, the process will not be immediate or complete. In Egypt, this process unfolded according to its own
time frame; now, too, Israel must be patient. Is Moses warning them—
and us—that the process of land redemption, and human redemption,

will proceed slowly? Can we take our time? Will God? What is the lesson of this encounter?

Taking a cue from midrashic technique, we can look very closely at the words used and gain some insight into our mandate. The words *me'at, me'at,*[8] used to explain how God will liberate our people from slavery in Egypt, do not mean slowly *(le'at, le'at)*. Rather, they refer to a process that progresses in small, measurable parts. Little by little we can do it. If we presume to accomplish it all, in one fell swoop, we shall fail. Redemption's fourth lesson demands of us small steps, limited projects, bounded goals. Though we may grasp the whole problem, see the enormity of the oppression and persecution, we can only tackle it piece by piece, person by person. Perhaps then God will help us as we bring divine redemption into our lives and world.

Thus, the story claims our attention and charges us to act based on this model of redemption. We can try to use our limited powers and accept our humble likeness to God. Conceivably, the biblical model imposes on us a message that together we can create an awesome redemptive force on earth. God awaits our engagement. So does our humanity.

All of which leaves one question: For whom is this model intended? Are women charged with these redemptive tasks? Can they be the recipients of redemptive acts? Are women part of this collective? Is their experience enshrined in the narrative? And most importantly, when we ritualize the telling, what part do women and their experiences play? The cumulative effect of the exclusion of women from our retelling of the story and from the public performance of ritual has left us invisible and with the erroneous impression that we are not ritually active or theologically significant. There are numerous examples of women's rich participatory ritual life, of women as ritual experts, confident in their skill, authoritative in their position. It is our task to excavate the record, extract women's different ritual experiences, and find the means of personal identification. That is one part of our small but important redemptive task. We must listen to and understand women's pain and suffering, but also their joy and strength. We must see their oppression wherever it occurs, as well as their self-sufficiency and independence. We must liberate and celebrate. We must find the strength to love, or at least to act lovingly.

Passover is a story of redemption that is meant for women, too. The biblical model for human redemption is found in the story of Ruth, which tells of redemption and love with and for women. Tradition claims that, in the future, Rachel's tears will move God to redeem her exiled children. It is intriguing—and imperative—to note the talmudic claim that Israel was redeemed because of the righteousness of the women.[9] Will the world today be redeemed because of the righteousness of Israel, of women? As we prepare for Passover, with food, family, and friends, let's think about freedom and liberation, just a little bit. Let's do one small act of redemption. Like God, let's save our world and ourselves.

I love Passover. It claims me and elevates me. Surrounded by family, ritually active, secure in my home, I can embrace these concepts and hold on to hope. I can begin to think of God's presence in my life. I wonder if I can carry that awareness forward? Isn't that the challenge?

≋

An Embrace of Tradition

TARA MOHR

Only three decades have passed since the first women's seder—a mere moment compared to the three-thousand-year history of the seder. Remarkably, during this brief period, women's seders have emerged as one of the most beloved and popular communal gatherings in contemporary Jewish life. Thousands of women attend the ritual each year,

---

Tara Mohr graduated from Yale University in 2000 with a B.A. in English Literature. The coeditor of *The Women's Passover Companion* and *The Women's Seder Sourcebook* (both Jewish Lights Publishing), Tara works on Jewish outreach and organizational change programs as a Koret Synagogue Initiative Consultant in the San Francisco Bay Area. Currently, she is also writing a study of Shakespeare's comedies.

participating with enthusiasm and often taking leadership roles in creating it. Participants speak about women's seders with excitement and fondness, commonly remarking that it is among their most significant forms of Jewish involvement. And organizations hosting the ritual report that they are among their most well-attended events, drawing many participants who attend few if any other programs.

Understanding the factors underlying the ritual's success, we can better support women's seders, and offer Jewish women the kinds of ritual and communal experiences they need and want. What accounts for the popularity of women's seders? What draws women to the ritual, and what makes them return year after year?

Speaking to women about why they attend women's seders, one hears many different ideas. It is a rare chance to gather with the women of the community; it is a chance to find personal, spiritual meaning in a Jewish ritual. It is a way to be Jewish; it is a way to be feminist. It is a powerful religious event; it is a lovely celebration. Similarly, women's haggadahs vary widely in content and style. Some emphasize external sources of slavery, while others explore internal forms of oppression. One community haggadah proudly deems itself feminist; another is resistant to using the term anywhere on its pages. Many hardly mention the women of the Exodus story, and others feature their names on every page. Are there common elements among these diverse women's seders? And how does this diversity play into the rituals' popularity?

At its most fundamental level, the Passover seder is about recounting the story of our people's enslavement and redemption. So, too, women's seders, even in their diversity, share the common core of remembering slavery and celebrating liberation. And this is perhaps the greatest factor contributing to their appeal. The themes of freedom and oppression, revolution and liberation are deeply relevant to women of our era. Indeed, the feminists who created the earliest women's seders in the mid-1970s were primarily secular political activists who could not ignore the extraordinary irony of celebrating their freedom on one night while throughout the rest of the year they were engaged in a fight for women's liberation. These women transformed their celebration by refusing to divorce their feminist concerns from their approach to and practice of the Passover ritual. Using the basic framework of the Passover narrative, they explored a feminist journey:

> We will be slaves to no nation and before no man.
> We can find our way through the wilderness.
> We can find our way through thicket and stone.
> We can find our way under hot desert sun to our home.[1]

At the seders, they discussed political issues ranging from racial strife to domestic violence. Among the "plagues" named by this group were the "cutback in social programs," "deserting fathers" and the "opening of the ozone."[2] More significantly, these innovators experimented with using the seder as a fertile ground for examining the ideas at the center of their activist work. Looking at social problems as plagues, for example, provided a novel context bearing the gravity of religious ritual in which to name and discuss these issues.

The women of those first seders saw themselves as the struggling Israelites, enslaved by patriarchy. Today, women living with far greater freedoms feel less comfortable drawing parallels between the Jews' oppression in Egypt and women's oppression in patriarchal societies. But questions about the meaning of liberation, the experience of wilderness, the legacy of oppression, and the landscape of the Promised Land are equally resonant and urgent for these women. At a women's seder, the attendants contemplate these questions in new ways, often on a more personal level than at their family seders, and in relation to their status as Jewish women as well as to the situation of women around the world. Thus, while women's lives have changed dramatically in the years since the first women's seder was held, the themes of Passover, as explored in the haggadah, continue to offer a rich and provocative paradigm for Jewish women to explore their personal, spiritual, and political concerns.

Beyond this, Passover is a holiday with which most Jewish women are deeply familiar. It is the most widely celebrated holiday in the Jewish year, and, because it takes place at home, nearly all women have had an intimate experience of it. For some, this experience may be centered on participation in the family seder—of reciting the Four Questions, tasting the *maror*, discovering the hidden *afikomen*. Other women carry the memory of not participating at all, of busily preparing food in the kitchen while overhearing the men debating and discussing around the seder table. These women bring to a women's seder the memory of their exclusion as well as recollections of their exhausting work cleaning for Passover and preparing the seder. Women's seders respond to such memories: some focus on honoring women's traditional work, others affirm a commitment to an equal division of labor when it comes to preparing for—and leading—the Passover seder.

Further, the Passover story features something quite rare in our traditional texts: a fascinating group of female biblical figures who play a crucial, positive role in the narrative. The first women's seders noted—and deplored—the absence of women in the haggadah and their relative obscurity within traditional texts. The 1976 *The Women's Haggadah* asks, "Who are our mothers? Who are our ancestors? What is our history?"[3] Today's women's haggadahs draw on the feminist Judaic scholarship and women's rabbinic commentary that have developed in recent decades to answer these questions.

These contemporary feminist haggadahs often focus on highlighting the righteous women of the Exodus story—the midwives Shifra and Puah; Yocheved, mother of Moses; Pharaoh's daughter, Batya; Tziporah, Moses' wife; the prophet Miriam; and the wise Serach bat Asher. This is an extraordinary group of biblical figures, each playing a key part in the story of our liberation, each nearly invisible in traditional accounts of the Passover story. Exploring and honoring these women, women's seders have offered participants inspiring Jewish heroines, a connection to their foremothers, and, importantly, a sense of women's long-standing importance in Jewish history and tradition.

Thus, the content of women's seders has a particular power in drawing participants to the ritual. A second group of factors related to the way in which the seder approaches this content—the "how" of the seder as opposed to the "what," we might say—is of equal significance.

This approach allows for—and indeed encourages—innovation, discussion, personal expression, and learning. For despite the rigidity of its overarching "order," the seder focuses on its themes in an extremely open and mutable framework. Key passages of the haggadah are understood by many women's seder participants to legitimize and encourage supplementing the traditional text with new interpretations, discussion, ritual and textual innovations, and personal reflections. We are instructed that, while there are four scripted questions, asking our authentic questions, whatever they be, will suffice. We read that "whoever expands on the story of the Exodus is praiseworthy," and many women do expand on the customary telling at their seders. The injunction to see ourselves as if each of us had personally gone forth from Egypt inspires women to explore their own experiences of internal and external oppression and liberation at the seder. The importance of this is made clear in women's haggadahs, which often highlight these touchstones from the traditional text. Further, all haggadahs possess a shared pedagogical mission: learning the story—by telling it, hearing it, tasting it, and discussing it—is the fundamental purpose of this highly participatory ritual.

On a practical level, because it is lay led and traditionally held in the home, the seder can be modified without the sanction of the rabbi or even the community at large. Jews understand the seder to be flexible because they have experienced it as such, having attended different or evolving seders over a lifetime.

Thus, despite the variations in the ways they incorporate even their most common elements, women's seders all share the traditional seder's way of approaching that content: learning its fundamental message by questioning and discussing it, sharing personal opinions and stories that relate to it, reinterpreting it, and putting it in a contemporary context. This approach makes the seder the kind of space where novel ideas are proposed, new questions and interpretations are welcomed, and new understandings can be developed. For Jewish feminists bringing new perspectives and interpretations to the tradition, this kind of space is extremely valuable. Further, because a women's seder is a *separate women's space*, participants are able to more freely and authentically question, interpret, share, and engage in a dialogue.

Thus, the creation of a women's educational and exploratory *space* is the defining feature of women's seders. Embracing innovation, the women's seder allows women to ask new questions and create new interpretations, liturgy, and rituals. Promoting discussion, it offers participants an opportunity to have a voice, to be heard, to draw on the strength of other women's voices. And because it has a pedagogical focus, the seder offers women something very valuable: a Jewish feminist education. Whether through the sharing of new interpretations, rituals, midrash, feminist history, or personal stories, women take home much-needed education that they are unlikely to receive at any other community event.

Women's seders are too often defined by a kind of shorthand about their content—a women's seder is Miriam's Cup, an orange on the seder plate, or a group of women dancing with tambourines. But these designations reduce the active, exploratory process that women are undertaking together to its most common and easily recognizable expressions.

The women's seder is not a single, coherent revision of texts and tradition guided by feminist principles; there is no one "women's seder." Women's seders are, in all their forms, a kind of space—for questioning, recovering, creating, healing, and discovering. In this separate space, women begin to develop an authentic relationship to the texts, ideas, and traditions of the holiday. We must reframe our understanding of women's seders from a feminist transformation of a traditional ritual to what they in fact are. In all their myriad forms, women's seders are the fruits of something new: women's communal, sustained, authentic embrace of a Jewish tradition.

≈≈≈

2

Reclaiming and Re-creating Passover Rituals for Women

All the prayers I make you are flashy
Like new silver
It's too much
Being alone with you. I want a
Rebbe, a minyan, a
Thousand generations to put
A patina on these words—
I want a crowd around this mountain.

—RACHEL ADLER, *THIRD HYMN TO THE SHEKHINA*

The Passover seder is one of Judaism's oldest, most powerful, and most widely observed rituals. As with so many rituals, part of its power lies in the accumulated weight of the collective memory and loyalty of all those who, over thousands of years, have performed the seder. The rituals of the seder evoke for us not only the experiences of our ancestors in Egypt but also the lives of Jews throughout history who have sustained this ancient ritual and

45

imbued it with their own meaning. At the same time, a part of the power of ritual lies in its capacity to elicit and express new layers of meaning that come from our own lived experience. These connections are immediate, urgent, and often unexpected. Jewish tradition teaches us the importance of both *keva* (structure) and *kavanah* (intention) in our ritual practice: our observance must be both fixed and fluid, structured and spontaneous. Ritual must be at once fresh and familiar.

The Passover seder encompasses these opposing elements of ritual practice. The seder, after all, is deliberately an act both of remembering and of imagination. The items on the seder plate are intended to evoke the memory of our ancestors' slavery in Egypt in the most visceral way: as we taste the symbolic foods we link their lives to our own. Further, we are commanded to see ourselves as if we personally had gone forth out of Egypt: the story we tell at Passover is both the story of our people and the story of our own lives.

The authors in part 2 grapple with the ongoing challenge of balancing tradition and change, preserving a connection to the past while creating a sense of relevance in the present. Some have reinterpreted traditional Passover rituals to address their own contemporary experiences, concerns, and religious aspirations. Others have invented new rituals, grounding them in ancient texts and inherited traditions. Each offers a model of how we can approach traditional—and innovative— aspects of the seder. Beginning with the practice of cleaning for Passover, the writings in part 2 address several aspects of the seder and holiday, including reclining at the seder table, Miriam's Cup, the Four Children of the haggadah, the orange on the seder plate, opening the door for Elijah, Passover music, and, finally, the days of Passover that follow the seders on the first and second nights.

In the opening reflection, Orthodox feminist and rabbinical candidate Haviva Ner-David suggests that women can enrich their Passover experience by reclaiming the work of our foremothers, the domestic preparations for the holiday. In "Thoughts on Cleaning for Pesach," she argues that women's Passover preparations have been devalued largely because they are considered to be merely "women's work." Ner-David describes how she has learned to experience this task as a spiritual cleansing, equally significant to the other *mitzvot* (religious duties) of the holiday.

And yet, reclaiming a traditional Jewish practice can be a deeply complex endeavor. In "We Can't Be Free Until All Women Are Important," feminist activist Leah Shakdiel examines the rabbinic injunction to recline at the Passover seder—a requirement that was not originally extended to women. Noting that the act of reclining is a physical embodiment of the freedom that we are meant to experience on the seder night, Shakdiel raises a fundamental and painful question: From a traditional perspective, does Passover's promise of freedom extend to women? Through a provocative historical analysis of Jewish law, Shakdiel argues that the rabbis' selective application of this requirement to women perpetuates an age-old division of women into patriarchal categories that ultimately continue to enslave us all.

While Shakdiel's examination uncovers new layers of meaning in the traditional act of reclining at the seder table, the next piece explores a recently established ritual that has been created and embellished by Jewish feminists of our own generation. In "Setting a Cup for Miriam," religious studies scholar Vanessa Ochs analyzes the origins and significance of the Miriam's Cup ritual and recounts the experience of incorporating the ritual into her family seder. Ochs examines a crucial question for Jewish feminists: How does the community come to feel that a new ritual is an authentic part of the tradition?

Leora Eisenstadt's "The Celebration of Challenge: Reclaiming the Four Children" revisits one of the most familiar aspects of the traditional haggadah, offering a novel reading of the Four Children. Recasting the traditional four sons as daughters, Eisenstadt offers new interpretations of their questions and draws on the stories of women from the Bible as she crafts innovative responses to them.

In "Orange on the Seder Plate," Susannah Heschel shares memories of her childhood Passovers, discussing how these family experiences of the holiday led her to create the ritual of including an orange on the seder plate. Heschel recounts the origin of the ritual and analyzes how and why its meaning has been transformed as it has become increasingly popular at women's and family seders. Urging us to return to the custom's intended meaning of expressing solidarity with Jewish gays and lesbians, Heschel provides a provocative critique of the evolution of this new Passover ritual.

In "The Open Door: The Tale of Idit and the Passover Paradox," Rabbi Sandy Eisenberg Sasso offers a powerful retelling of the biblical account of Lot's wife, Idit. What emerges is a redemptive vision that embraces Idit—honoring her, rather than condemning her, for her compassionate and grief-stricken gaze upon the doomed cities of Sodom and Gomorrah. This vision finds expression in an innovative, entirely original ritual designed to accompany the opening of the door for Elijah at the Passover seder.[1]

Like Sasso, musician Judith Wachs asks us to bring the words of women's wisdom to the seder table. In "A New Song for a Different Night: Sephardic Women's Musical Repertoire," Wachs discusses the forgotten repertoire of Sephardic women's music. Her reverence for this music redeems the undervalued and underappreciated women's songs—and the history they capture—from relative obscurity. She introduces songs from a vast oral tradition preserved by Sephardic women and suggests them for inclusion in our seders.

Carol Ochs's "I Will Be with You: The Divine Presence on Passover" examines the ways in which we understand God not only at our seder table but throughout our celebration of the Passover holiday. She offers eight meditations for use during the week of Passover that can deepen our sense of God's presence in our lives throughout the Passover holiday.

Ritual has the capacity to address and engage our whole being in a way that has particular power and resonance for Jewish women. To the extent that we have been taught that there must be a split between our spiritual and physical lives, ritual provides the healing of integration and wholeness. It offers us a way to not only explore, but to embody, in a sacred context, our questions, critiques, hopes, and values.

Thoughts on Cleaning for Pesach
HAVIVA NER-DAVID

When I was a child, my mother expended a lot of energy cleaning for Pesach. Our whole suburban New York home was turned upside down. Each room was cleaned in a search for *chametz* and for the dirt and junk that had piled up since the last big cleaning the year before. And all of this had to be done at least a few days before Pesach itself, in order to leave enough time for the cooking required to prepare for two seders.

As I came into my own as a young feminist I resented the fact that my mother (with the help of our house cleaner) was the one to do all of this cleaning and cooking, while my father was the one who led the seder. I told myself that I would never be subject to this inequity. I saw my mother as enslaved to an exaggerated notion of what was required by Jewish law in terms of ridding one's home of *chametz,* which I thought was totally antithetical to the notion of Pesach as a holiday of freedom. I decided that I would do the minimum amount of cleaning required by Jewish law and spend the rest of my precious pre-Pesach preparation time studying in order to be able to contribute to the content of the seder. I would stress the intellectual and spiritual side of Pesach preparation rather than the mundane, physical side.

However, as I grew as a religious feminist, married, had children, and set up a Jewish home in Jerusalem, I realized that this cleaning did have to get done by someone. Even if my husband and I (and our house cleaner) shared this work, I still had to focus much of my pre-Pesach energy on cleaning. The truth is, even if a search for *chametz* does not halakhically require turning one's entire home upside down, with small children it practically does—the chances of finding a half-eaten cracker almost anywhere in the house are pretty high with a toddler

---

Haviva Ner-David is the author of *Life on the Fringes: A Feminist Journey towards Traditional Rabbinic Ordination.* She is studying for rabbinical ordination with an Orthodox rabbi in Jerusalem and for a doctorate in philosophy of halakhah at Bar Ilan University.

walking around. Therefore, once we were already cleaning to that degree, my husband and I figured we might as well do a real spring cleaning. I began to appreciate, then, my mother's motivations for turning Pesach preparations into a meticulous spring cleaning.

Moreover, when I began studying feminist theory seriously, I was exposed to the idea of gendered division of labor and introduced to the concept that societies often place a higher value on the work that those of a higher social status perform. As Judith Lorber explains in her book *Night to His Day: The Social Construction of Gender:*

> In a gender-stratified society, what men do is usually valued more highly than what women do because men do it, even when their activities are very similar or the same. In different regions of southern India, for example, harvesting rice is men's work, shared work, or women's work. A gathering and hunting society's survival usually depends on the nuts, grubs, and small animals brought in by the women's foraging trips, but when the men's hunt is successful, it is the occasion for a celebration. Conversely, because they are the superior group, white men do not have to do the "dirty work," such as housework; the most inferior group does it, usually poor women of color.[1]

Lorber's analysis suggested that the issue of Pesach cleaning was not as simple as I had assumed. I began to understand that I too had fallen into the trap of devaluing women's work simply because it was women who were doing it. I was underestimating the halakhic and spiritual significance of the work that my mother, her mother, and her mother's mother had been doing for generations of Pesachs. Ironically, my feminism had led me to disparage my own mother and the labor of her hands. The fact that I was not alone in having fallen into this trap did not convince me that I was vindicated in having done so. If it was the men who were cleaning the house for Pesach, perhaps I would have considered *that* the essence of the Pesach experience.

This realization did not lead me to accept all of women's traditional roles in Judaism nor to defend woman's status or the way society has traditionally been divided along gender lines. Rather, it helped me to understand that all *mitzvot* are important: both lighting Shabbat candles and going to shul on Friday night, both cleaning for Pesach and participating in the seder. Of course, women should get more involved in the *mitzvot* and practices they have not traditionally considered their own, but that does not mean that they should abandon the customs of their mothers. And on the flip side of the same coin, men should become more involved in the spheres of Jewish life in which they have not traditionally been engaged, like cleaning for Pesach.

So there I was, doing a thorough spring cleaning before Pesach, much as my mother had done before me. And much to my surprise, I did not find it as burdensome as I had imagined it would be. In fact, I found it quite spiritually powerful—even transforming. As I sorted, wiped, and scoured I felt a spiritual cleansing taking place within me. Although I was engaged in an activity I had seen as an expression of women's servitude, I felt myself being psychologically and spiritually freed, much like the Jewish slaves were after they left Egypt.

I decided then to look in the Bible, where the prohibition against having *chametz* in your possession on Pesach originates, for some kind of reinforcement of what I was experiencing. But when I looked in Exodus 12 and Deuteronomy 16, where the explanation for this prohibition is found, all that I read about *chametz* and matzah was related to remembering the Exodus, when Jews had to leave in such a hurry that they didn't have time to let their dough rise. In order to reenact this experience each year, we eat no *chametz,* no dough that has risen. The Torah explains that we perform this *mitzvah* so that we can remember a national historical moment. I found nothing in the text to support the sense of personal, spiritual, and psychological freedom I felt in the actual act of ridding my home of *chametz*—the feeling that this cleaning was an important religious expression of one possible meaning behind Pesach.

Then I turned to the *Zohar,* a mystical commentary on the Bible that is the central text of Kabbalah. There I found much material to validate what I had experienced. In its commentary on *parshat Titzaveh,*[2] the *Zohar* associates *chametz* with the *yetzer harah,* the evil inclination, and *avodah zarah,* idol worship: "And such is the evil inclination like yeast in dough, because it enters into the insides of a person, slowly, slowly, and then it multiplies and grows more and more until all of the body becomes enmeshed in it. And that is idol worship, which is likened to the evil inclination." As we rid our homes of *chametz* we are ridding ourselves of the evil inclination, of all of the drives that are preventing us from being who we strive to be.

Then, when I did some reading to prepare for the seder, I came across a beautiful insight of the late Rabbi Shlomo Carlebach in the *Carlebach Haggadah*:

> What keeps us from becoming free sometimes is a very small thing. *Chametz* is *assur b'mashehu* [forbidden even in the smallest amount]. It's forbidden for us to have even the smallest amount of it in our possession, because sometimes one crumb can destroy your life. You know, friends, most married couples that get divorced do it not because of a major event, but because of small events, tiny crumbs. As Pesach comes we're getting rid of all those tiny crumbs. Between redemption and slavery is a *mashehu*, something so tiny. Real redemption comes when we walk around with a candle and find this tiny trait that's holding us back from being what we could be, this little thing that's in essence ruining us, when we find it and burn it.[3]

On that note, I would like to share a personal custom of a ritual that I perform each year before Pesach. As I clean I compile a list of all of my own personal spiritual and psychological *chametz*—the things that keep me enslaved to my evil inclination, the foibles that I hold on to that keep me from total, unencumbered, unfettered faith in the Almighty, the things that prevent me from being what I would like to or could be. Then, when I burn the *chametz* on the eve of Pesach, I toss that list into the fire and watch it burn.

However, I always keep in mind the difference between what is required by Jewish law and what is driving me to go overboard in my cleaning in order to reach the spiritual heights to which I aspire (as well as the level of spring cleaning I desire). I am not required to rid our home of particles that a dog would not eat. So, for instance, crumbs that are covered with dust are not *chametz*, and I do not need to buy toothpaste or dishwashing detergent stamped "Kosher for Passover." There is no need to cover the shelves in the pantry with contact paper. A good cleaning to get rid of any visible pieces of *chametz* is enough— unless, of course, I were to cook directly on my pantry shelves! However, if you choose to cover your shelves because it reminds you of your own childhood Pesach experience, that is fine. You should just be aware that the halakhah does not require this of you. That way, you will be able to make educated decisions and prioritize appropriately in your Pesach cleaning if you begin to feel overwhelmed.

One helpful reminder rings in my head as I clean: Dirt is not *chametz,* and we are not the paschal sacrifice. If going overboard with the cleaning gets in the way of our ability to fully participate in the seder, then we are sacrificing our own souls spiritually, because we are preventing ourselves from the positive commandments associated with Pesach, such as remembering that we were slaves in Egypt, reenacting the Exodus, and eating matzah on the first night of Pesach. This is what the seder is about. But if we are too exhausted from weeks of cleaning to really participate fully in the seder, then we have missed out on an important aspect of Pesach. That is why it is crucial to remember what is actually required of us by Jewish law when doing our search for *chametz.* Perhaps the Rabbis realized that one can go overboard when cleaning and thus miss out on other important *mitzvot* related to Pesach; perhaps this was why they delineated exactly what is *chametz* and what is not, what one must be sure to find and expel from the house before Pesach and what one can leave alone. And so, while doing a thorough spring cleaning before Pesach can be spiritually fulfilling, we should keep the other positive commandments associated with Pesach in mind. If we don't, if we get so caught up in the cleaning that we lose perspective of the broader meaning of Pesach, have we really freed ourselves of the enslavement to idol worship that the *Zohar* talks about? Idol worship comes in many modern forms, and turning Pesach into nothing more than a spring cleaning may be one of them.

We Can't Be Free Until
All Women Are Important

LEAH SHAKDIEL

The Passover seder most likely evolved over many generations, until it crystallized after the destruction of the Second Temple into its present format: an annual family dinner that reenacts the original Exodus through symbolic food and consciousness-raising text.[1] Thus, the cultural context of the time helped shape the laws enacted in the Mishnah and then further elaborated in the Talmud.[2]

One such law in the Mishnah refers to the required body posture at the seder: "Even a poor Jew shall not eat other than while reclining."[3] The Babylonian Talmud further clarifies what was probably obvious to its contemporaries—that this posture during a "symposium" can be enjoyed only by free people, who can afford to eat and drink from tables set in front of the beds on which they are lounging.[4] Like a dramatic, exaggerated gesture that functions as a visual aid to identify the different characters in an ancient morality play, reclining emphasizes the sharp contrast in status between participants and slaves. This understanding is implied in the talmudic text, which clearly distinguishes the ethos of seder night from that of the surrounding culture: all Jews are free and are therefore required to recline—even the homeless man who would not count as a citizen of the polis and the grown man who is living at his father's.

In the midst of these radical rabbinic challenges to Hellenistic notions of social hierarchy, it is especially unsettling to find the following short comment about women and the requirement to recline: "A woman at her husband's is not required to recline, and if she is an

---

Leah Shakdiel heads *Be'er* (well), a new program for women that combines Torah study with community work, in Yeruham, Israel. In 1988, she became Israel's first female member of a local religious council, following a successful struggle that ended with a landmark Supreme Court decision. Shakdiel is a social and political activist for peace, empowerment of the disadvantaged, civil and human rights, and feminism. She is married to Moshe Landsman and is the mother of three children: Rachel, Tzvi, and Pinchas.

important woman, she is required to recline." The first half of this statement establishes that the man is at the center of the seder. He owns the space and the event in its entirety. He is the natural bearer of the eternal message of freedom embedded in the ritual, whereas the woman seems to exist only as his wife. As such, she is quite naturally excluded from the symbolic body posture: while on her husband's turf, she is not free, neither in the eyes of God nor in the eyes of the Jews present, family and guests. She is not even imagined apart from a husband's authority. His claim on her constitutes her as a person, as a Jew.

The Jewish woman, then, is seen as a dual creature. First, she is a Jew who shares the historical fate of the Jewish man as well as the national and spiritual consciousness that derives from that special history. She is expected to be present at the commemoration of her people's liberation, the Passover seder. But because she is also a woman, she is subject to the secondary and subservient role—at the seder and elsewhere—of women to men in all patriarchies. Despite all its efforts to instill in the people a concept of a freedom transcending political and cultural circumstance, rabbinic Judaism—as a vision, a project, an aspiration—clearly gives in at this point. The Rabbis tell us that we, Jewish women, are free as Jews but not free as women.

Perhaps the preservation of the strict social gender hierarchy is related to the unquestioned association of freedom with lordship over something or someone. In a world where hierarchies are considered both natural and intrinsically good, the free man is likened to a king. His very freedom is thus contingent on his having a domain. In this context, to challenge a man's dominion over his wife would be to challenge his very freedom; his freedom is inversely linked to her subordination. At most, a woman can be her king's queen or his princess—wife of, daughter of—a treasured possession who knows her place.

This image of the treasured—and subordinate—married woman may indeed have been important as a means of bestowing status and "freedom" upon the husband. Yet, the power of this image goes deeper still. It is one side of an imagined split that has been perpetuated in many different cultures since antiquity: the split between "good

women" and "bad women." The good women are those worthy of
matrimony and motherhood, whereas the bad ones are those whom
men entertain out of wedlock. Images of reclining women have been
commonly used in literature and art to represent the "bad women"
only: the silhouettes on Greek urns that inspired Renoir's *Large
Bathers,* the various odalisques, Rembrandt's *Danae.* Small wonder our
very own Queen Esther included a seductive sprawl on the festive bed
in her scheme to evoke her husband's anger against Haman.[5]

In light of this, how are we to understand the second half of the talmudic statement: the qualification requiring "important women" to
recline at the seder? We can understand the mishnaic and talmudic
statements surrounding the obligation to recline at the Passover seder
as a subtle reflection of the abusive splitting of women into two categories: the pure ones and the impure objects of pornographic desire.
The difference between subsequent Sephardi and Ashkenazi halakhic
traditions in interpreting this talmudic statement reflects two different
strategies that were available to the Rabbis in resolving this matter.

In Sephardi halakhic literature, the Talmud is quoted almost ver-
batim, with one significant omission: the husband. This implies that
all women, married or not, are exempted from the expression of freedom, and the "important" ones remain the exception to this rule.[6] The
women's nonreclining posture at the seder differentiates them clearly
from the lounging courtesans who join the men in, say, coffee houses,
where the serious discussion of arts and politics is generously spiced
with pleasures of the flesh. Sephardi rabbis, it seems, protect the purity of women by ensuring that they remain distinctly apart from the
philosophic "symposium" of the men, despite their presence at, and
participation in, the seder.

By contrast, in Ashkenaz, there is an obsessive effort to define what
makes a woman "important." She is mistress of her own house, as she
has no husband; or she is not subordinate to her husband, is not under
his awesome authority; or she makes a significant contribution to the
family's livelihood through craft, commerce, or inheritance; or she is of
important paternal lineage; or she has maids and servants enough to

wait on the table, so that she is not busy doing this herself and there-fore can sit at leisure; or she is used to reclining like that during the rest of the year, single or married; or she has a husband who does not feel superior to her but understands that he needs her as much as she needs him—and she is aware of all of this.

Listing the numerous circumstances that qualify a woman as "important" highlights a significant point: the exemption from the obligation to recline is seen as exclusion from privilege and honor that these women deserve to share with the men. Most probably, the Rab-bis' understanding of the place of women in Jewish families was chang-ing by this time, in view of the pivotal role that Jews played in the creation of the proto-modern middle class in Europe.[7] Indeed, the defi-nition of an "important woman" became so expansive as to render the original exemption from the obligation to recline virtually irrelevant and obsolete. What was in talmudic times the exception—"important women"—became more and more the norm in many communities, a gradual process culminating in a notable declaration that summarizes earlier sources: "All our women are important."[8]

In other words, Ashkenazi halakhists faced, in some sense, a new gender. The New Woman was a creature who defied the age-old essen-tialist dichotomy of wife and mistress, the one who could be a partner in homemaking and in matters of the spirit at the same time, while both men and women present were trusted to control their sexuality even when they mixed on an equal footing.[9]

The Ashkenazi Rabbis' ambivalence toward this new reality is reflected in their rulings. They often added that, even though the origi-nal cause for the nonreclining posture of married women had admit-tedly been canceled out, the custom remained unchanged by most Jews. It was apparently one thing to transcend social mores long gone and quite another to challenge existing etiquette. Perhaps even more importantly, broadening the definition of "important women" at the seder table did not inspire most Jews to institute an equal share of freedom for women in other spheres of life. No one seemed to take any action toward educating communities to treat women differently, until the spirit of egalitarianism took root in post-Emancipation Europe and America. Even today, while many of us already celebrate a Judaism that offers an equal share of freedom for women, Ultra-Orthodox rabbis react by rejecting this change outright, issuing halakhic decisions forbidding women to recline at the seder: this could only result in licentiousness and therefore should be avoided with as much care as *chametz* on Pesach.[10]

When I visit my neighboring Bedouins, I am considered an "important woman." I am entertained in the guests' tent; I am directed to sit on the mattress and recline on my left on the pillow while food and drinks are served for me to hold up in my right hand. For I am an important woman—a stranger, a gender apart, the untouchable and unmarriable woman—and therefore I can participate in the formal event in full. The core of the event is, of course, the discussion that develops among those allowed to have a voice. The women of the household are nowhere to be seen; in fact, they are more tucked away when I am around than in their everyday life. It's the closest I get to understanding the Talmud's perspective on this issue.

I call upon us all to think about this when we recline at the seder. Have we done away with the ancient division of women into two camps so that we can be ruled and exploited more efficiently for the various services we can supply? I am afraid not. Those of us privileged enough to be allowed into the still patriarchal world of respectable occupations and roles are not only often silenced and marginalized there but also forced to pay a price for our presence. For as we take our place as the "good women"—those allowed to have some kind of voice at the table—we legitimize this world, and its systems, by our participation within it. And meanwhile, many women—many of us—are being abominably abused as sex objects, trafficked, raped, or humiliated in the media.

When I recline at the seder, I renew my commitment to work toward mending all these wrongs.

≋

Setting a Cup for Miriam

VANESSA L. OCHS

It goes without saying that every Jewish object was once new. But how do we—Jewish women engaged in the creation and development of new rituals—come to experience a new ritual object as authentic? In this reflection, I explore this question, both as an anthropologist studying Miriam's Cup and as a Jewish feminist incorporating the ritual into my own Passover seder.

Miriam's Cup honors the prophetess Miriam, highlighting her role in the Exodus story and invoking her healing and creative presence. Containing water, it evokes and accesses the sustaining waters of Miriam's well. The object and the ritual are central to the developing Passover practice of honoring Jewish women, historical and familiar, by telling their stories; recalling their contributions as guides and liberators; and seeing oneself as their heir, an inspirational force in the lives of others.

Which came first—the cup or the ritual? According to folklorist Penina Adelman, a scholar of this new ritual and one of its innovators, the answer is neither. Miriam's presence came first—a presence that appeared and appealed to Jewish women born into a historical period in which Jewish women grasped the authority to ritualize their own experiences and to remember Jewish women of the past, those silenced or forgotten.[1]

Adelman tells the story of the origin of the Miriam's Cup rituals. In 1978 in Philadelphia, she joined a group of Jewish women for a "women's night in the *sukkah*." It is customary to "invite" biblical guests *(ushpizen)* into one's *sukkah*, but instead of inviting the traditional guests—who have always been male—this group invited their

---

Vanessa L. Ochs is the author of *Words on Fire: One Woman's Journey into the Sacred* and *Safe and Sound: Protecting Your Child in an Unpredictable World*. She is coauthor with Elizabeth Ochs of *The Jewish Dream Book: The Key to Opening the Inner Meaning of Your Dreams* and coeditor with Irwin Kula of *The Book of Jewish Sacred Practices* (both Jewish Lights Publishing). She is Ida and Nathan Kolodiz Director of Jewish Studies at the University of Virginia and is associate professor of religious studies.

"illustrious female ancestors." All agreed to invite Miriam, the expert in celebrations, who had the foresight to bring bells and tambourines out of Egypt. Miriam joined them, bringing the gift of visions. After all the women shared the visions they had received from Miriam, their host poured everyone a glass of water, and they drank to Miriam, "savoring the sublime taste of water which had been graced by her presence."[2]

Following this experience, Adelman wrote a Rosh Chodesh ritual honoring Miriam in her book *Miriam's Well: Rituals for Jewish Women Around the Year*. Adelman later recounts that in 1989, an ongoing Boston Rosh Chodesh group adapted this ritual, centering it on the legend of Miriam's well. Stephanie Loo and Matia Angelou, members of the Rosh Chodesh group, created "the ritual of drinking from the cup of Miriam in their own homes. Thus, the constant interplay between written word, spoken word, and ritual act generates ever-evolving forms of the ritual."[3]

Looking back, Adelman remembers how naturally and spontaneously this particular symbol came into being. As one of the initiators recalls, "... it was as if *Kos Miryam* already existed and was just waiting to be discovered." It was there, ready to meet the ritual needs of the group.

This sentiment links the initiators of Miriam's Cup to a larger trend among Jews creating new rituals. Jewish innovators and reformers have always attempted to obscure the newness of a truly new or newly borrowed ritual object. As religious historian Erwin Goodenough explains, "[t]he most successful religious reformers have invariably insisted that they were bringing in nothing new but were discovering the true meaning inherent from the first symbols of the religion they were reforming."[4]

This process is in keeping with historian Eric Hobsbawm's formulation of the "invented tradition," in which inventors of new traditions dip into the vast repositories of a culture's rituals and symbols, obscuring the "break in continuity" actually intended.[5] Emphasizing the link to the past, it becomes possible to simultaneously disguise and legitimize such innovation. The Miriam's Cup ritual evokes traditional rituals such as Elijah's Cup and familiar ideas like Miriam's well. It focuses on connections to the past, as participants imagine themselves as daughters of Miriam, and it affirms the continuing presence of the ancient well. Still, it is an entirely new ritual—a ritual as much about change in the present and future as continuity with the past. Yet, the Miriam's Cup ritual serves to preserve, at least, the illusion of continuity, even when—or especially when—it masks radical departures.

The introduction of a new ritual object allows Jewish women to resolve complicated issues that would potentially provoke arguments if they were approached in a more direct way. Scholars of folklore call this practice coding, referring to ways in which women in many cultures have both addressed and resolved important issues subtly, avoiding detection. By placing a Miriam's Cup on the table without discussion, a woman avoids asking her family, "May I introduce a new women's ritual? Is it permissible according to Jewish law and our family's practice for me to introduce a new Jewish practice that has been coined by contemporary women and that celebrates women's activism?" By placing the cup on the table as a fait accompli, the woman avoids arguments and debates and yet changes the status quo.

New ritual objects, in particular, can make ritual innovation more readily acceptable to tradition-bound, conservative individuals or communities, those particularly anxious about innovation. In this context, objects disguise the novelty of a ritual by building it within some familiar artifact, something that looks and feels "traditionally" or "authentically" Jewish.

When the ritual began to spread from Rosh Chodesh groups to homes, where it was used to meet private needs, Miriam's Cup became the property of the community. There, it became linked to one particular holiday and to one particular Passover ritual: the seder. The dissemination of the ritual occurred primarily through the proliferation of women's seders, which began first in the feminist centers of the East and West Coasts and eventually moved into Jewish community centers, synagogue sisterhoods, and Hadassah groups all over the country. At first, versions of the ritual were passed from one group's handmade haggadah to the next; now, they are available in several published haggadahs. Today, the ritual hardly looks innovative. Once the cup became connected to the Passover seder, its stronghold increased dramatically.

American Jewish families now experience Miriam's Cup alongside other venerable traditions, such as eating matzah or dipping a green vegetable in salt water, rather than as a new-fangled, fringe, feminist, or political gesture to be easily dismissed. Whether they first encountered Miriam's Cup in someone else's home, in a new haggadah, in an article from the Jewish media, or in an Internet search, this new ritual has found its way into a growing number of seders.

Miriam's Cup entered my own family's seder on Passover of the year 2000. I had planned to attend the seders of relatives, but at the very last minute I needed to stay at home and to make my own family seders—something I had not done for years. Being at my own seders with just my immediate family and any guests we chose to invite (at this last moment, they would invariably be Christian friends without Passover plans) meant that I, as the member of my family who leads rituals, would be in charge. I was positioned to introduce a new Passover ritual—something I would not have felt comfortable doing at someone else's seder, given how strongly people feel about maintaining control over their own family traditions. The urge to have a Miriam's Cup ritual in our seder welled up in me.

I had hoped I could quickly turn to one haggadah in my collection of homemade, feminist, and new haggadahs and find a Miriam's Cup ritual that appealed to me. But, like Goldilocks, I found something not "just right" about each one. In one case, the liturgy was moving, but the placement in the order of the seder felt wrong. In another, the ritual action seemed appealing, but the liturgy sounded too feminist for a mixed-gender group. In another, the liturgy was not feminist enough for me. In the end, I gathered together bits and pieces of ritual actions and liturgy into my own Miriam's Cup text.

Next, I had to decide where in the seder to place the new ritual.

But before I'd decided, the night of the seder arrived, so I resolved to spontaneously find the proper moment in the seder—one that just felt right. Having forgotten to buy spring water, I used Brita filtered water instead. For the cup, I searched my basement and found a red-stemmed plastic champagne goblet that had caught my eye at a Pier One sale years before. Since I had never used it, it was kosher for Passover, and, because the women in my family value items that are on sale and purchase them even when they're not necessary, I thought—with a wink—that this bargain of a cup would be our Miriam's Cup, as it would honor the women in my line who are smart shoppers.

But then I recalled that I had bought a ceramic Miriam's Cup from Betsy Platkin Teutsch at the Yale Jewish women's conference the year before. At the time, I didn't buy it because I needed it. I didn't know whether I would ever perform a seder ritual with it. I bought it because I wanted it. It matched my Miriam's tambourine. It was a new thing on the market. It was made by an artist whose work I like to collect. Unlike the Miriam's Cups I had seen and coveted at exhibitions, this was one I could afford. Maybe, in the back of my mind, I imagined that if I owned the cup I might desire to perform the ritual—perhaps having the necessary props would be the impetus I needed. And if my desire was strong enough, I could figure out how to introduce it at a seder sometime. But I had no specific plans. Like the doggie in the pet store window, the cup would not let me leave without taking it home.

Once home, I put the cup away in my cabinet for Jewish ritual objects, not knowing whether I would one day use it as it was intended or just save it as a Jewish artifact of a certain time, a certain place, and a certain sensibility.

Thus, Miriam got her proper cup, and Elijah—whose beverage needs I had yet to consider—ended up with the red champagne goblet (which was just fine, as the men in my family are equally fond of sales). During the first and second seders at our home, I led slightly different Miriam's Cup rituals. One night there was water already in the cup and we drank from it, toasting Miriam herself and the Miriams in our own lives. The next night, we each poured water from our cups to fill Miriam's Cup, and we waited for her to drink from it, inviting her and Elijah to our door simultaneously so that, together, they could bring healing to our world.

I improvised both nights, but—masking my tentativeness and anxiety about introducing something new—I facilitated the rituals with all the authority I could muster, as if I had been doing this ritual for years, as if Jews had been doing this from the beginning of time. What I did know for sure was that I was *not* the only person introducing or observing a Miriam's Cup ritual for the first time that Passover. I was not the only person using a newly purchased Miriam's Cup or pressing another cup into service. I was emboldened by this sense of being part of a community of novice celebrants. Even at the first seder, the ritual already felt quite right to me. By the second seder, I felt as if we had been performing a Miriam's Cup ritual for years with this very cup and would naturally continue to do so for years to come. As our guests had never been to a seder before, they accepted the ritual as one apparently ordained by my God and my tradition, along with all the others. My family opined that "we did it the right way."

There is a Jewish expression, "Three times is a *chazaka*," which means that once ritual practice is carried out three times, it acquires the status of *minhag,* a tradition that has all the weight of law. If, in the spirit of "Three times is a *chazaka*," I were to observe the ritual of Miriam's Cup just one more time in the future, it might become our family tradition—one observed by my children, by theirs, and by theirs after them—because not doing it would feel wrong to the family, as if something were missing from the seder that made it less real, less complete. When a new Jewish tradition is experienced as being authentic, not just by one person but by a "community's willingness to affirm it,"[1] then it *is* authentic.

The Celebration of Challenge: Reclaiming the Four Children

LEORA EISENSTADT

The Torah speaks of four types of children: one who is wise and one who is wicked; one who is simple and one who does not even know how to ask a question.[1] *The wise child asks, "What is the meaning of the laws, statutes, and customs, which the Lord our God has commanded to us? And you shall explain to him all the laws of Passover, to the very last detail about the* afikomen.*"*

The wicked child asks, "What is the meaning of this ceremony to you?" Saying "to you," he excludes himself from the group and thus denies a basic principle of our faith. You may therefore set his teeth on edge and say to him, "This is done because of what the Lord did for me when I came forth from Egypt." For me and not for him; had he been there, he would not have been redeemed.

The simple child asks, "What is this about?" To him, you shall say, "With a strong hand the Lord brought us from Egypt, from the house of bondage."

As for the child who does not know to ask, you must begin/open him, as it is written, "And you shall tell your child on that day, 'This is done because of what the Lord did for me when I came forth from Egypt.'"[2]

At the traditional seder we read this memorable passage about the Four Children, both the questions and the scripted responses to them: questions and answers that Jews have shared around the seder table for centuries. It is a midrash in which the author elaborates on four biblical passages indicating questions "your children" will ask in the future. The author of this passage names these questioners as sons, and, according to each son's question, attributes to him a distinct personality and relationship to Judaism.

Leora Eisenstadt graduated from Yale University in 1999 and is currently studying law at New York University. She plans to pursue a career in women's rights and civil rights law.

In this creative revision, I use the same midrashic method and the same biblical quotations to create an alternative interpretation of the Four Children. Reinventing the four questioners as daughters, I examine their questions and explore the personalities from which these questions might have emerged, thus expanding our understanding of this sparse yet evocative passage.

The haggadah's portrait of the wise child is based on a biblical passage from Deuteronomy that foresees a future son asking, "What mean the testimonies, and the statutes, and the ordinances, which the Lord our God has commanded you?"[3] The haggadah venerates this child as the son who desires to learn about the laws and rules of the tradition and understand the need for them. Yet, the haggadah—and, indeed, much of our Jewish tradition as a whole—also celebrates his question, balancing the importance of our "laws, statutes, and customs" with a validation of questioning itself. In this spirit, our midrash on the wise woman, the *chachama*, will celebrate the woman who asks questions of both the laws and the boundaries handed down to her.

In modern Hebrew, *chachama* has two meanings: "wise woman" and "midwife." The midwife, the wise woman—what does she ask, what does she challenge? For the answer, we look to the midwives of our own tradition, Shifra and Puah, the first heroines of the Book of Exodus:

> The king of Egypt spoke to the Hebrew midwives, one of whom was named Shifra and the other Puah, saying, "When you deliver the Hebrew women, look at the birthstool: if it is a boy, kill him; if it is a girl, let her live." The midwives, fearing God, did not do as the king of Egypt had told them; they let the boys live. So the king of Egypt summoned the midwives and said to them, "Why have you done this thing, letting the boys live"? The midwives said to Pharaoh, "Because the Hebrew women are not like the Egyptian women: they are vigorous. Before the midwife can come to them, they have given birth." And God dealt well with the midwives; and the people multiplied and increased greatly.[4]

What do these *chachamot* ask? Whom do they challenge? They challenge the ruler of Egypt. They challenge a culture of total obedience to the king. They challenge the notion that we should abide by the rules and guidelines no matter the human cost. Without their willingness to question the ideology of those in power, we would not have survived to tell our story.

The *chachama* in our midrash asks about the laws and rules and, in so doing, asks us to teach her about our relationship to those rules. We can answer the *chachama* at our seder table by explaining that she can act in the tradition of Shifra and Puah. We can share with the wise daughter the lessons that Shifra and Puah teach: that questions are at the heart of movements for freedom, that questioning the powerful is the first seed of liberation. The wisdom of the *chachama* is that she knows when, whom, and what to challenge.

Traditionally, the wicked son is understood as the one who does not know what to challenge; he brings an unacceptable question to the seder table. This child is based on a verse in which God instructs the Israelites that their children will one day ask the question, "What does this service/work mean to you?"[5] The haggadah emphasizes "to you" and thus interprets this question as evidence that the child does not view himself as a member of the community. His separation from the community is seen as grave and dangerous, meriting a severe response. The original midrash hears anger and alienation in the child's question and offers a harsh response, stating that, had the child been present at the redemption, he would not have been redeemed.

But we can read this question differently. Perhaps the "wicked" daughter is not isolating herself from the community but merely challenging her elders. "*Is* there meaning for you?" she asks. "Do you simply follow blindly without questioning? What is your connection to this tradition and its rituals?" We choose not to hear exclusion in the question, and we are therefore able to respond with inclusion. We can hear this child's question as a genuine search for meaning, and we respond by embracing and internalizing it. Our own observance is enriched, not threatened, by her question.

Although each of us must answer the "wicked" daughter's question from our own hearts, we can look to our tradition to encourage us to craft our response with sensitivity and compassion. The biblical women who also dared to ask a question that was not supposed to be asked are our inspiration. The "daughters of Zelophehad"—Mahlah, Noah, Hoglah, Milcah, and Tirzah—pushed their tradition to recognize and include them.[6] When their father died, leaving no sons as heirs, these five women insisted to Moses that, although it was contrary to the customs of their patriarchal society, they should have the right to partake of the inheritance. Zelophehad's five daughters questioned the patriarchy of Jewish society in ways that no woman or man had ever done before. And God agreed. God endorsed the challenge that they raised and, in this way, also supported the very act of questioning. Just as the difficult question asked by Mahlah, Noah, Hoglah, Milcah, and Tirzah forced their community to confront a problem, so too can the question of the "wicked" daughter, which asks us to articulate our relationship to our tradition, help us to improve ourselves. In this spirit, we reclaim this child and interpret her words anew, recognizing her courage and internalizing the challenge she puts forth.

While the "wicked" child teaches us to ask the questions we are not officially sanctioned to ask, the simple child teaches us to ask another important question. The haggadah's portrayal of the third child, the simple son, draws on the Exodus verse that foretells, "There shall come a time when the child shall ask, 'What is this?'"[7] The haggadah describes this child as "simple" because of the seemingly simple nature of his question. But, in the biblical text, "What is this?" immediately follows these words: "That thou shalt set apart unto the Lord all that openeth the womb; every firstling that is a male, which thou hast coming of a beast shall be the Lord's...and all the first born of man among thy sons shalt thou redeem."[8] What does this child ask? She asks, "What is this?" Why are only the males redeemed by God? Where am I in this tradition? The simple daughter asks the most fundamental and difficult of questions.

To answer this most fundamental of questions, we turn to our most fundamental beginning: "And God created humans in God's own image, in the image of God created, male and female God created them.'"[9] In the first chapter of the Torah, we read a profound statement of the parity of male and female. While the rest of the Torah's lessons and stories may not include equality between women and men, we find strength in these earliest moments. We can respond to the simple daughter's painful question and her feeling of absence in her own tradition by recalling this time of gender equality. We explain that we understand the anger and hurt implicit in her challenge. We tell her that we share her question and continue to search for an answer. We thank her for teaching us to ask the questions so fundamental that we may forget to ask them at all.

The fourth child, the son who does not know how to ask, raises perhaps the most difficult and personal challenge. This child moves beyond the questions we may forget to ask to remind us of the questions we are unable to articulate, though they remain inside us. In creating the fourth child, the "child who does not know how to ask," the haggadah responds to a biblical passage that provides only the answer, with no accompanying question.[10] Why create this child at all? Why not simply include the three questions actually quoted in the Torah? The fact that we are asked to formulate a response to the child who cannot even ask a question only further highlights the absolute necessity of the process of questioning. The haggadah assumes that behind any child's silence there are valuable, unasked questions.

How do we respond to a daughter without questions? What do we do for the child who cannot engage in our celebration of questioning? The haggadah states, *"At ptach lah!"* You, *woman,* open her! This injunction forces us to open not only our children but also ourselves to this process, finding the strength to bring forth new questions and challenges. In this midrash, we learn that, even when we feel incapable of asking our questions or voicing our challenges, we must not give up. We must simply push harder to find the strength, courage, and knowledge within ourselves.

There are times when we all resemble the child who does not know to ask, when our silence overwhelms us. It is, perhaps, this child's role to remind the seder participants of our own silences and the people who gave voice to our silent questions. She reminds us that we find comfort in voicing our questions, whether or not we find answers. In response to this child who does not know to ask, we can take a moment in the seder to remember the parent, friend, teacher, or whomever it was who was able to alleviate some of our pain by creating the space for our questions.

In reinterpreting this ancient passage of the haggadah, we address the questioner in each of us: invoking the wise daughter to guide us in discerning who, what, and when to question; welcoming the "wicked child" to ask the questions that we have been conditioned to turn away from or repress; honoring the simple child who shows us the fundamental questions at the core of all our learning and discovery; and, above all, opening the silent child within us, learning to define and articulate questions that we have not been able to ask before. As we question and engage with our texts and traditions, our relationship to them grows stronger. We can learn from the four daughters how to celebrate both the question and she who asks it.

≈≈≈

Orange on the Seder Plate
SUSANNAH HESCHEL

Passover was high family drama in my childhood. Preparations began weeks in advance, with meticulous scrubbing, shopping, and organizing. Strong emotions came out in the two days before the holiday, when the kitchen was half kosher for Passover, half *chametz,* and everyone had to tread very carefully. One mistake could bring calamity. One year, the Passover dishes were mistakenly washed with the wrong

---

Dr. Susannah Heschel is the Eli Black Associate Professor of Jewish Studies at Dartmouth College. She is the author of numerous studies of modern Jewish thought, including *Abraham Geiger and the Jewish Jesus,* which won the National Jewish Book Award, and a classic collection of essays, *On Being a Jewish Feminist.*

sponge, prompting an emergency trip downtown to buy a new set of dishes just hours before the seder.

Then came the cooking. My mother ground the fish in a hand grinder, ground the liver and onions in another grinder, washed the masses of vegetables, separated dozens of egg yolks for ten sponge cakes, and put the right ingredients in the right pots—but it was up to my father to add the spices. He was the seasoning expert who would appear in the kitchen every few hours; taste the boiling sweet and sour carp, the chicken soup, the chopped liver; and determine which pots needed pinches of cloves, salt, garlic, sugar, and pepper.

The two days before Pesach were the most intense part of the holiday for our family. Searching with a candle for the *chametz* the night before the holiday, burning it in the morning, and then making anxious last-minute runs to the store until, in the afternoon, panic set in. My mother always became frantic. At that point, husband and daughter became too much, so she banished us from the apartment. We went across the street to Riverside Park, where we joined the sad, quiet parade of husbands and children banished from their homes while frenzied wives did their last-minute cooking in the hours before the holiday began. We walked for an hour or two, feeling our exile, worried about when we could return home and be welcomed, and feeling guilty that my mother was exhausting herself.

When we finally sat down at the table for the seder that evening, we heard the same liturgy from my mother every year: If the men had to do all this work, the Rabbis never would have made these laws! Only women understand the true meaning of Egypt; only women have to slave away for weeks of preparation for Passover!

No Exodus quite yet for my mother. While my father presided over the seder, with a dozen friends and colleagues present, my mother was back in the kitchen, hovering over the pots: preparing, serving, washing.

I never quite knew where I belonged. I wanted to be with my father, listening to his explanations of the haggadah, reading the Hebrew texts, enjoying the splendor of the beautiful table. But I also wanted to stay in the kitchen, helping my mother and urging her to sit down with the guests, to rest, and to enjoy the seder. Wherever I was, I felt guilty for abandoning the other parent.

There were, in effect, two seders taking place: the liturgical seder led by my father, and the seder of the meal and of serving the guests. Passover is about liturgy *and* food; both reenact slavery, the Exodus, and the promise of redemption. How could they be brought together? At the ritual commemoration of the Exodus, what could we do to recognize the slavery created by the obligations of the seder itself?

Frankly, recognition alone was not what I wanted. My mother once told a pious professor of Talmud, "If I met the Rabbis who created the Passover laws, I'd give them a piece of my mind." The male gender privilege is enacted each year as the men interpret the laws of preparing for Passover and preside as kings over the seder, without participating in the scrubbing, shopping, cooking, serving, and washing. Only a radical change, a social revolution, will change that.

My own experience of radical change came after the death of my father. I suddenly found myself in both positions—in charge of the kitchen work and also leading our family seder. I looked for various ways to bring the experience of preparation to the seder table. Preparing for Passover is an essential *mitzvah,* as important as the seder itself, but it has become for so many of us simply a chore, devoid of liturgical attention. When the matzah is baked before Passover (usually by men), the task is accompanied by the recitation of psalms. But women's food preparation for the holiday has come to be devalued as a secular activity, rather than respected as a *mitzvah.* I had long known that Chasidim understand setting the seder table and arranging the seder plate as religious acts, accompanied by kabbalistic meditations. I decided to share this idea with my guests and asked them to arrive early and participate in that process.

Yet, overcoming the gap between kitchen and seder table was only a small gesture of social change. I also wanted the seder guests to be aware that while, on the one hand, we were celebrating the collective liberation of the Jewish people from Egyptian slavery, on the other hand, Passover was reinforcing gender and sexual enslavement. How could we bring that reality to our consciousness?

During the years just after my father's death, I started reading some wonderful feminist analyses that helped me understand the enslavement my mother experienced and the conflicts I felt between kitchen and seder. Mary Daly's book *Beyond God the Father* rescued me from my confusion about the way Judaism honored religious study and synagogue observance while at the same time excluding women from full participation in these arenas. From Daly I learned that the problem was not laws relegating women to second-class status but rather a symbol-system that placed holiness in the male domain. "If God is male, then the male is God," Daly observed.[1] At the same time, I learned from Adrienne Rich about "compulsory heterosexuality" and the connections between social and sexual regulation of women.[2] I knew, from my own experience, that women who asked too many questions and rebelled against their prescribed status used to be charged with witchcraft and now were likely to be called lesbians—as if that were a status of shame. I also understood that women without husbands or fathers (like my mother and me) were left in a kind of social limbo in the Jewish community. "Lesbian" had become a whip in society's disciplinary regimen used against any woman who deviated from the strict gender rules.

In the early 1980s, the Hillel Foundation invited me to speak on a panel at Oberlin College. While on campus, I came across a haggadah that had been written by some Oberlin students to express feminist concerns. The haggadah included a wonderful story about a feminist *rebbe* at her *tisch* (table), surrounded by her disciples, celebrating the seder. One disciple asked her, "*Rebbe,* why is there a crust of bread on the seder plate?" She sighed and answered, "Years ago, a family of women was preparing for Passover, cooking and cleaning, singing and rejoicing, and the youngest, Puah, aged fifteen, announced, 'I have a question, and I'm going to ask the rabbi!' She went to see the rabbi of the town, known for his strictness and learning, and he was delighted to see her: a question just before Passover usually meant that a crumb of *chametz* had fallen into the chicken soup pot, and he could then pronounce that everything had to be thrown out—the soup, the pot, the whole kitchen—instructing the family that they had to start all over again. 'Ask, my child,' he said. She asked, 'Rabbi, what room is there in Judaism for a lesbian?' 'What!' screamed the rabbi, outraged. He jumped up, grabbed her by the shoulders (forgetting that he shouldn't touch a woman), and shouted, 'There's as much room for a lesbian in Judaism as there is for a crust of bread on the seder plate!'"

"And that," the feminist *rebbe* said, "is why we have a crust of bread on the seder plate."

The Oberlin story was wonderful, and the ritual of placing a crust of bread on the seder plate in response to it was inspiring to me. But I couldn't follow it literally. Including bread on the seder plate destroys Passover—it renders everything *chametz*. And its symbolism suggests that being a lesbian is being transgressive, violating Judaism, which is not true. I wanted to celebrate being gay or lesbian as one of many great ways to be Jewish and to mark the fruitfulness created in human society by the diversity of our sexualities. I also wanted to call attention to the links between the homophobia that has made the lives of gays and lesbians so difficult and the gender discrimination experienced by Jewish women.

So at our next Passover, I decided to place an orange (actually, I used a tangerine!) on our family's seder plate. I chose an orange because it suggests the fruitfulness for all Jews when lesbians and gay men are contributing and active members of Jewish life. "Be fruitful and multiply"[3] is the Bible's first commandment, and we need to recognize the fruitfulness of gay and lesbian presence, and encourage that presence to multiply.

Early in the seder, I asked everyone to take a segment of the fruit, say the blessing over it, and eat it to symbolize our solidarity with Jewish lesbians and gay men as well as with others who are marginalized within the Jewish community. Since each tangerine segment has a few seeds, we added the gesture of spitting them out at that seder, recognizing and repudiating the sin of homophobia that poisons too many Jews.

During the ritual I also mentioned widows, thinking of my mother, whose experience of social marginalization following the death of my father was painful to watch. No longer part of a couple, she was not invited to friends' homes or to evenings at the theatre. While I didn't say anything, I wanted to mention orphans, thinking of myself. In Jewish tradition, the loss of a father makes you an orphan, even if your mother is still alive. That is certainly also true in patriarchal societies. The death of my father had suddenly and radically altered my position—something I felt acutely in every social situation from the synagogue to interactions with friends. Losing a husband and father meant that our household had lost much of its status in patriarchal society.

And, thinking about my own family experience, I also saw the orange as representing the fruitfulness that results when women lead the seder. In so many ways, my life was one of struggling to be part of Judaism—struggling for a bat mitzvah, an *aliyah,* the right to say kaddish, inclusion in the *minyan.* All the barriers that my generation of feminists was able to pull down needed public markers. Yet, celebrating women's inclusion in the synagogue had become, even at that time, a mainstream, conventional act, whereas gay and lesbian Jews were still behind barriers. While the feminist movement was reaching a stage of acceptance in the Jewish community that made it unacceptable to ridicule its efforts, Jewish attitudes—even in the years after the Stonewall riot (the major gay revolt against homophobia, in New York City in 1969)—remained hostile and mocking toward gay liberation.

The connections between my struggles for recognition as a woman, my mother's social banishment as a widow, and the erasure of gay and lesbians within the Jewish tradition were clear. The place for women is small and narrow, and sexual options are confined, and—if limited to heterosexuality only—unnatural.

Thus, while I originally placed an orange on my family seder plate for a combination of reasons that were indeed related to women's marginality in Judaism, my fundamental message was clear: we ate the orange to express our solidarity with gay and lesbian Jews. To speak of slavery and long for liberation demands that we acknowledge our own complicity in enslaving others.

Over the years, when lecturing, I often mentioned my custom as one of many new feminist rituals that had been developed in the past twenty years. I always identified it as an act of solidarity with lesbians and gay men. I talked about the celebration of homosexuality in medieval Hebrew poetry, about homoeroticism in classical rabbinic and kabbalistic texts, and about the ways in which a homosexual hermeneutic might help us understand some of the experiences underlying male-authored Jewish theology, which expresses passionate love of a male God. I drew parallels between the experiences of closeted gays and Jews who have hidden their identities in different historical eras, from the enslaved Israelites in Egypt to the Marranos who concealed their religious practices to modern Jews striving to assimilate. And I was ashamed when gay and lesbian Jews thanked me for naming homophobia a sin, because, they said, rarely did anyone in the Jewish community do so.

After a few years, I discovered a strange and disturbing phenomenon: strangers started telling me that they were placing an orange on their seder plate because they had heard a story about me. The story went like this: After a lecture I delivered in Miami Beach, a man stood up and angrily denounced feminism, saying that a woman no more belongs on the *bimah* than an orange belongs on the seder plate. After hearing this tale dozens of times, all over the country, I realized that my story had fallen victim to a kind of folktale process in which my custom was affirmed but my original intention was subverted. My idea— a woman's words—were attributed to a man, and my goal of affirming lesbians and gay men was erased.

For years I had read studies by feminist scholars about women who had ghostwritten men's books or whose scientific discoveries were attributed to men. I read such studies with a kind of distance, sure that such things could never happen today—and certainly not to me. Yet, I had experienced that same, typical patriarchal maneuver.

Nowadays I know of lots of people who place an orange on their seder plate, and I have even seen new seder plates designed with a place for the orange. The explanations given for including this ritual in the seder are usually far removed from my original intentions. The orange has come to signify a general affirmation of Jewish women, rather than Jewish lesbians and gay men. While I am delighted by any effort to recognize women in a Jewish context, I worry about the process that led from my original goal to the present, more watered-down version. I certainly support the inclusion of women and the empowerment of women, but nowadays, outside the Orthodox community, that is hardly radical or controversial. What does remain a deep and intractable problem, however, is the pervasive homophobia in Jewish life. The issue is not merely one of inclusion but also one of removing a toxin that has infiltrated our minds and souls.

Passover remembers enslavement and celebrates liberation. The matzah itself is double-valenced—a symbol of slavery and of freedom. I would hope the orange can also have a double significance, reminding us of the ways homophobia poisons our lives and the ways homosexuality enriches our community.

The transformation of the orange's significance might itself prompt us to consider how deeply ingrained patriarchy remains in our modern society. But beyond that, my hope is for the orange to once again bear the meaning I originally intended for it: a ritual object that helps the Jewish community to take an important first step—speaking into existence gay and lesbian Jews.

≈≈≈

The Open Door: The Tale of Idit and the Passover Paradox

SANDY EISENBERG SASSO

On Passover evening, when we celebrate the Exodus from Egypt, we open the doors of our homes at the conclusion of the seder meal to welcome the prophet Elijah. But at this observance, called in the Bible a night of vigil, we greet Elijah not with words of blessing but with scriptural verses that invoke God's wrath upon those nations that have threatened us. As we open the door we are instructed to recite: "Pour out Your wrath upon those who do not know You..." declaring to the world that we will seek vengeance against our enemies.

In the Genesis narrative of Sodom and Gomorrah, we also encounter an open door. Usually intended as a sign of hospitality, here the door is opened to a violent mob, which threatens the rape of Lot's daughters. This moment is the precursor to another exodus—not the flight of Israelite slaves from Egypt, but the flight of Lot's family from the wrath of God poured on Sodom and Gomorrah. The open doors of the seder and of Sodom connect the two stories of exodus.

This is the retelling of the story of that other exodus: the exodus of a family and, in particular, of a woman—the wife of Lot.

A pillar of salt lost in a dead sea was once a woman, named Idit. Now her warm embrace, her painful witness is frozen in salt and cattle lick it all day long. It seems to melt away, but when morning dawns, it stands there still, as large as before.[1]

Who was this woman, biblically nameless, but identified in a rabbinic source as "Idit,"[2] "the chosen one"?

She followed her husband, Lot, from her home in Haran to

Rabbi Sandy Eisenberg Sasso has been rabbi of Congregation Beth-El Zedeck in Indianapolis since 1977. She is the author of several nationally acclaimed children's books. *But God Remembered: Stories of Women from Creation to the Promised Land* and *Noah's Wife: The Story of Na'amah* (both Jewish Lights Publishing) were selected as Best Books of the Year. Most recently, she is the author of *Cain and Abel: Finding the Fruits of Peace* (Jewish Lights Publishing) and the editor of *Urban Tapestry: Indianapolis Stories.*

Sodom. She followed Lot and did not turn back—not once. Lot journeyed on the promise made to his uncle Abraham that he would become a great nation and be richly blessed, but Idit never heard this promise. Lot traveled on that vision, and Idit traveled only on a donkey. Yet, she went with Lot to a strange land and did not turn back.

Idit gave birth to five daughters in Sodom, but Sodom was not what Lot's distant vision had promised. There, stones sparkled with sapphires and the earth with the dust of gold. But the people of Sodom stole from one another and murdered for the sake of gain. No birds came to Sodom. The people took all the fruit from the trees, and the birds could not find food. It was in this cruel land that Idit and Lot made a home.[3]

When Idit's first child, Palotit, learned of a poor man begging in the streets of the city, she offered to help. Nurtured with loving-kindness, she had no fear of Sodom's rules, which punished those who showed compassion to the poor and the stranger. For the crime of giving bread to the hungry, the people of Sodom took her, bound her, surrounded her with kindling wood, and lit a fire.

Idit was grief-stricken, but she remained with Lot and her four other daughters. Two were married, and two were betrothed to men of Sodom.[4]

One night, Lot came home late in the evening. He was trembling, but his voice was strong: "Idit, strangers have arrived in the city. We must open our door to them. They are to be our guests." With that, Lot invited the strangers to enter their house. It was then that Idit's silence broke into rage.

She and Lot quarreled fiercely.[5] "Lot, listen to me. Hospitality to strangers cannot take precedence over the saving of life. Remember what happened to our beloved daughter, Palotit. Who knows what will happen to us? Tell our guests why they must leave. This is no ordinary city, no ordinary rules apply."

Lot refused to listen.

Idit and Lot had not yet gone to sleep when the townspeople, the men of Sodom, gathered about the house. Idit knew what they would demand. Did she know as well what her husband would do?

Lot opened the door to his home and went out to the townspeople. He pleaded with them not to rape his guests. He offered instead his daughters.

His daughters cried to him in terror and disbelief: "Father, we are your daughters, born of your seed. Have you still a mouth to plead for the people who make these demands?[6] Remember your firstborn, Palotit. Do not abandon us. Be our shield and protector. Deliver us from this madness."

Lot's brow was wet with sweat; yet, he stood his ground. He weighed the sins and upheld his code of hospitality, believing that the rape of his daughters was less an offense than the violation of his guests. Lot always lived according to the rules.

The outcry of Idit and her daughters reached to the heavens, to the God of Idit and Palotit. "Will not the Judge of all the earth deal justly with us? We have appealed to our father, but he is unwavering. We plead our case before You. Pour out Your wrath upon these people who do not know You. Heed the tears of our mother, Idit, who intercedes on our behalf. Listen to the cry of our sister, Palotit. Do justice in Sodom."

In an instant, a bright light blinded the men of Sodom. They stumbled over one another and could not find the entrance to Lot's home. It was then that Lot's guests, the ones he had protected, revealed that they had a divine mission. They informed Lot that the city of Sodom would be destroyed. They urged him to gather his family and escape. But when Lot told his sons-in-law of the divine decree, they mocked him. His married daughters would remain in Sodom.

When dawn broke, God's messengers led the way outside the city. Lot took the lead; Idit, as always, followed a step behind, her two unmarried daughters walking behind them both. As the sun began to rise, sulfurous fire poured out of the heavens upon Sodom, and the ground quaked.

So often before, Idit had followed Lot and had not turned back. This time was different. This time she turned back. She could no longer follow Lot, who only a few hours earlier had been ready to sacrifice the honor of her daughters. No longer sustained by the secret visions in Lot's eye, she could not follow the God of Abraham without question, without challenge. Her heart swollen with compassion for her daughters, she looked back, out of mother love, to see if they were following.[7] She lingered out of sympathy, out of lament for human life destroyed. She turned out of regret and anguish for life's grandeur wasted. She looked back for Palotit and for her two daughters, who remained within the city, now reduced to smoke and ashes.

She turned back and saw the wrath visited upon Sodom. Her turning was also a question, like Abraham's to God. Is this the birthing of redemption or the world's final kaddish? She turned and beheld the back of the Divine Presence and was consumed in tears.[8] Were her tears for Sodom or for God?

Her two daughters ran to hold her. Their mouths were filled with smoke and their legs trembled from exhaustion and fear. By the time they reached their mother, nothing remained but salt, as if she had been completely dissolved in her tears. The fire and the smoke of the city burning behind them forced them to leave her there—a pillar of salt on a once fertile plain. Lot never looked back. No one saw with Idit's eyes the wrath of God poured upon Sodom. Only her daughters bore witness to the reflection in their mother's eyes. From the descendants of Idit's daughters came Ruth, the great-grandmother of David; Naamah, the mother of Rehoboam; and from these kings, we are told, the promise of the Messiah.

Tradition records the day of Idit's death on the sixteenth of the month of Nisan.[9] This date coincides with the time when, centuries later, Israel would be freed from Egyptian bondage. As our sources connect Idit's death with the Feast of Freedom, we must bring her remembrance, her exodus, to the seder table.

Idit alone witnessed God's wrath poured upon the nations, spilling sulfurous fury on Sodom and Gomorrah.[10] At the conclusion of our seder meal, as we prepare to welcome Elijah, we pray for the pouring out of such divine wrath:

Shefoch chamatcha—Pour out Your wrath upon the nations that know You not, and upon the kingdoms that call not upon Your name; for they have consumed Jacob and laid waste his habitation. Pour out Your wrath upon them and let Your fury overtake them. Pursue them in anger and destroy them from under the heavens of the Eternal.[11]

How curious that as we open our doors in almost childlike wonder, anticipating the arrival of the legendary prophet Elijah, we recite this curse. How strange, as we open our doors to the promise of redemption, that our greeting is a jarring admonition. Medieval Jewish history recounts the evening of the seder as an occasion for pogroms and charges of blood libel. Jews were accused of kidnapping Christian children, murdering them, and using their blood to bake matzah. The door was opened out of the practical need to prove wrong the accuser. It was a night of watching, a vigil against the forces that threatened the community. Praying for Elijah's coming, our ancestors opened the door with apprehension over the destructive forces that gathered around them.

When our children run to open the door for Elijah, they anticipate a moment filled with promise. But maturity makes the door seem heavier and the open entry more ominous and foreboding. For Lot, the open door was a sign of hospitality; for Idit, it invited the rape of her daughters. At the seder we, incurable dreamers, open the door expecting Elijah, the promise of redemption. And yet, we, perennial realists, open the door, guarding against danger.

For women, open physiologically, an open door holds both the fear of being raped and the prospect of love fully given and received.[12] How can we open our doors to promise but not to violation? How can we remain open with the right to refuse entry?

This paradox of promise and fear remains central to the seder. Like Idit, we are at once angered over the forces that seek our destruction, saddened by the brokenness of life, and hopeful that redemption will yet come. If but one of these components is missing, the ritual fails. Anger—even righteous anger—with no hope of redemption, is corrosive and ultimately debilitating. Sorrow over the failures of humanity without outrage and the promise of change is the seed of depression and cynicism. Uncontrolled, it ultimately defeats us. And hope without the awareness of shattered lives and the reality of evil is wishful fantasy. Poised before the open door, about to recite *shefoch chamatcha,* we confront our deepest desires and most profound fears.

Much like Idit's daughters, exhausted and conscious of our vulnerability, we express our rage in the face of the darkness. We acknowledge our powerlessness before forces we cannot control. Yet, standing before the open door, our bodies and souls nourished by good food and ritual, we express our hope in the face of the unknown. We recognize our power over what we can change.

Let us join *shefoch chamatcha* to the sobering witness of Idit. As we open our doors at the close of the seder and prepare to recite the verses invoking God's wrath, we must see with Idit's eyes the horror of destruction. Perhaps if we turn with Idit to witness the wrath visited upon Sodom, we may be less likely to invoke it.

For Idit teaches us that the promise of Elijah does not follow necessarily from the destruction of the oppressor. The promise lies in her tears, in the sorrow of a woman pained by all that is annihilated and aching for all whom she cannot save. After Sodom and Gomorrah, there follows no messianic age. Divine wrath brings a reprieve, not a rebirth.

All too often, evildoers perish, but the systems of evil continue, only to give birth to a new generation of oppressors and victims. Yet, Idit's daughters, out of Sodom, go forth to create a new generation that bears the promise of redemption.

When Idit confronts, in all its ugliness, that which brings death and destruction, she refuses to give her consent, to turn away, to follow the vision of another's eye and the path of another's foot. She becomes a witness. We have become accustomed to seeing the pillar of salt on a barren plain as an eternal symbol of punishment for disobedience. In light of Idit's story, that pillar becomes a monument of tears—the tears of Idit, an eternal symbol of loving-kindness. Idit's daughters saw her act of love and her defiance. They saw the way of Idit—the recovery of the soul with a raging kindness. From the descendants of the daughters of Idit comes the promise of the Messiah.

As you open the door for Elijah and recite *shefoch chamatcha* at your seders, I invite you to remember Idit, the salt of her tears, and the promise in her story.

≈≈≈

A New Song for a Different Night: Sephardic Women's Musical Repertoire

JUDITH WACHS

She who took the ark
The sun and the moon shine upon her.
—FROM *"PAR'O ERA ESTREYERO"* ("PHARAOH WAS STARGAZING")

Despite the *kol isha*[1] stricture, which forbids women to sing when men are present, it is well known that in times of travail the voices of women have been called upon to inspire, nourish, and fortify the spirit of the community. Perhaps one of the most resonant musical images in literature is that of Miriam singing and dancing with her *tof* (tambourine) at the shore of the Reed Sea, leading the women in celebration of the escape from slavery in Egypt.[2] And when the Jews were expelled from Spain in 1492,[3] the rabbis encouraged the women and children to sing—with tambourines and drums—because they recognized the ability of music to alleviate the pain and suffering of all the people.

For more than five hundred years, Sephardic[4] women, the descen-

---

Judith Wachs is the founder and artistic director of Voice of the Turtle, a quartet that has been specializing in Judeo-Spanish musical traditions for twenty-four years. She also created and performed "Kitchen Archivists—The Role of Sephardic Women in Preserving Oral Traditions." She has created several radio scores, including the WGBH radio drama "Tell Me a Riddle" and *"Kol Ishah*—Voices of Jewish Women" for WMBR. She has been a performer of medieval, Renaissance, and traditional music for twenty-eight years.

dants of this traumatic exodus, continued to sing in exile to lift the spirits of their communities. Music was central to their daily lives, and this enabled them to create and preserve an astonishing musical heritage for five centuries. They were also able to maintain their language, Judeo-Spanish,[5] because women's traditional, home-centered lives were insulated from the larger society in which the men worked.

The nonliturgical Sephardic musical repertoire is composed of an enormous aggregate of Judeo-Spanish treasures transmitted through centuries primarily from mother to child, from grandmother to grandchild, from woman to woman, and from women to the community. This collection could be compared to a *genizah*—the hidden archive of old, sacred texts or community documents that are no longer of use and that are usually preserved within the synagogue. But this musical *genizah* was a living part of daily life. It was created and maintained despite—and perhaps in defiance of—the enormous upheavals and challenges that Jews of Spanish descent faced over the centuries. But, as it was "women's music," its importance was virtually hidden, its significance rarely recognized.

This precious cache—stories sung, remembered, carried, created, adapted, and adopted in all the new homelands of the Sephardic community—provided a unique form of historical documentation for many communities of Spanish Jews who had endured the Inquisition, forced conversions, displacement, exile, dispersal, reversals of fortune, and war. The songs, directly or obliquely, by metaphor or allusion, in a general or personal voice, addressed the subjects of personal and community loss, joy, love, war, history, geography, Bible stories, food, life-cycle celebrations—in short, everything experienced in life. But until the past twenty years, few people outside of Israel, even among Sephardim themselves, knew of or appreciated the extent, the value, or the significance of this repertoire. Even fewer studied how the women were able to perform this remarkable feat of preservation.[6]

I first heard Sephardic music, *"Skalerika de Oro"* ("Ladder of Gold") to be exact, in 1976, at a rehearsal for a concert of European medieval and Renaissance music. It is a song from the wedding repertoire traditionally sung by women. "A ladder of gold, and ivory...for the bride...even if she has no *dinero,* we still wish her *mazal bueno*!" I was dumbstruck, not only by the poetic imagery and the beauty of the song[7] but by the fact that I—well versed, I thought, in Jewish music—had no idea that this repertoire existed. This song resonated so strongly within me that it catalyzed a search for more, but I was surprised to learn that almost nothing—in English, at least—was readily available on the subject.

After digging through academic channels, I located in London one collection of the songs, *Chants Judeo-Espagnols,* edited by Isaac Levy.[8] It was relinquished to me with the caveat that I would promise to "guard it closely and use it wisely," as there were very few copies in existence. Shortly thereafter, I came upon a slim volume at the Harvard Music Library edited by Leon Algazi.[9] Both books include the melodic line of each song and the lyrics in Judeo-Spanish; the Levy volume also has a French translation of the songs. These songs had been passed down entirely through oral tradition, and as a result, there was no information in the collections on their origins.

Levy dedicates the book to his mother, "who in my childhood rocked me [in the cradle] with these songs and from whom I inherited my love of music." A few sentences in the introductions to Algazi's volume acknowledge the women who preserved these songs; elsewhere in the book Algazi remembers his mother singing while rocking an infant's cradle, as well as the voices of young girls singing Spanish love songs. Remembering the destruction of the entire community in Salonika during the Holocaust, Algazi also emphasizes the importance of not losing these Sephardic traditions.

While continuing my research over the years, collecting material directly from informants in Israel or in the United States and listening to field recordings,[10] I often heard elderly Sephardic women say: "This isn't important" (meaning that only liturgical songs were important) or "The real singer is the cantor." This self-deprecation was prevalent despite these women's extensive knowledge of a repertoire preserved entirely by memory, including hundreds of songs with complicated ornamentation requiring enormous vocal and aural sophistication. Deeming this unimportant meant denying not only their expertise and skill but also the critical role that their sung memories fulfilled.

Why these women didn't realize the value of their contribution is obvious to any feminist today. While women's traditional spheres of influence were admired, what men did—in this societal construct—was what was "really" important. This attitude was in part responsible for the devaluation, and ultimately the near disappearance, of something remarkable.

The Judeo-Spanish musical repertoire, preserved primarily by women, is largely represented by three genres often described as *romançes, coplas,* and *canciones.*[11] These genres are distinguished by a variety of poetic structures, musical forms, subjects, social functions, and performance practices. For the most part, the *romançes,* the old ballads from medieval Spain, told tales of kings and queens and knights and damsels in distress. But among the Sephardim, these ballads also recounted biblical stories and midrashic tales. For example, the popular Moroccan-Sephardic ballad *"Mosé salió de Misrayim"* ("Moses Went Out of Egypt") recounts the story of how Moses heard the voice of God instructing him to tell King Pharaoh to "let my people go." Through these songs, women were able to learn biblical stories.

One reason the *romançes* were preserved so thoroughly in exile was that they functioned as lullabies, sung nightly by mothers to their children. These were not, for the most part, of the "sleep my child" variety, but rather tales of the old country—bedtime stories from medieval Spain. While falling asleep, the children could imagine their own history and thus to some extent identify with the community's continuing affection for Spain, despite the trauma and injustice of the Inquisition and expulsion.

Coplas, a second genre of Sephardic poetry and song, focused on teaching Jewish history and holidays through midrash and biblical stories. This genre was widely considered to be a men's repertoire, but it is evident from the collections that women played a large role in their conservation.

"Kuando Moshe Rabeynu" ("When Moses Our Teacher"), a *copla* transmitted through an informant from Bulgaria,[12] recounts the biblical scene of Moses receiving the Ten Commandments. *"Mosé, Mosé, Mosé"* ("Moses, Moses, Moses") contains a rare allusion to Miriam as well as to the daughter of Pharaoh:[13]

> And Miriam the prophetess
> who was so wise
> ordered that an ark be built
> and thousands of wonders
> into which to put Moses
> to throw him into the sea.
>
> The daughter of Pharaoh
> came to bathe
> and because of Moses
> avoided the curse [of God].

In *"Par'ó era estreyero"*[14] we also find reference to Miriam, as well as unusual acknowledgment of the heroism of the midwives and the role of Pharaoh's daughter:

> Pharaoh was stargazing,
> went out one night to the night air
> and saw a star
> which foretold the birth of Moses.
>
> He sent for the midwives
> as many as were in Egypt
> asking them
> to foreswear delivering a Jew.
>
> The midwives were Jews
> beloved of God
> who received and delivered
> and thus, Moses was born.
>
> His sister the Levite
> made an ark
> coated it with pitch
> put it into the Nile.

The daughter of Pharaoh Batya
went to the shore of the sea
saw the ark
and took it from the water.

She who took the ark
the sun and the moon shine upon her

She who took the ark
the sun and the moon shine upon her.

In *"Kuando d'Aifto"* ("When in Egypt"), we see again the powerful image of women lifting the spirits of the community in adversity, through song: "When we went out of Egypt with children and women, with six hundred thousand singing…" These references occur very rarely, and yet their presence is significant.

Passover songs such as *"Tenia yo"* ("Once I Had") are conjectured to be "code songs," which may derive from the time of the Spanish Inquisition. Referring to traditional haggadah customs, the songs may have been sung out of context to fool spies who were looking for signs of Judaizing during the Passover week. For example, *"Tenia yo"* tells the story of a man and his donkey and his vineyard as a diversion, a ruse to distract the listener—the subsequent verses become the traditional *Chad Gadya* when the coast is clear.

Women also sang *canciones,* which included folk songs, love songs, and humorous songs. *Canciones* often featured Judeo-Spanish lyrics paired with melodies from new homelands, incorporating tunes, rhythms, and scales from Turkey, Bulgaria, Yugoslavia (Bosnia), Greece, Rhodes, and Morocco. The Sephardim also adopted and adapted folk songs of their Arab neighbors in Jerusalem.

Women sang all aspects of this repertoire at community occasions—births, lamentations, circumcisions, weddings—and among themselves, washing, cooking (many songs are actual recipes), and sewing. *"El rey de Fransia"* ("The King of France"), for example, which tells the story of a young daughter who embroidered a vest for the king, was sung on the sewing day. During laundry day or a visit to the *mikveh* (ritual bath), the women sang ballads that referred to the sea or contained water imagery. The oldest women passed down children's songs, which recalled their own childhoods and the children's games that accompanied the songs. One such song remembers the holiday ritual in which the children of Salonika went from house to house to collect flour and oil in order to make *burmuelos* for Hanukkah.

Every aspect of love and emotional life appeared in the texts: advice from mothers to daughters; rejection of mothers' advice; a young bride's discomfort with her mother-in-law with whom, by custom, she was obligated to share living quarters; or competition between mothers-in-law to show off their generosity to the young couple. Songs were often jokes about community characters or even just plain gossip. Many referred to magic, astrology, or potions for health.

The extraordinary repertoire has been shaped by the complicated history of the Jews, and of the Sephardim in particular. It reflects the unique Judeo-Spanish perspectives gained by surviving amid a fluctuating reality. In this vast musical collage, women, in a process unique to women, were largely responsible for documenting this history.

These "documents" deserve a place of honor at any table, and the women responsible for them deserve recognition, honor, and celebration. For a women's seder, I suggest that we create a "new song" by including relevant selections from the Sephardic musical repertoire, which tell of Moses and Miriam, the midwives, and the daughter of Pharaoh, Batya— a name we rarely hear. We enrich the seder by bringing to the table music and poetry whose resonance—both historical and personal—amplifies the sound and spirit of women, and of the holiday of Passover.

The Songs

The songs featured below have been gathered together for the first time here.[15] This coherent suggestion of women's Passover repertoire is my "midrash," as it were. This collection offers the opportunity to envision and incorporate images of Jewish women singing through the ages—singing to and for their community, to and for each other.

With the exception of *"Pesah a la mano,"* composed recently by Flory Jagoda (the only Sephardic woman whom I know of who is continuing to write text and music in this tradition),[16] these songs were learned through field recordings or from written, notated collections that almost never reveal authorship, as they are part of an oral tradition that derives from all parts of the Sephardic diaspora. They reflect but a few pieces of a vast panorama.

From the incredible repertoire of Sephardic women's music—and from its preservation and survival—it is clear to me that, despite the traditional lives led by Sephardic women, they openly and consistently defied the strictures that discouraged the female voice. They carried on musical traditions in their daily lives with joy, accompanying themselves on tambourines, on drums, and occasionally on melody instruments. They preserved a repertoire that could not have survived without some individual and personal commitment to, and understanding of, the importance of these pieces of Jewish history.

Kuando Moshe Rabeynu (When Moses Our Teacher)

It is thought that songs about Moses were preserved by *conversos*—crypto-Jews, or forced converts—to the Ottoman Empire. This *copla* tells of Moses going up to the heavens to receive the Ten Commandments and is based on midrashic sources. It is usually sung during the feast of Shavuot, which commemorates the giving of the Torah.[17]

> *Kuando Moshe rabenyu kijo ereynar,*
> *los sielos i la tierra ampezo a temblar*
> *ke grande sinyor era Moshe Rabbenu*
> *ke abashava i asuvia los siete sielos*
>
> *Elohenu y avotenu*
> *el sinyor del mundo 'ntero*
> *lo veamos en la siya*
> *ke se alegre la juderia.*

When Moses our teacher wanted to reign
the skies and the earth began to tremble
What a great lord was Moses our teacher
who descended and ascended to the seven heavens.

Our God and our Father
Lord of the whole world,
let us look upon Him on his throne
to the joy of all the Jewish quarter.

Mosé salió de Misrayim (Moses Went Out of Egypt)

This biblical *romançe* from Morocco recounts the Exodus narrative of Moses' escape to Midian and his marriage to Jethro's daughter, and tells the story of Moses hearing God's voice on Mount Horeb. The song closes with Hebrew used in traditional liturgy.[18]

Mosé salió de Misrayim
huyendo del rey Par'o
fuese derecho a Midian
encontróse con Yitro.

Dió le así por la su hija
porqu'era temiente de Dios;
Mosé pasaba el ganado
que su suegro le entregó.
Y al pasando su ganado
al monte de Horev llegó
asentóse en una piedra,
esperando ver a Dio.

Oyó una voz que decía:
—Mosé, Mosé mi siervo,
Descalza de tus zapatos,
qu'en lugar santo estás tú.

Vete derecho a Misrayim
dile al rey Par'ó
que te entregue a mi pueblo
a mi pueblo hebreo.
Y si no te lo entregaré
castigarle quiero yo
con diez plagas que le mande
Pa' que sepa quien soy yo.

(Hebrew):
Hodu l'Adonai ki tov

ki le'olam hasdo
(Judeo-Spanish):
Alabado sea su nombre
por que siempre bien
nos dió.

Moses went out of Egypt
fleeing from King Pharaoh
and went straight to Midian
and met Jethro.

He was given his [Jethro's] daughter
because he was a God-fearing man.
Moses tended his flock;
which his father-in-law assigned to him.

While working
he came to the mountain of Horeb;
he seated himself on a rock,
waiting to see God.
He heard a voice which said:
—Moses, Moses my servant,
take off your shoes,
you are in a holy place.

Go straight to Egypt
tell King Pharaoh
to send out my people
my Hebrew people.
And if he will not let them go
I will punish him
with ten plagues which I will send him
so that he will know who I am.

(Hebrew):
Give thanks to the Lord for his goodness
for His everlasting graciousness
(Judeo-Spanish):
Praised be His name
because of His continuing goodness.

Mosé, Mosé, Mosé (Moses, Moses, Moses)

This *copla* tells the story of how Miriam saved Moses from the doom of Pharaoh's edict to kill all male babies born to Jews.[19]

> *Mosé, Mosé, Mosé*
> *nuestro Rabbenu Mosé*
> *Voy a contar un maaseh*
> *de nuestro Rabbenu Mosé.*
> *Y Meriám la nevia*
> *la que mucho sabía*
> *mandó hazer un arca*
> *y a las mil maravillas*
> *para meter a Mosé*
> *para echarle a la mar.*
> *La hija de Par'ó*
> *viniera se abañar*
> *Y de zehut de Mosé*
> *se la quitó la maka.*

Moses, Moses, Moses
our teacher Moses
I will tell of the deeds
of our teacher Moses.
And Miriam the prophetess
who was so wise
ordered that an ark be built
and thousands of wonders
into which to put Moses
to throw him into the sea.
The daughter of Pharaoh
came to bathe
and because of Moses
avoided the curse [of God].

Kuando d'Aifto fueron salidos (When We Went Out of Egypt; Adrianopoli)

Collected through field recordings, these lyrics invite the singer to imagine himself or herself as part of the "we" that went out of Egypt singing.[20]

Kuando d'Aifto fueron salidos
kon ijoz y kon mujerez
kon shishim ribos kantando
kon shishim ribos kantando
detraz lez korryo Par'ó
kon un pendon kolorado

Onday moz trushitez Moshe
a morir sin siboltura
y a morir en despolvado
ke voz haray miz keridos
hazed tefila al Dio
y yo haray por otra vanda.

When we went out of Egypt
with children and women
with 600,000 singing
with 600,000 singing
the Pharaoh in pursuit
with a red banner

—Where did you take us Moses
to die without proper burial [without a gravestone],
to die in the sands of the desert
—What can I do, my beloved people?
Make a prayer to God
And I will make another plea.

Par'ó era estreyero (Pharaoh Was Stargazing)

This Turkish song recognizes and lauds the heroic acts of the women of the Exodus story.[21]

Par'ó era 'streyero
salyo una noche al sereno
vido una 'streya divina
tenya ke naser Moshe.

Mando yamo a laz komadrez
kuantaz en Aifto son
a todaz laz akonjuro
ke no resivan a judio.

Las komadrez eran Judiaz
del Dyo eran keridaz
arresivian y fuivan
empero nasyo Moshe.

Su ermana la Levia
izo hazer una arka
entera la pezledeo
al rio Nilo la echo.

Ija de Par'o Batya
salyo al bodre de la mar
vido venir una arka
metyo lo mano y la kito.

Eya ke la arka avyo
el sol y la luna esklaresyo
eya ke la arka avyo
el sol y la luna esklaresyo.

Pharaoh was stargazing,
went out one night to the night air
and saw a star
which foretold the birth of Moses.

He sent for the midwives
as many as were in Egypt
asking them
to foreswear delivering a Jew.

The midwives were Jews
beloved of God
who received and delivered
And thus, Moses was born.

His sister the Levite
made an ark
coated it with pitch
put it into the Nile.

The daughter of Pharaoh Batya
went to the shore of the sea

Saw the ark
and took it from the water.

She who took the ark
the sun and the moon shine upon her
She who took the ark
the sun and the moon shine upon her.

Tenia yo (Once I Had)

Also a "code song," which mimics *Chad Gadya*. The song opens with nonsense but then continues with the traditional story.[22]

Tenia yo
Tenia yo un viejo,
ke kavava vinyas
vinyas tan ermozas
enchidaz de rozaz.
Tenia yo tenia yo un azno
ke yevava'l viejo
ke kavava vinyas
vinyas tan ermozas
enchidaz de rozaz.
Tenia yo
tenia yo un palo
ke kharvava'l azno....
Tenia yo
tenia yo una agua
ke matava'l fuego...
al buey ke bevya l'agua...
...un shohet ke degoyo al buey...
...malakh-hamavat ke degoyo al shohet....

Once I had a donkey that carried the old man
who cared for my vineyard
a beautiful vineyard
swollen with roses.
And along came a stick
which beat the donkey
a fire which burned the stick
the water which put out the fire....

Pesah a la mano
(Passover Is at Hand, composed by Flory Jagoda)

Flory Jagoda, writing at the end of the twentieth century, describes some of her Bosnian family's experience preparing for the Passover holiday. I have included Jagoda's contemporary piece as the end to this collection, to affirm that Sephardic women's music will not only be preserved but also created throughout the twenty-first century.[23]

Purim, Purim, Purim, lano
Pesah, Pesah a la mano
Las masas si stan faziendo
Los japrakis si stan koziendo

Refrain (2x):
Aman, aman, aman, aman
Il Dio Bendicho mos da mazal

Purim, Purim, Purim lano
Pesah, Pesah a la mano
La Nona sta diziendo a lows nyetos
Alimpia il puelvo, kontones I loz techos

Refrain (2x)

Purim, Purim, Purim lano
Pesah, Pesah a la mano
Il Sinyor Rubi disho a las tiyas
No kumer il pan ocho diyas

Refrain (2x)

Purim is over
Passover is at hand
Matzot are being made
The stuffed leaves are being baked

(Refrain)

Aman...
Almighty God gives us good fortune
Aman... Almighty God gives us good fortune

Purim is over
Passover is at hand
The grandmother is telling the grandchildren
Clean the dust—corners and ceilings

Refrain

Purim is over
Passover is at hand
The Rabbi tells the aunts
Not to eat bread for eight days

≈≈≈

I Will Be with You:
The Divine Presence on Passover

CAROL OCHS

The Israelites sought God, whom they thought of as a father, king, and shepherd, on a mountaintop and in the Holy of Holies in the Temple. But we need to look only as far as our own seder tables to discover manifestations of God throughout the Passover ritual: in nourishment, beauty, love, and the story of our Exodus from Egypt.

God Nourishes and Sustains

During the Festival of Freedom, our homes become the Temple and our tables serve as the altars. Instead of turning to a priestly authority and a distant house of worship in our observance, we each undertake the cleansing and preparation for this holiday. As we ready our homes and our tables for the Passover celebration and prepare the nourishing

Dr. Carol Ochs is director of graduate studies and adjunct professor of Jewish religious thought at Hebrew Union College, New York, where she teaches and provides spiritual guidance for rabbinic students and Doctor of Ministry candidates. The most recent of her seven books are *Our Lives as Torah, Jewish Spiritual Guidance,* and an expanded edition of *Women and Spirituality.* She holds a Ph.D. in philosophy from Brandeis University and is a professor emerita at Simmons College, Boston.

foods that our loved ones will enjoy at the seder, we can contemplate all the ways that God nourishes and sustains us. As we chop the nuts to make the sweet *charoset,* we can let it remind us of the way God has sweetened our trials with hopes for eventual liberation. And even as we mix the salt water, we can take a moment to remember that God sees and numbers all our tears.

God is continually nourishing and sustaining our world. The plagues described in the Passover story are traditionally understood as a terrible scourge that Adonai visited on the Egyptians, but we can see them in a different light. What if we contemplate the plagues not as God's destructive acts but rather as the consequences of the withdrawal of God's nourishing presence? Let us consider the possibility that the water becomes undrinkable because God has withdrawn the gift of divine nourishment. Without God's support, the fruitful land of Egypt cannot even fend off frogs. The Egyptians, whose advanced society was a model of cleanliness when blessed by Adonai, become overrun with lice and flies when God's sustenance is withdrawn. Health also recedes as God withdraws: the cattle become diseased, the people experience boils. The bountiful land, once nourished and protected by God's presence in the crops, is destroyed by hail and then by locusts, which lay to waste the enduring productivity of the land. Finally, God is revealed as both light and life when God's withdrawal engulfs Egypt in darkness and life gives way to death.

As we prepare foods to nourish our loved ones, and as we participate in the seder ritual, we can remember all of the ways that God continues to nourish us.

God Is Revealed in Beauty

The candles gleam, the silverware sparkles, and we know that God calls to us in beauty. The table linen is snowy white; the flowers scent the room. The seder plate is stunning. The *karpas* and the horseradish remind us of the beauty of the earth in which they grew. Grandfather's *kiddush* cup is old—and even has dents in it from when the children used it for teething—but it too is beautiful, for it connects the table to three generations of seders. All of the beauty surrounding us at the seder points us to truth and goodness. This beauty reminds us that every part of life itself is a blessing. When we are in the presence of beauty, the world seems charged with a new vitality, with a splendor that does not belong to it. It is as if beauty is poured through our world, as light pours through a stained-glass window. We realize that what is sacred is not each exquisite object or scene, but God, the beautifier, to which all forms of beauty point.

God Is Made Manifest in Love

Friends and family find their seats around the seder table. As we search the faces of loved ones and guests we see God shining through their eyes. And when, at last, we tell the story of our Exodus from Egypt, it confirms what we have already experienced in our lives: God is found in the love between human beings. We find God in the love of Yocheved and Amram for their son Moses, and in the care and concern of Miriam, who lovingly watched over him. We find God in Bat Pharaoh's rescue and love of the infant Moses and in Shifra and Puah, the midwives who loved every life enough to disobey Pharaoh's orders. Finally, we find God in Moses' awakening to his love for his own people. The capacity to love amidst all the terrors of slavery is only possible because of the abiding presence of God.

God Is Found in the Birth of the Jewish People

The story of Passover is a story of deliverance. We are thrust out of the narrow place, *mitzrayim,* through the birth waters of the Sea of Reeds, and born as the People of Israel. Just as the birth of a child is preceded by a long gestation, by strange new signals coming from within the mother's body, by anxious waiting and watching, and finally by labor and delivery, so the central images in the haggadah depict a long gestation, many signs and wonders, a long night of waiting, and finally, the birth of the People of Israel. As we contemplate the story of the birth of the People of Israel we can remember our own experiences—and witnessing—of pregnancy and giving birth. Pregnancy is a kind of covenant—a promise whose full implications we cannot understand but that will change us as we try to fulfill it. We promise to see a human being from infancy through to maturity. Regardless of how many other children there are in the world, each child is unique, and caring for our own children will transform us. In the story of our Exodus from Egypt, God is present as progenitor, midwife, and nurturer. The manna that the Israelites were fed in the wilderness resembles mother's milk: however much or little is taken suffices. It cannot be stored, but each day there will be enough.

Reflecting on our experience of Passover leaves us with themes for meditation over the course of the festival. To bring a greater awareness of God's presence into your Passover observance, you can read and reflect on one of the meditations below on each of the eight days of Passover.

Day 1. God is immanent. We feel God's presence strongly in our sense of freedom and gratitude as we prepare for the seder. Suddenly, Miriam's song at the sea feels like our very own: "Sing to Adonai, for God has triumphed gloriously."[1]

Day 2. God is known experientially. God is not a stranger but appears in and through our own lives. In the Ten Commandments, we read, "I am Adonai your God who brought you out of the land of Egypt, the house of bondage,"[2] not "I am Adonai, Creator of heaven and earth." The Israelites did not experience Creation; they needed a definition of God that would relate to their own lived experience. We too find that the God who engages our supreme loyalty and belief is the God we meet through our own experience.

Day 3. God is trustworthy. We recall that God is not a stranger, that the God we have personally experienced is one we love and trust. And yet, as we reflect on these words we are forced to confront why people suffer—perhaps the most difficult question in theology. We do not understand why there is suffering, but we can say, with Job, "I had heard You with my ears, but now I see You with my eyes; therefore, I recant and relent."[3]

Day 4. God connects us to others. We find God in and through our relationships to others in love, friendship, joint worship, shared festivals, and the communal celebration of life-cycle events. "When two sit together and interchange words of the Torah, the *Shekhinah* abides between them."[4]

Day 5. God connects us to the goodness of the material world. "Taste and see that Adonai is good."[5] The beauty of our homes as we prepare them to receive guests, the delicious aromas of cooking and baking, the special fatigue from all the work we have done for Passover, the warmth of the freshly ironed clothes we will wear at the seder—in all these sensory experiences, we find God. God is inextricably tied to the material world.

Day 6. God performs traditional women's work. "I led you through the wilderness for forty years; the clothes on your back did not wear out, nor did the sandals on your feet; you had no bread to eat and no wine to drink."[6] Nurturing and nourishing, caretaking and guiding are the same activities God undertook when God delivered us from Egypt and cared for us in the wilderness. Let us remember that the tasks that patriarchal societies have trivialized as "women's work" are sacred, godly endeavors.

Day 7. God models parenting for us. "The Law is very close to you, in your mouth and in your heart."[7] God raises, leads, and teaches, and finally places the Torah in our hearts and mouths. We too raise, lead, and teach our children, giving them all we can, including a framework for making their own decisions. Then we must trust them to live their lives based on these models; we hope to follow God's model of blessing and then releasing them.

Day 8. As Passover comes to an end we meditate on "I will be with you,"[8] God's oft-repeated promise in the Torah. This sense of abiding presence during the holiday forms the foundation for our fundamental understanding of God's role in all the seasons of our lives. Each year, we renew our faith in God's presence as we take down the Passover dishes and begin, once again, the journey that delivers us from bondage and reminds us that God is in our midst.

3

Women of Exodus

Feminist history is history charged with meaning. . . .
Memory is nutriment and seeds stored for centuries can
still germinate. Feminist history is not simply contribu-
tory; it demands that we turn the questions upside down,
that we ask women's questions where they have not been
asked before. —ADRIENNE RICH, *BLOOD, BREAD, AND POETRY*

If you want to understand any woman you must first
ask about her mother and then listen carefully. . . . The
more a daughter knows the details of her mother's
life—without flinching or whining—the stronger the
daughter. —ANITA DIAMANT, *THE RED TENT*

The Torah teaches us that the boundaries between past, present, and future are permeable, that history is significant only insofar as it has meaning for us. The historian examines the past in order to determine what happened; we, as Jews, look at the past and ask: "What does this mean for us, and what claims does it make on our lives?" These questions inspire and inform the entire interpretive tradition within Judaism. Scholar of biblical and rabbinic literature Avivah Gottlieb Zornberg succinctly describes the traditional Jewish preoccupation with questions of collective meaning and memory rather than questions of simple historical truth: "'What really happened in Egypt?' becomes a less important question than 'How best to tell the story? Where to begin? What in the master story speaks to one and therefore makes one speak?'"[1]

In the vast body of rabbinic literature known as midrash—the interpretation of biblical texts through story, parable, or commentary—voices of commentators speak to one another across vast distances of time and place. Commentaries from different generations and different Jewish communities around the globe sit together on the pages, as if at the same table. All are engaged in the sacred process of revealing the "seventy faces of Torah."[2]

Our generation has witnessed a revolution in this sacred process as Jewish women have joined, shaped, and expanded this conversation in significant ways. Each of the authors in part 3 is a part of this revolution. Focusing on the women of the Exodus story, they weave new stories out of the spaces of women's silence, offer novel interpretations of the text, extract new lessons from traditional commentaries, and address marginalized aspects of our heritage. The insights revealed in their reflections do more than enrich our history—each also demonstrates a unique approach to the work of shaping it.

The word *midrash* comes from the root *lidrosh*, to seek or to ask. The authors in part 3, in a sense, draw their inspiration from the "search" that lies at the heart of the midrashic enterprise. They too are searching—for new layers of insight and meaning in the biblical text—and they use a variety of tools in their search. Excavating, analyzing, reading, imagining, intuiting, and listening, they struggle to find and understand the lives of these women.

Judith Rosenbaum explores the lives and deeds of the women of the Exodus story, identifying a key value embodied by each. In "*Shiru l'Adonai:* Widening the Circle of Memory and History," Rosenbaum gives voices to the biblical women, who each step forward to speak about their lives. Rosenbaum powerfully articulates the numerous ways in which the community gains from incorporating these figures—and the values they embody—into the narrative of our people's history.

In "Miriam's Leadership: A Reconstruction," scholar Lori Lefkovitz focuses on Miriam, perhaps the most celebrated female biblical figure. Lefkovitz offers an original analysis of each of the biblical passages in which we meet Miriam, looking closely at her approach to leadership. Her insightful reading uncovers the important role Miriam played in the liberation from slavery and highlights the ways in which these passages offer a rare account of a female leader who functioned in the public, rather than the domestic, sphere.

Rabbi Margaret Moers Wenig's "Their Lives a Page Plucked from a Holy Book" considers what happened to the women of the Exodus story during the times when they are absent in the text, imagining what came to pass in each of their lives. Her moving exploration of the untold lives of these biblical women offers us a provocative model for how contemporary midrash can confront the spaces of women's omission from the traditional text.

In "With Strong Hands and Outstretched Arms," Rabbi Sharon Cohen Anisfeld probes the biblical text of Exodus for a deeper understanding of the divine-human partnership that makes liberation possible. She weaves together traditional commentaries and personal reflections in an analysis that celebrates the compassion and courage of the women of Exodus and highlights their role in our people's journey from despair to hope.

While the early writings in this part focus on the individual women of the Exodus story, the closing pieces approach the topic of "the women of Exodus" differently. In a close reading of a traditional midrash, scholar Avivah Gottlieb Zornberg explores the Israelite women's response to Pharaoh's decree against sexual relations between the male and female slaves. "The Secret of Redemption: A Tale of Mirrors" highlights the extraordinary collective actions of the Israelite women. Analyzing the women's seduction of the men through the use of "the mirrors," Zornberg shows how this "mirror work" led to a transformation of the slaves' self-perception.

Feminist scholar Bonna Devora Haberman returns to the Book of Genesis, adding a new figure to the circle of women who play a crucial role in the Exodus story. "'Fixing' Liberation, or How Rebecca Initiates the Passover Seder" is a provocative midrash establishing Rebecca as the initiator of the Passover seder. Haberman asks us to include Rebecca's story in our Passover celebration "and pass on the blessing of her fervent desire and courage for liberation to our daughters and our sons forever."

Why is it important to tell these stories? Surely, our understanding of Torah and of our heritage as Jewish women would be incomplete without them. Yet, the writings in part 3 do more than merely add to this understanding. The women of the Book of Exodus convey a vital legacy. They teach us what it means to revere God, to resist violence, to work together. They show us how, in the midst of oppression, to make choices; how, in the face of a death decree, to honor life; how, in the face of illusion, to adhere to the truth.

To create a history that teaches us these important lessons is indeed to create a history charged with meaning.

Shiru l'Adonai: Widening the Circle of Memory and History

JUDITH ROSENBAUM

Despite its central command to remember, the Book of Exodus begins with forgetfulness. The new king does not remember Joseph, and it seems as if God has forgotten the Children of Israel.[1] The tension between remembering and forgetting in this story calls our attention to the incompleteness of history; while some stories of our past are highlighted, revisited again and again, others were omitted from our his-

---

Judith Rosenbaum is a Ph.D. candidate in American civilization at Brown University, writing a dissertation on the women's health movement. She graduated from Yale University in 1995.

torical narrative and have been forgotten. At the Passover seder, we gather as a community of family and friends and turn history back into memory, for together we retell the story of Exodus from Egypt—a collective experience that forged a free people from a band of slaves—as if it had happened to each of us personally.

At a women's seder, we extend the imperative to tell our history by reintroducing the women of Exodus, who have fallen into the margins of our traditional Passover story. They bring to our table faith in God, respect for common humanity, belief in the centrality of family and community, and understanding of the power of memory and ritual. Recalling their roles in the Exodus gives us an opportunity to honor and explore the values that they represent. These values challenge us to see our own acts in the context of our communities, our history, and our humanity. Embracing their deeds as part of our heritage not only expands our historical view but reminds us of the role we each play in making history.

They sit in a circle on a rug laid down on the sand. Two women—midwives—squat on the ground, leaning protectively on their birthing stools, prized possessions. A mother rests cross-legged with her daughter beside her, absently playing with the rug's frayed edge. Another holds a baby at her breast. One woman, so old her skin is leathered and her hair white, and wispy as a baby's, sits still and dignified, supported at the elbows by great-granddaughters. The women are quiet but for the low hum of a lullaby sung by the new mother. Some children sway to the music while their mothers listen to the wind. When the wind dies down and the baby dozes, the women look deeply into one another's eyes and bring their stories to the tight circle. Two women begin to speak in unison.

"Our names are Shifra and Puah. We are midwives. We greet new life as it arrives in the world with its bold cry. Despite the orders of our mighty ruler, we could not ignore our calling and drown a newborn's first breaths in the rushing waters of the Nile. When others quaked in fear of Pharaoh, we were struck with awe of God. And God brought many strong babies into our hands."

The first mention of God in the Book of Exodus occurs in the story of the midwives Shifra and Puah, who defy Pharaoh's orders to drown male Hebrew babies because they are in awe of God: *"va-tirena ha-miyaldot et ha-elohim."*[2] It is not clear from the text whether Shifra and Puah are Hebrews themselves or merely the midwives to the Hebrews; some midrashic sources argue that they are, in fact, Miriam and her mother, Yocheved. But whatever their identities, we know that these women have great faith in God, despite God's apparent neglect of the people. It is for the midwives' act of remembering God as a power above Pharaoh that the Children of Israel are made strong: "Therefore God dealt well with the midwives and the people multiplied and grew very mighty."[3] Thus, Shifra and Puah bring God into this story and create the conditions for Israel's survival. In remembering God, they help God remember Israel.

"I am Yocheved, mother of Miriam, Aaron, and Moses. Every day, for three months, I stifled my baby's cries, marveling at his strong lungs and sturdy little body that relaxed against me when I held him. When he grew too big, I built for him a tevah *that could cradle him, save him, even in the waters of the Nile. I prayed that this ark would save him as Noah's ark had once saved all living creatures."*

Yocheved remembers miracles. The mother of Moses, Yocheved hides her son for three months, and when she can no longer conceal his presence, builds him an ark, a *tevah,* in which to float him on the Nile.[4] Her sense of history is revealed through the language that the text uses to describe this attempt to save her son. The word *tevah* is only used in one other place in the Torah: in the story of Noah. Noah builds a *tevah* in order to save himself, his family, and the animal kingdom from the flood. A *tevah,* then, is a vehicle of salvation in waters of destruction. Yocheved's use of this particular word and method to save her son reflects her keen memory of God's role in history, calling on the powers of the first *tevah* to protect her infant son on the waters of the Nile.

"I am Miriam, called a prophetess because I can find water; my true gift is that I can hear water, understand its message, and bring it to the community. As a young girl, I heard the lapping waters of the Nile reassuring me that my brother was rescued, and I brought him back to our mother's breast. As a woman, I shared the song that the Sea of Reeds sang when it rose up before us and then bowed down at our feet as we reached the other shore. In the desert, I have heard the water beneath the sand, running below our feet to the Promised Land."

Miriam teaches us that the best leaders place community at the center of their work. Miriam keeps her family together and creates communal rituals to mark the miracles she experiences with the people. As a child she is sent to watch over Moses as he floats down the Nile. It is she who offers to find a Hebrew woman—Yocheved—to nurse the baby Pharaoh's daughter has found, thus reconnecting her family by returning Moses to their home. Later, at the Sea of Reeds, Miriam gathers the women to sing and dance with her. Although the text places Miriam's celebration after Moses' song, hers is inclusive—*"shiru l'adonai,"* "sing to the Lord"—using a plural form of the verb to invite the entire community to sing.[5] Moses, on the other hand, sings in the singular—*"ashira l'adonai,"* "I will sing to the Lord."[6] Moses celebrates by himself; Miriam brings the entire Jewish community into her celebration. Creating a ritual of singing and dancing together with timbrels, Miriam builds on the miracle they have just experienced to deepen a sense of community among the terrified and relieved people.

"You may not know me, or want to include me in your family, but I, Pharaoh's daughter, am a mother to your people. When I heard the baby squalling among the reeds, I knew immediately that he must be a Hebrew baby. And I knew just as quickly that I could not let him die. I drew him from the water and sent him home with the girl who peered at me from among the reeds."

The daughter of Pharaoh is a bold but mysterious figure. Pharaoh's own daughter defies his commandment to kill all male Hebrew babies, bringing her father's ultimate foe into his household. She never questions who this baby is—she must know he is a Hebrew—and she does not falter in her decision to save him. In a time of hatred and strife, Pharaoh's daughter upholds the most basic values of common humanity and respect for life. Her role in saving Moses makes the redemption of the Children of Israel possible. For this, the Rabbis include her among the righteous women of the Bible, and some commentaries suggest that she left Egypt with the Israelites during the Exodus. Her assertion of a common humanity with the Hebrews admits her to their fold.

"I am so old that my name has already faded from your lips. I am Serach bat Asher, recalled only by my genealogy. I came down to Egypt with Jacob, my grandfather, and I leave today with you. When your memories of our miracles are faint and cloudy, I will make them clear to you."

Serach bat Asher is a woman mentioned only in passing in the Exodus story, but midrashic literature hands her the weighty role of bearing collective memory. Serach is granted eternal life by Jacob after she tells him—gently and kindly so that he survives the shock—that his beloved son, Joseph, is still alive. As a figure who spans the ages, she takes on the important task of providing continuity from one generation to the next. Serach recalls the secret phrase, *"pakod pakaditi"* "I will redeem you," that will identify God's messenger to the people, thus reassuring the elders of Israel that Moses is in fact their redeemer. She also locates Joseph's bones, without which the Children of Israel could not have left Egypt. In the time of the Mishnah, Serach is credited with describing the transparency of the waters at the splitting of the Sea of Reeds for the Rabbis. Her acts of memory make redemption possible and keep its miracles accessible to the following generations.

By bringing the women's stories into our women's seder, we take into our own hands the delicate balance of memory and forgetfulness at the heart of the Exodus tale. We not only expand the historical record by including the forgotten women of Exodus but also broaden the spectrum of values that form the legacy of this story. Coming together as a community, creating our own rituals, celebrating our common humanity by applying the Passover message of liberation to a wider context, we put into practice the values that the women of Exodus represent. These women remind us that as we fashion new communities, new rituals, new stories—new memories—together, we hold the potential to make history. If we, like Serach bat Asher, uphold our responsibility to carry certain memories for the community, we can help make possible our next journey. The process of redemption begins with remembering.

We sit together in a circle. We may not look the same; we may not speak the same language. We look from face to face, peering deep into each other's eyes to ask for the stories that have not yet been told. We open our mouths, we raise our timbrels, and together we sing.

≈≈≈

Miriam's Leadership: A Reconstruction

LORI LEFKOVITZ

The Reed Sea parts. This miracle is the stuff of legends, paintings, and dramatic movie scenes. Moses leads the people through the parted waters and then sings a beautiful song of victory and gratitude. Only after this dramatic scene, with its bold poetry, do we come to the more understated sentences that describe the women following Miriam in instrumental dance. She leads them in a chant that scholars observe is a one-sentence summary of *Shirat Hayam,* "The Song of the Sea." Scholars also speculate that the song of Miriam[1] is among the oldest passages of the Hebrew Bible. In dating Miriam's song as an older

---

Dr. Lori Lefkovitz is Sadie Gottesman and Arlene Gottesman Reff Professor of Gender and Judaism and academic director of Kolot: the Center for Jewish Women's and Gender Studies at the Reconstructionist Rabbinical College. Her most recent book, coedited with Julia Epstein, is *Shaping Losses: Cultural Memory and the Holocaust.*

version of the poem that precedes it, source critics of the Bible suggest that *Shirat Hayam,* the long poem, may actually be a later elaboration of what had begun as Miriam's song.

Although we are familiar with Miriam from before this moment—we met her at the Nile when she hid her baby brother Moses in a basket—this is the first time she is named. She is identified as Miriam the prophet, sister of Aaron. Why, a rabbinic midrash asks, is she named as the sister of Aaron? This medieval Rabbi responds that it is to indicate that she was a prophet even before the birth of Moses.[2]

Aside from incidental mentions of her name, Miriam appears four times in the Bible, and these appearances contain valuable information about her role as a leader of the people. When Pharaoh decrees that all baby boys born to Hebrew slaves must be killed, the midwives Shifra and Puah disobey the death decree. What follows is the story of Moses' mother Yocheved, who creates a waterproof basket and sends her young daughter Miriam to place the baby Moses in the basket in the Nile. Yocheved orders her child to hide in the bulrushes and discover the fate of the baby who will grow up to be the reluctant hero of the Hebrew people.

While Miriam stands watch, Pharaoh's daughter, the princess herself, comes to bathe and takes pity on this floating baby. She declares her intention to adopt him, and Miriam steps forward, offering Yocheved as the wet nurse for the child.

This is a remarkable conspiracy among women. The midwives, a slave mother, her daughter, and a princess cross boundaries of age, race, and class to save the life of a baby. The male realms of politics and economy loom large in the Bible—with decrees against whole populations—while in a smaller female domestic space, a single baby is saved. And in this act begins the redemption.

One rabbinic midrash suggests that Shifra and Puah are none other than Yocheved and Miriam.[3] I suspect this is partly because in the world of the Bible, we see very little of the community of women that must have existed. Instead, we meet women alone or in pairs. And so, the idea of five distinct women making history in so short a space of time seems unrealistic to the commentator, who reduces the size of this extraordinary group. In addition, he increases the heroism of Moses' relatives—and thus of Moses—by collapsing the identity of the midwives into that of the leader's mother and sister.

Even more remarkable than the fact that we see Miriam in the company of other women (both as a child and then as the leader of the dance at the Reed Sea) is the fact that we have a story about her as a child. No other woman in the Bible has a recorded childhood. And Miriam's story is a miracle story set at the shores of the Nile River. Even the etymology of Miriam's name brings us to the sea. As Ellen Frankel suggests in *The Five Books of Miriam,* Mir-Yam derives from the Hebrew words *mar* and *yam,* "bitter sea." Alternatively, "Mir" comes from the Egyptian word *mer,* beloved, making her name "Beloved Sea."[4]

We meet Miriam for the second time when she leads the women in dance with timbrels. My first childhood encounter with this line struck me with some surprise. I was not surprised that Miriam led the women in celebration. That seemed natural. But I had been told often enough about the extreme haste with which the people left Egypt—such haste that they did not have enough time to let their dough rise. This, after all, is why we are forever commanded to eat matzah on Pesach. How is it, then, that women who were so busy rushing, and could hardly pack decent food, all packed their *toopim*—their timbrels?

I later learned that women are depicted elsewhere in the Bible celebrating victories with dance and with timbrels. We can only imagine that these timbrels had the status of religious ceremonial objects. Were we to leave home in haste today, we might remember to take the family candlesticks. Back then, a good Jewish girl made sure she had her tambourine.

After the miracle of the Reed Sea, the people begin their long and arduous journey through the wilderness. A pillar of smoke leads and protects the people by day, and a cloud of fire accompanies them at night. A rabbinic commentary to the text adds that smoke and fire accompanied the people because of the merit of Moses and Aaron. The commentary goes on to say that the people were also accompanied through the desert by a well. The presence of this well of water, essential to their survival in the desert, was attributed to the merit of Miriam.

But the people, only minutes out of Egypt, begin to complain, as they will continue to do tirelessly in the desert. The first complaint is that the desert water is bitter, and Moses uses his magic rod to sweeten it. Still later, when there is no water, God will tell Moses to hit a rock with his rod to get water.

The third time we meet Miriam is when she and Aaron have a complaint to lodge against their brother, Moses. The text in this story is rather unclear, but it seems to suggest that the elder siblings think that their little brother is arrogant. They ask: "Aren't we prophets, too?"[5]

God responds angrily by calling the team of Aaron and Miriam outside. Then, God appears as a cloud upon them. When the cloud lifts, it is Miriam who is leprous, covered in white. The female body is a kind of drawing board upon which God's messages are written.[6]

More interesting than the fact of the leprosy, however, is the way Miriam's brothers, and indeed all the people, respond. Aaron and Moses see Miriam, and they panic. Moses utters the shortest and the most urgent prayer in the Bible. He calls out to God: "*Ayl Nah, Refah Nah Lah.*"[7] In staccato rhyming Hebrew, he calls, "Please God, heal her." God replies: "If her father had spat in her face, would she not bear her shame for seven days?"[8] Miriam's leprosy turns out to be a version of divine spit.

The people won't budge without Miriam. She is quarantined, and only when she recovers and rejoins the leaders are the people willing to continue their journey.

Miriam is mentioned only once more. In the passages leading up to the Israelites' entry into the Promised Land, God declares that Aaron will not enter Israel. In a detailed description of the removing of Aaron's vestments and the investiture of his son Elazar, Aaron's death is reported, as is the people's thirty day period of mourning.[9] By contrast, Miriam's death is reported with no comment at all.[10] The text says simply, "Miriam died there and was buried there."[11] The next verse, in an apparent non sequitur, reads, "and the land was without water."[12] It seems as if the earth itself was mourning, that Miriam's death brought drought. And indeed a rabbinic midrash recounts that Miriam's well disappeared upon her death but returned because of the merit of Moses.[13]

After Miriam dies, the people yet again decry their fate and rail against their leader, Moses, for taking them out of Egypt to die of thirst in the desert. Again Moses prays, and again God tells him to go to the rock. This time God says, "Lift your rod and tell the rock to give you water."[14] Moses strikes the rock (as he had been instructed to do in the past), and although the people do get their water—lots of it— Moses is punished for his disobedience. Because he struck the rock instead of talking to it, God declares that he will not be allowed into the Promised Land.

Of all the Bible stories I learned in Hebrew school, this one troubled me the most. So small a crime, I thought, and so big a punishment. Moses, who put up with so much, who twice climbed a mountain to get the law, who led this endlessly cranky people through wars and wanderings, who was ever humble and ever great, would not get into the Promised Land because he had hit a rock? It wasn't as if he had hit a person. Moses was the hero who had risked his life and his position because he couldn't bear to see a slave beaten.

Thinking of Ilana Pardes's work on what she calls countertraditions in the Bible, it has since occurred to me that something else is going on here.[15] Miriam, whose name means either Bitter Sea or Beloved Sea, is always associated with miracles and water. In mythology and legend, gods and goddesses, heroes and heroines often have a miracle story associated with their childhood. Miriam saves her baby brother from drowning at the Nile. Later, she leads the women in triumphant celebration after the parting of the Reed Sea. When she and God get into a power contest, God makes her leprous, but neither her brothers nor anyone else will proceed without her. One begins to sense some fear among the people that without Miriam there will be no water.

When she dies, this fear is confirmed. God reassures Moses, but Moses nevertheless panics, for the first time. He doesn't talk; he strikes. Perhaps he too thinks that without Miriam there cannot be water, and perhaps this is the serious crime: the reason why Moses' faith is questioned.

Rivkah Walton offers another interpretation.[16] She observes that the text says that God tells Moses to talk to *the* rock. Which rock is *the* rock? And then Walton remembers that in the ancient world, as we know well from the Christian Scriptures, great people were buried in caves, and the mouth of the cave would be covered by a huge boulder. God says, "talk to the rock," and Walton interprets this to mean, "Go to the rock that blocks Miriam's grave and ask for water." According to this reading, Moses' crime is against the memory of Miriam, and God is defender of her honor. Angry that even after her death they must depend upon Miriam for water, Moses impatiently strikes the stone before her grave. God punishes the little brother's impertinence.

Our Bible is a layered document, and in it we can find hints of more complete stories hidden at the lowest levels of the text. Ours is a Bible with one God as the hero and a long series of brave men who lead God's people. But here we have Miriam, whose name means Beloved Sea, whose song is the oldest piece of the text, who performs a sea miracle as a child, who claims leadership after the parting of the Reed Sea, who competes with God and wins—the people won't go anywhere without her—and because of whose death the earth goes dry. If brother Aaron the prophet is High Priest, sister Miriam the prophet was perhaps the Water Priestess, with special access to the divine water pipe.

Most of the heroines codified in biblical stories are important in relation to their roles as mothers, wives, or seductresses (the matriarchs, Sarah, Rebecca, Rachel, and Leah; and Hannah, Yael, Esther, Judith, Ruth). So, too, in subsequent literature have women been represented in domestic roles more often than as leaders in the public sphere. In a time before women were confined by our stories into roles as mothers and seductresses, we have hints that they could be leaders in other ways: priestesses, celebrants, judges, and prophetesses. History

narrowed women's sphere of action, overempowering them in the bed-
room and disempowering them in political and religious realms.

But what history has done, history can also undo. And that brings
us to our own day. Judaism teaches us that history is made by people
but that God and the sacred transcend time. Outside of the constraints
of mortality and physics is a timeless universe, one that insists that you
and I were present for the miracles of the Exodus and for the miracle at
Sinai. In that time before and after time, the workings of history that
separated women's and men's sacred jobs had not yet been effected.
If we place ourselves in that transcendent place, we can stand up with
Miriam today, hearing her victory chant and dancing our joy and gratitude for the blessings that are ours and the miracles that have been
wrought on our behalf.

Bimhayra biyamaynu, speedily and in our day, may the prophets
Elijah and Miriam lead the generations of Israel to the waters of
redemption, to the time and place where there is always peace.

≈≈≈

Their Lives a Page Plucked
from a Holy Book

MARGARET MOERS WENIG

The piece that follows is a midrash.[1] Midrash is usually commentary
on the Torah in the form of a story. For those who may be unfamiliar
with rabbinic midrash, I have outlined below a few of the basic oper-
ating principles that the Rabbis employed and which I use here as well.

First, in order to clarify unexplained aspects of the biblical narrative,
the Rabbis granted themselves license to invent conversations between

---

Margaret Moers Wenig is rabbi emerita of Beth Am, The People's Temple, and
instructor in liturgy and homiletics at Hebrew Union College–Jewish Institute of
Religion. She is the coauthor, with Naomi Janowitz, of *Siddur Nashim: A Sabbath
Prayer Book for Women,* the first to use female images for God.

biblical characters and even to invent characters altogether and insert them into the biblical story. The Rabbis imagined, for example, that Satan visited Sarah and informed her of Abraham's intention to sacrifice their son Isaac.[2] Of course, there is no evidence in the biblical text of Satan's visit to Sarah; nonetheless, through this imagined conversation, the Rabbis endeavored to account for the timing of Sarah's death, so soon after the binding of Isaac. Like the Rabbis, I too invent conversations in this reflection to account for elements of the text that cry out for explanation.

Second, the Rabbis took the liberty of weaving together verses from a wide variety of sacred sources, often without identifying them. Sometimes, before a verse, a midrash will note that it is quoting by using the phrase *"k'mo shecatuv"* (as it is written). At other times, however, a midrash simply quotes without acknowledgement or attribution. Similarly, at times rabbinic insights are attributed with a phrase such as "Rabbi Ishmael taught...." Often, however, a midrash speaks anonymously. I too will weave together verses from numerous sources, ancient and contemporary, usually without identifying them (except in notes). No part of this midrash is attributed to such a person as R. Ishmael or R. Elazar, for it is entirely my own.

Finally, it was not unusual in midrash for the Rabbis to project a custom or an institution from their own time back into an ancient story. They did this for the sake of filling in an ellipsis in the text. For example, immediately following the story of the binding of Isaac, the biblical text says, "Abraham returned to the lads and they went to Beersheba and dwelled there." The Rabbis asked, Why does the text say that Abraham alone returned to the lads; why is Isaac's name omitted? A midrash suggests that Isaac did not accompany his father to Beersheba because Isaac went to study Torah with Shem.[3] That might seem like a reasonable suggestion—except that there was no Torah in Abraham and Isaac's day! Yet, the Rabbis insisted: "*Ein mukdam v'ein m'uhar batorah.* There is no early or late in Torah." The truths of Torah transcend chronological time. In midrash, therefore, it is altogether possible to say that Isaac studied in the yeshiva of Shem, for what else ought a young man to do but study Torah? I too assume the liberty of projecting elements of contemporary culture back into ancient times.[4]

Their Lives a Page Plucked from a Holy Book

The opening portion of the Book of Exodus provides us with a stunning collection of women who resist and defy, women celebrated in feminist haggadahs for the role they played in freeing the Israelites from slavery, seven clever and courageous women: Shifra, Puah, Yocheved, Miriam, Bat Pharaoh, Tziporah, and Elisheva.

Shifra and Puah, *ham'yaldot,* the midwives, defy Pharaoh's order to kill all newborn Israelite boys and are rewarded by God with great houses;[5] Yocheved bat Levi, the mother of Moses, hides her son until he can be hidden no longer, places him in the river Nile in an ark lined with pitch and then suckles him as a paid wet nurse;[6] Miriam *achoto,* sister of Moses, who stands watch over her brother and offers to find a wet nurse for him;[7] Bat Pharaoh, Pharaoh's daughter, draws baby Moses out of the water and chooses to raise him;[8] Tziporah, the Midianite wife of Moses, the mother of his two sons, saves Moses' life by performing an emergency circumcision on her baby;[9] Elisheva, daughter of Aminidav, sister of Nachshon, wife of Aaron, is the mother of Aaron's four sons.[10]

What happened to these seven brave women when the men they birthed, nursed, raised, saved, and nurtured were leading the fight for freedom that resulted in the Israelite exodus from slavery and the mass destruction of Egyptian land, livestock, and population? In the opening chapters of the Book of Exodus,[11] these seven women risked death to save the lives of their own male babies or to save the lives of sons of their enemies.[12] How could it be that these same women remained silent during the plagues? Where were these women during the plagues? And what became of them after the Israelites left Egypt?

Just as Miriam had stationed herself at a distance to watch her brother Moses in the bulrushes,[13] so too Miriam stationed herself at a safe distance to watch her brothers Moses and Aaron negotiate with Pharaoh. When Pharaoh refused to let the Hebrews go, *"Vayarem b'mateh vayach et hamaim asher bayaor....* Aaron lifted up the rod and struck the water in the Nile in the sight of Pharaoh and his courtiers and all the water in the Nile was turned into blood and the fish in the Nile died. The Nile stank so that the Egyptians could not drink water, and there was blood throughout the land of Egypt."[14]

"What are you doing?" Miriam asked her brothers when they returned home.

"Pharaoh ordered every male Israelite child thrown into the Nile," Moses answered her. "Now the Egyptians will suffer when the Nile flows with blood. This is God's will."

"I don't believe it," replied Miriam, and she left them.

A week later, the negotiations resumed. Once again, Pharaoh refused to let the people go; this time, Aaron brought a torrent of frogs. Then it was lice. Then swarms of insects. Then a plague that killed Egyptian livestock. Then boils.

"Stop this craziness!" Miriam yelled at her brothers.

"The Egyptian people want us dead," Moses replied.

"Not *all* of them do," insisted Miriam.

Miriam sent a message to all the Egyptian women she knew, and they organized a letter-writing campaign to convince Pharaoh that the Israelite people were no threat. To no avail. Once again, Pharaoh refused to grant Moses' request, and heavy hail and fire rained down, striking all that was in the open: grasses of the field, and trees as well. Intensifying their efforts, a coalition of Egyptian and Israelite women— led by Shifra, Puah, Yocheved, Miriam, Tziporah, Elisheva, and Pharaoh's own daughter—gathered an unprecedented number of women, in front of Pharaoh's palace, in a demonstration of protest against the escalation of the conflict. Pharaoh was not moved. And a thick mass of locusts ate all of the grass, all of the fruit of the trees not already felled by hail. Egyptians were starving. Insect-borne diseases were rampant, and darkness engulfed the land. But Pharaoh would not let the Israelites go.

Vayomer Adonai el Moshe v'el Aharon ba'eretz Mitzraim lemor....
The Lord said to Moses and Aaron in the land of Egypt: This
month shall mark for you the beginning of months. It shall be
the first of the months of the year for you. Speak to the whole
community of Israel, and say that on the tenth day of this month
each of them shall take a lamb to a family, a lamb to a household.... You shall keep watch over it until the fourteenth day of
this month, and the entire community of Israel shall slaughter it at
twilight.... *Velakchu min hadam venat'nu al shtei hamezuzot ve'al
hamashkotf al habatim....* They shall take some of the blood and
put it on the two doorposts and the lintel of the houses in which
they are to eat it.... For that night I will go through the land of
Egypt and strike down every firstborn in the land of Egypt, both
human and animal.... And the blood on the houses in which you
dwell shall be a sign for you: when I see the blood I will pass over
you, so that no plague will destroy you when I strike the land of
Egypt.[15]

Miriam spoke to her brother Moses: "How can you go along with
this plan? When God threatened to destroy all of Sodom, Abraham
argued with him, 'Will you destroy the righteous along with the
wicked?'[16] Surely you will not allow the innocent to die?!" Moses
answered her: "Please, if you can obtain our freedom through non-
violent means, this plague will be averted. Be my guest. You have fourteen days."

In many regions of Egypt, Israelite and Egyptian women dressed in
black and held vigils, marches, sit-ins. Men were among the demon-
strators, too. Moses and Aaron joined an Israelite hunger strike.

But whenever Pharaoh showed signs of softening, his right wing
threatened him, and he was forced to hold fast.[17]

Miriam failed to obtain agreement from Pharaoh to release the
Israelites. Nothing was left for her to do but to warn the Egyptians
and try to protect them: On the thirteenth day, *"Veyishalu ish me'eit
rei'eihu ve'isha me'eit re'utah klei kesef uklei zahav."* As Israelite men
and women went from Egyptian house to Egyptian house, ostensibly
to ask for objects of silver and gold from their Egyptian neighbors,[18]
they secretly warned the Egyptians of the impending danger. And as

the Israelites left each Egyptian home, they put blood on the lintel and the two doorposts of each Egyptian house. *"Vayitein Adonai et cheyn haam b'eyney mitzrayim."* The Egyptians were deeply grateful.[19]

When word reached Pharaoh that the Israelites were seen leaving Egyptian homes with sacks of silver and gold and marking Egyptian doorposts with blood, Pharaoh immediately dispatched his army to arrest the thieves and vandals and to wipe clean the markings of blood from off the Egyptian doorposts. Yocheved and Elisheva were among those arrested and thrown in prison.[20] The next day, their families left Egypt without them.[21]

Miriam had wanted to warn Pharaoh's daughter herself. But she arrived too late. *"Vayehi b'chetzi halaila v'Adonai chika kol b'chor b'eretz mitzrayim mebechor Paroah hayoshev al kiso ad bechor hashevi asher beveit habor vechol bechor beheimah.* In the middle of the night the Lord struck down all the firstborn in the land of Egypt, from the firstborn of Pharaoh, who sat on the throne, to the firstborn of the captive who was in the dungeon...."[22] *"Mi bechor Paroah...."* The Torah never mentions that Pharaoh had a son. Pharaoh's daughter was his firstborn. (Lest the masculine noun *b'chor* lead you to believe that only male firstborn were felled, the haggadah suggests otherwise: *"dam, zefardeya, kinim, arov, dever, shechin, barad, arbeh, hoshech, makat bechorot:*[23] blood, frogs, lice, beasts, cattle disease, boils, hail, locusts, darkness, slaying of the firstborn." Pharaoh's daughter was among them.)

Miriam failed to arrest the destructive course of the plagues. Moses, on the other hand, finally succeeded in freeing his people. On the far shore of the Reed Sea, he sang:

> *Ah shira l'Adonai ki gao ga'ah*
> *sus v'rochvo rama vayam.*
> I will sing to the Lord for He has triumphed gloriously
> horse and driver He has hurled into the sea.
> The Lord is my strength and my might
> He is become my salvation.
> This is my God and I will glorify Him.

The God of my father and I will exalt Him.
The Lord, the Warrior, the Lord is His name.
Pharaoh's chariots and his army He has cast into the sea;
and the pick of his officers are drowned in the Sea of
    Reeds....[24]

When the men finished singing their song, *"Vatikach Miriam haneviah et hatof be'yadah."* Miriam the prophetess, Aaron's sister, took a timbrel in her hand, and all the women went out after her in dance with timbrels, and Miriam chanted for them: "Sing to the Lord for He has triumphed gloriously; / Horse and driver.... He has hurled.... Into the sea...."[25]

Her voice trailed off. She did not echo the rest of the verses her brother had sung. She was heard only to whisper, "Praise to life though it crumbled in like a tunnel on ones we knew and loved."[26]

Miriam withdrew from politics after the Exodus from Egypt, emerging only once to challenge Moses' sole authority as a prophet. She was stricken with scales, and Moses himself prayed for her recovery.

A midrash in *Sifrei Bamidbar* teaches that Miriam became the wife of Caleb, foremother of Bezalel, or King David. But that's not how I imagine the rest of Miriam's life.

I think Miriam spent the remainder of her days as a teacher, a teacher of girls and of her nephews, Nadav and Avihu, Elazar and Ithamar, whose father had ceased to show any emotion[27] after the arrest and disappearance of his wife, Elisheva. Miriam used to tell her nephews stories about their mother, arrested before they were old enough to remember her. "My heart is moved by all I cannot save," sighed Miriam, "so much has been destroyed [and yet] I have to cast my lot with those who age after age, perversely, with no extraordinary power, reconstitute the world."[28] Aaron blamed Miriam for the death of Nadav and Avihu.[29] Some days she blamed herself.

No longer did Miriam place herself in the middle of the great conflicts of her time:[30] the battles with Amalek, the building of the golden calf, the report of the spies, the rebellion of Korah. It was the

day-to-day work of sustaining a community that drew her in. She used
to recite to her students the words of Marge Piercy:

The people I love the best
jump into work head first
without dallying in the shallows
and swim off with sure strokes almost out of sight.
They seem to become natives of that element,
the black sleek heads of seals
bouncing like half-submerged balls.

I love people who harness themselves, an ox to a heavy cart,
who pull like water buffalo, with massive patience,
who strain in the mud and the muck to move things forward
who do what has to be done, again and again.
I want to be with people who submerge
in the task, who go into the fields to harvest
and work in a row and pass the bags along,
who stand in the line and haul in their places
who are not parlor generals and field deserters
but move in a common rhythm
when the food must come in or the fire be put out.

The work of the world is common as mud.
Botched, it smears the hands, crumbles to dust.
But the thing worth doing well done
has a shape that satisfies, clean and evident.
Greek amphoras for wine or oil,
Hopi vases that held corn, are put in museums
but you know they were made to be used.
The pitcher cries for water to carry
and a person for work that is real.[31]

Tziporah, the Torah tells us, survived the plagues in safety in Midian, where Moses had sent her and their sons when the trouble started.[32] They saw Moses, once again, briefly, when Jethro brought them
to visit at Rephidim. "*Vayetzei Moshe likrat Yitro chotno vayishak-lo.*
Moses bowed low and kissed his father-in-law. They asked after each
other's welfare and went into Moses' tent."[33] But Moses had no words

or embrace for his wife. There was no longer any love between them. Tziporah took the boys back to Midian. They never inherited their father's mantle.[34] They didn't even mourn his death. But Tziporah went on to become a physician, saving lives as she had once saved her husband's life. And her sons, after her, became doctors in Midian as well.

Shifra and Puah did not fare as well. After the death-of-the-first-born, Shifra went mad and took her own life. Puah died a year later of cancer.

Yocheved and Elisheva? No one knows whether they were ever released from prison. Miriam tried to find them after *yetziat mitzrayim* (going out of Egypt). She never did. "All these lives—like pages torn from a holy book."[35]

"At night I dream the women of our family come to me and say: 'We who modestly carried our pure blood through generations, bring it to you like wine kept in the kosher cellars of our hearts.'"[36]

When Miriam was dying, her mother's words came back to her—words Yocheved once said as her husband was reciting *Eshet chayil*.[37] "Miriam, my *mamelah,* when they say, 'A woman of valor who can find; her worth is far above rubies,' I want you always to remember: a woman's worth is not measured only by what she does in her lifetime. A woman's worth is measured also by what she inspires others to do years, generations after she has died."

A man's worth is not measured only by what he does in his lifetime. A man's worth is measured also by what he inspires others to do years, generations after he has died.

So, too, the value of a movement is not measured only by what it accomplishes during its lifetime. The value of a movement is measured also by what it inspires others to accomplish years, generations after the movement has died.

Miriam never married and never had daughters of her own. But among her students, and the students of her students, and the students of her students' students are numbered: rebels and radicals, legislators and lawyers, poets and painters, teachers and organizers, nurses and doctors, scientists and rabbis. And your worth is far above rubies.[38]

With Strong Hands
and Outstretched Arms

SHARON COHEN ANISFELD

At the heart of our telling of the Exodus story on Passover lies this simple statement: "Once we were slaves in Egypt, but God brought us out from there with a strong hand and an outstretched arm."[1] The words are etched into our consciousness as Jews; our defining memory as a people is bound up with a sense of our utter dependence on God. We are meant to remember our liberation from Egypt not primarily as a drama of human heroism but as a story of divine compassion and power.

The image of God's strong hand and outstretched arm simultaneously comforts and challenges us. No place, no matter how desperate, is beyond the reach of God's redeeming hand. Yet, confronted with the urgent problem of human suffering, then and in our own time, we must struggle to understand our own place in the story. What was and is the role of human beings in bringing an end to suffering and injustice? How do we cultivate a sense of gratitude and humility, without encouraging passivity and helplessness in the face of an unredeemed world? A closer look at the opening chapters of Exodus reveals that the image of God's "strong hand and outstretched arm" has reverberations throughout the story of our departure from Egypt and that, in fact, it bears not a simple message of human powerlessness but a complex message of interdependence between human beings and God.

This story begins with a cry—the deep, inarticulate cry of pain and longing that rises up from the bellies of the Israelite slaves and ascends to heaven. It is this cry, at the end of the second chapter of the Book

Rabbi Sharon Cohen Anisfeld is director of education and programming at Harvard Hillel. While associate rabbi at Joseph Slifka Center for Jewish Life at Yale from 1993 to 2001, she was an adviser to Jewish Women at Yale. She has been a faculty member of the Bronfman Youth Fellowships in Israel since 1993. She lives in Boston with her husband and two children. She is coeditor of *The Women's Passover Companion* and *The Women's Seder Sourcebook* (both Jewish Lights Publishing).

of Exodus, that—after generations of slavery—finally evokes a response from God and sets the process of liberation in motion.[2]

> The Israelites were groaning under their bondage and cried out; and their cry for help from the bondage rose up to God. God heard their moaning, and God remembered the covenant with Abraham and Isaac and Jacob. God looked upon the Israelites, and God took notice of them.[3]

The cry of the Israelites at this point in the story is particularly significant when we consider the profound silence that it pierces. For the horror of Pharaoh's Egypt is epitomized by the effort to stifle, muffle, and silence the human cry. The following midrash brings that horror into full relief:

> Rabbi Akiva says: Pharaoh's police would strangle the Israelites in the walls of the buildings, between the bricks. And they would cry out from within the walls and God would hear their moaning, as it is said, "And God heard their moaning and God remembered the covenant..." (Exodus 2:24).[4]

In the biblical text itself, there are other intimations of the stifled human cry. Indeed, the quintessential human cry is the cry of the newborn. Great pains are taken by the women of Exodus to ensure that this cry is not heard, lest it be silenced forever. This is implied in the text when we learn that Yocheved could no longer hide Moses at three months—presumably because there was too great a risk that his cries would be heard. The following midrash elaborates on this poignant image:

> R. Hanan said, "What did the chaste and virtuous Israelite women do? They took their infants and hid them in holes [in their houses]. So the wicked Egyptians would take their own young children, bring them into the homes of the Israelites, and pinch their young until they cried. When the Israelite infants in their hiding places heard the Egyptian children cry, they cried with them. Then the Egyptians would seize the Israelite infants and cast them into the Nile."[5]

Pharaoh creates a world in which mothers have to stifle the cries of their own babies, and yet here we also see how irrepressible the cry of life is. An infant hears another infant crying and cannot help but respond with her own cry. Life cries out to itself—it cannot be silenced. Ultimately, the only perfect silence is death. In this context, the crying out of the Israelites can be more fully understood as the beginning of our liberation, for it is the irrepressible welling up of life within us that again and again gives birth to hope.

But why is it that God does not intervene to bring an end to the suffering of the Israelites until they cry out? Is God unaware of their suffering before this point? Is God indifferent to their suffering before this point? This is a troubling aspect of the story, for we cannot help but wonder where God was when slaves were being ruthlessly beaten and babies were being thrown into the river to die.

This question stands now as it always has. But part of the answer is suggested by the Chasidic commentator Sefat Emeth, who writes: "Before this, they were so deep in exile that they did not even feel they were in exile. Now that they understood exile and groaned, a little redemption began."[6]

The awareness of suffering is the beginning of longing, and longing is the beginning of redemption. To cry is, at some level—however inarticulate—to reach out. It is to take the risk of exposing one's own lack, and it is to take the risk of asking for help. While the text specifically does *not* say that the Children of Israel cried out *to God,* we are told that their cries ascended to heaven. It was enough for them to cry out, even without knowing why and to whom, for God to hear them and respond.

Shortly after this moment in the text, Moses encounters God in the wilderness of Midian at the Burning Bush. They have a dialogue there, which begins with God calling out to Moses, "Moses Moses!" And Moses responds, *"Hineini."* Here I am.[7]

An extraordinary midrash from *Exodus Rabbah* comments on God's call to Moses in this encounter:

Moses Moses. Here the Hebrew text provides no stop equivalent to a comma between the two occurrences of the name Moses.[8] Why not? This question may be answered by the parable of a man overloaded by an excessively heavy burden, who cries out all in one breath, "Somebody somebody, come quickly, take this load off me!"[9]

The claim of the midrash is astonishing. God's emphatic double call to Moses is a cry for help—a cry that echoes the cry of the Israelite people just a few verses earlier. These cries, together, bear the urgent message of radical interdependence, for God teaches Moses at the bush that the cry for help does not only link human beings to one another; it also links heaven and earth.

In this midrash, God—as it were—takes the risk of acknowledging a lack, a need for help. And in so doing, God teaches Moses, and us, that the suffering of another demands not sympathy but empathy, the recognition of shared vulnerability. God shows Moses that the path to redemption is not a path of autonomy and grand isolation. The burden of liberation must be shared. This is a lesson that Moses—whose career as a leader begins in lonely flight—will struggle with all his life.

This lesson was brought home to me one evening when my son Daniel was first adjusting to kindergarten, and a friend of his was over at our house for dinner. At some point during the meal, Daniel suddenly began to cry, and his friend James asked me what was wrong. I explained that Daniel was feeling a little scared about going to kindergarten the next day. In a moment of generosity that I will never forget, James immediately said to Daniel, "Do you want to hear some things that I'm afraid of?" And without self-consciousness, he began to list some of the things that frightened him. Soon, we were going around the table, each of us telling what made us afraid. Daniel was comforted in a way I had not been able to comfort him myself.

What James intuitively understood was the power of recognizing our shared vulnerability. Why is this so powerful? Because to know that others are as vulnerable as we are is both to feel safer about sharing our own weakness and to know our own strength—to know that others need us, even as we need them.

Shortly after the Israelites finally leave Egypt, they again find themselves in what seems to be a desperate situation, and again they cry out. This time, they stand at the threshold of freedom. They have witnessed great "signs and wonders"; they have survived the final night of passage out of Egypt. But, after a three-day journey out of Egypt, the Israelites find themselves caught between the pursuing Egyptian army and the sea. When they realize they are trapped, they panic:

> And they said to Moses: "Was it for want of graves in Egypt that you brought us to die in the wilderness? What have you done to us, taking us out of Egypt? ... It is better for us to serve the Egyptians than to die in the wilderness"![10]

Moses responds by attempting to reassure them: "Have no fear! Stand by, and witness the deliverance which the Lord will work for you today.... The Lord will battle for you; you hold your peace!"[11]

But God responds by admonishing Moses:

> Why do you cry out to Me? Tell the Israelites to go forward. And you lift up your rod and hold out your arm over the sea and split it, so that the Israelites may march into the sea on dry ground.[12]

God's response is fascinating. What, precisely, is the nature of the rebuke? I would like to suggest that Moses has misunderstood what the people need; he has misunderstood the relational imperative of the moment. The people's cry demands not his piety but his presence. God will indeed part the seas for the Children of Israel to pass through. Moses is right about that. Where he is wrong, God's response suggests, is in his intuition about what the people need to hear. It is as if God is saying: I'll take care of the sea, Moses. You take care of the people. Tell them to go forward—in other words, don't tell them that you have faith in *Me*, tell them that you have faith in *them!*

Significantly, God—the God who redeems us from Egypt with a "strong hand and an outstretched arm"—tells Moses to stretch forth his own arm and tell the people to go forward. Why does Moses have to stretch forth his arm? Surely it is not because he possesses magical or supernatural powers; we know it is God, not Moses, who must split the sea.

Moses must stretch forth his arm because, ultimately, the out-stretched arm *is* the response to the human cry. If the cry is one way of reaching out across the chasm between us, the outstretched arm is another. This is what liberation requires; this is what will enable the people to move forward; this is what will transform the waters of despair into the waters of redemption.

This is the greatness of the daughter of Pharaoh, whose compassion earns her the name Batya, daughter of God. According to a midrash in the Babylonian Talmud, tractate *Megillah,* the arm of Pharaoh's daughter "miraculously stretched to sixty *amot* when she extended her hand to reach for the baby Moses as he lay in a basket in the Nile River."[13] We are told that Pharaoh's daughter sees the baby and hears him crying. Her compassion miraculously extends across the vast distances of class and nationality and religion that separate her from the Hebrew child. She is called the daughter of God because she acts in the image of God—extending a strong hand and an out-stretched arm to protect this crying infant, the very embodiment of human vulnerability.

This is also what the midwives Shifra and Puah understand deeply, intuitively. Indeed, it is the essence of the midwife's work. For the midwife responds to the moans of the woman in labor; the midwife responds to the insistent, robust cry of the newborn child, with strong, skillful hands and a gentle, outstretched arm.

Perhaps this is why God is portrayed as midwife in the following midrash on the Song at the Sea. The commentary is responding to the verse *"Zeh eli v'anveyhu,"*[14] This is my God and I will praise Him.

R. Judah said: It was those babies whom Pharaoh had sought to cast into the Nile that sang praises to the Holy One, blessed be He, whom they recognized at the Sea. Why was this? Because when Israel were in Egypt and a Hebrew woman was about to give birth, she would go to a field and be delivered there; and as soon as the child was born, she would forsake him and entrust him into the hands of God, saying, "Lord of the Universe! I have done my part; now do Thine." R. Johanan said: Immediately, God would descend in His glory—can one say thus!—cut their navel, and wash and anoint them.... When the Israelites came to the Sea, and their children with them, and the latter beheld God at the Sea, they said to their parents: "This is the one who did all those things for us when we were in Egypt," as it says, "This is my God, and I will glorify Him"(Exodus 15:2).[15]

The midrash places the words of the song into the mouths of the Israelite children, now grown. The infants, whose cries once had to be stifled and hidden, now sing aloud! *Zeh eli v'anveyhu!* This is my God and I will praise Him! With all the patience, tenderness, and skill of a midwife, with a "strong hand and an outstretched arm," God has transformed the cries of the children of slaves into the song of free women and men.

The journey out of Egypt is not simply a journey from despair to hope. It is a journey from despair to hope and back again many times over. Such is our nature as human beings. The Children of Israel will weep and rejoice again many times on their long journey through the wilderness.

But the real-life process of liberation requires no less than this: that we reach out again and again, in spite of the great risks, in spite of the inevitable disappointments—that we reach out to one another, again and again, with strong hands and outstretched arms.

This is the wonder that God performs for us on our journey out of Egypt. This is the miracle that transforms our weeping into song.

≋

The Secret of Redemption:
A Tale of Mirrors

AVIVAH GOTTLIEB ZORNBERG

A classic statement in the Talmud focuses on women as the redeeming force in Egypt: "In reward for the righteous women in that generation, Israel were redeemed from Egypt."[1] Redemption, says the Talmud, came only because of "righteous women." Does this refer to the particular, courageous women singled out in the narrative—to Yocheved, Moses' mother, to Miriam, to Pharaoh's daughter, to the Israelite midwives? Or does it gesture toward a more general feminine power that, working at first in semidarkness, finally releases the people from the spiritual paralysis of Egypt?[2] This second, more radical view is adopted by *Midrash Tanchuma:*

> *"These are the records* (pikudei) *of the Tabernacle":* You find that when Israel were in harsh labor in Egypt, Pharaoh decreed *(gazar)* against them that they should not sleep at home nor have relations with their wives. Said Rabbi Shimeon bar Chalafta, What did the daughters of Israel do? They would go down to draw water from the river and God would prepare for them little fish in their buckets, and they would sell some of them, and cook some of them, and buy wine with the proceeds, and go to the field and feed their husbands, as it is said, "In all the labor in the field" (1:14).
>
> And when they had eaten and drunk, the women would take the mirrors and look into them with their husbands, and she would say, "I am more comely than you," and he would say, "I am more comely than you." And as a result, they would accustom themselves to desire, and they were fruitful and multiplied, and God took note of them *(pakad)* immediately.
>
> Some of our sages said, They bore two children at a time, others said, They bore six at a time, yet others said, They bore twelve at a time, and still others said, Six hundred thousand.... *And all these numbers from* the *mirrors....* In the merit of those mirrors

---

Dr. Avivah Gottlieb Zornberg is the author of the highly acclaimed *The Beginning of Desire: Reflections on Genesis* and *The Particulars of Rapture: Reflections on Exodus.*

which they showed their husbands to accustom them to desire, from the midst of the harsh labor, they raised up all the hosts, as it is said, "All the hosts of God went out of the land of Egypt" (12:41) and it is said, "God brought the Children of Israel out of the land of Egypt in their hosts" (12:51).

When God told Moses to make the Tabernacle, the whole people stood up and offered whatever they had—silver, gold, copper, etc.; everyone eagerly offered their treasures. The women said, "What have we to offer as a gift for the Tabernacle?" So they brought the mirrors to Moses. When Moses saw those mirrors, he was furious with them. He said to the Israelites, "Take sticks and break their thighs! What do they need mirrors for?" Then God said to Moses, "Moses, these you despise! *These mirrors raised up all those hosts in Egypt!* Take them, and make of them a copper ewer with a copper stand for the priests to sanctify themselves—as it is said, 'And he made the ewer of copper and its stand of copper, of the mirrors of those who created hosts....'" (38:8) [This is a free, midrashic translation of the verse].[3]

The midrash gains its momentum from the opening *gezerah:* Pharaoh issues a decree, a cut-and-dried (the root of *gezerah* means "to cut") formula that will separate men from women. In the context of the biblical narrative, the purpose is clear: "so that they may not increase" (1:10). Pharaoh has cut off the possibility of natural increase among the Israelites. But the midrash does not emphasize the effective purpose of the edict: merely that couples are sexually separated, since the husbands may not sleep at home.

The women enter the narrative as a question: "What did the daughters of Israel do?" The assumption is that the women, who are not most directly affected by the edict (since it is the men who are the laborers and who are prevented from going home at night), will adopt some measure against it. Since the edict is one of separation, of effective sterilization, the women's efforts naturally tend toward reunion. The little fish, archetypal symbols of fertility, become clear sexual signs as they providentially swim up in the women's buckets. They are transformed in the most pragmatic way—through cooking and the cash nexus—into a nourishing and stimulating meal for the exhausted husbands in the field.

It is striking that God appears twice in this narrative. First, God provides the little fish, the most "natural" of events. Thereafter, the women's planning takes over—the conscious use and reconstruction of the natural into the shape of desire. Having fed their husbands, the women contemplate themselves with their husbands as a couple in "the mirrors," which are described with the definite article, though we have not read of them till now. What follows is an intimate scene of erotic "boasting," shockingly unconventional in sentimental terms. Instead of praising each other, each praises her/his own beauty by comparison with the other. This "mirror work" produces desire and procreation; through processes that are complex and willful, they are "fruitful and multiply," fulfilling the original blessing/command to humankind (Genesis 1:28; 9:7).

And God acts a second time. God "takes notice"—*pakad*—of them. This one word, here most clearly signifying the mysterious gift of pregnancy, gathers multiple resonances. Its first use in the Torah was to narrate Sarah's pregnancy, after years of barrenness (Genesis 21:1). God's promise of redemption—*pakod yifkod*—is fulfilled here, in the most "natural" mode imaginable. For what could be more "natural" than the women's conceiving after they are reunited with their husbands? It is as natural as the shoals of fish that swarm up in the women's buckets. Yet, in these two moments, particularly in the fishing and in the conceiving of many children (and the midrash reminds us that the same word is used for both—*vayishretzu*—they "swarmed"), God enters the narrative and gives a surrealistic turn to the natural events: fish-becomes-wine-becomes-desire, and babies are born in multiples of (perhaps) six hundred thousand. Why does the midrash require God here? Why does it bring into play the epic resonance of *pakod yifkod*, of the secret of redemption? And why the mirrored narcissism of the couple at the visual heart of the midrash? On the "plot" level, it would have been sufficient to have the women feed their husbands well in order to achieve reunion and fertility.

The end of the midrash emphasizes the enigmatic character of events. The extraordinary fertility of the women leads to the Zen-like statement, "All these numbers were from the mirrors." The midrash deflects our attention from the "natural" level of reading, from the normal strategies of arousal of desire, the aphrodisiac function of wine and fish, although the calculated preparation of these delicacies was the opening subject of the narrative. Essentially, claims the midrash, it was all done with mirrors. The midrash finishes with a bizarre dialogue, in which Moses violently deplores the women's gift of these same mirrors to the Tabernacle, while God overrides his objections: "These mirrors raised up all the Israelite hosts in Egypt."

Subtly, the midrash yields its meanings. The mirrors are not simply the means by which women adorn themselves to set in motion the processes of desire, procreation, and the creation of a nation. A much larger claim is being made: Through these mirrors, each woman conceived *six hundred thousand* babies at a time. These mirrors, when God asks for gifts to the Tabernacle, to create sacred space, are *all the women have*. In Rashi's version, God concludes: "These mirrors are more precious to Me than any other gift."[4]

Moses' anger at the apparent frivolity, the inappropriate sexual associations of the gift, makes it clear that the gift is not a "giving up" of vanity.[5] It becomes an installation at the liminal point of entry into the sacred space: the mirrors are used to plate the priestly ewer, where hands and feet are washed. Giving their mirrors for this purpose, the women are making no ascetic immolation of the accoutrements of desire: Moses' outraged rejection indicates this quite unmistakably. "Break their thighs" expresses an anger at sexuality that transgresses boundaries. It is God who speaks for the women and their mirrors: "The mirrors *raised up* the hosts of Israel." The verb *he'emidu* is often used to mean "beget," so that God actually says: "These mirrors *begat* the hosts of Israel." It was all done with mirrors!

Mirror Work

The most direct effect of the mirrors, in the words of the midrash, is desire ("And they accustomed themselves to desire"). The drama; the action of husband and wife in front of the mirror; the four faces speaking, challenging, affirming beauty create a culture of desire. For one of the most arresting phenomena in the narrative is its fusion of intimacy and the most public perspective. The subject is the relation between husband and wife, in its most delicate moment; but in watching the couple in front of their mirror, we see multiple mirror reflections of the scene. Every woman in Israel is enacting the same drama. Our subject is not one particular woman, one extraordinary heroic figure, but "the daughters of Israel"—a title that gives honor and propriety to their acts. Strangely, there is a chaste, impersonal quality to the narrative: It tells, essentially, the story of redemption: "In reward for the righteous women of that generation, Israel were redeemed from Egypt" (BT *Sotah* 11b). In this way, a nation of six hundred thousand men was formed: this is the demographic, public product of the story. But, at the same time, each individual woman is described as having given birth to six hundred thousand. The very thought concentrates the mind wonderfully!

The enigmas of the story clearly center on the mirror. What is its role here in creating desire, fruitfulness, and the *pekida,* the transfiguring presence of God? Each woman says, "I am more beautiful than you." She initiates the boasting game. The midrash may well be evoking the verse from the Song of Songs: "I am black but beautiful—*na'avah*" (1:5). The word for beauty is the same as the one used in the midrash: *na'eh*—comely, harmonious. Literally, the verse reads, "I am black *and* beautiful," but since there is no alternative mode of indicating the disjunctive "but," a teasing ambiguity destabilizes the text. Clearly, in context, blackness is a reason for shame:[6] here, the beloved proudly claims a paradoxical beauty despite/within her swarthiness. This is no primary narcissism but the difficult project of seeing beauty in the blackened self.

Classic midrashim tell of the beauty that God sees in God's people, in their very blackness. In Rashi's commentary, for instance, although the lover has abandoned her because of her blackness, she asserts her *structural* beauty: the blackness is mere sunburn, but her limbs are well made. By analogy, even if her deeds are ugly, she affirms a true self, a genetic identity, in which beauty is always potential. To assert this, she must draw not on the assurances of a lover but on her own awareness of beauty-within-blackness.

She says, "I am more beautiful than you," not "You are more beautiful than I." Her boast, delivered as the two gaze together at their reflections in the mirror, is a challenge to her husband, grimy with clay and mud, to see beauty within that blackness. What she initiates is a dynamic, loving game. What she says is not a statement of fact but a performance of transformation. Against the *gezerah* of Pharaoh she sets up the mirror of desire. The hosts of Israel, the secret of redemption: it is all done with mirrors.

The peculiar nature of this gift of the women to the Tabernacle is discussed by Rambam.[7] Why was Moses so angry at this particular donation? After all, the women gave other female items associated with narcissism and sexuality—jewelry of all kinds. Rambam answers that the other gifts—gold, silver, copper—were melted down to make the accessories of the Tabernacle. Only the mirrors were preserved as mirrors and used for one specific object—the ewer. The burnished copper ("very beautiful," Rambam notes) was assigned to this one purpose, and so remains as an unmitigated reminder of the mirrors and their original uses, with all the erotic associations that Moses deplores. The ewer, at which priests consecrate themselves to the service of God,[8] retains the reflective surfaces, the form and function of the original gift.

There are even fascinating speculations in the midrashic literature that the ewer served as a kind of mirror-system, like a periscope or telescope, giving people a view of the interior of the Tabernacle, for example.[9] Mirrors thus function to allow vision at oblique angles, round corners, at a distance. With all the distortion of mirrors of that period (polished copper, we remember[10]), we may say that they function as revealers of the inaccessible: one's own face, the banned interior of the Tabernacle. They offer, in a sense, a counterworld to the world of the *gezerah*, of the "way it has to be." The natural limitations of vision are challenged and deflected by this instrument that distorts reality (even modern mirrors retain the right-left reversal) in order to extend perception.

A similar point is made by Rashi, in a comment on Isaiah 3:23. Here, mirrors are referred to as *gilyonim*—"revealers." Since this expression never recurs, Rashi explains: "These are mirrors, called so because they reveal the forms of the face." The plural perspectives of the mirror—each movement of the head produces a different form in the mirror, yielding a shifting, multiple revelation of self.

The diffracting, revelatory quality of the mirror is the gift of the women to the *mishkan*. It is not the object but the practice that is the gift: the mirror-practice, seducing with visions of possible futures. Such work with mirrors is finely performed by the righteous women of that generation, without whose righteous play redemption would have been impossible. We remember the talmudic claim with which we began: "In reward for the righteous women in that generation, Israel were redeemed from Egypt." The paradoxical elaboration of the midrash presents the feminine generative perspective, fluid and performative, as the force that ultimately releases the self from its rigid necessities. Against the *gezerah*, against Pharaoh's edicts, indeed against the sensibility of the lawgiver—Moses himself—the transformative vision of women breaks the deadlock of Egypt.

≋

"Fixing" Liberation, or How Rebecca Initiates the Passover Seder

BONNA DEVORA HABERMAN

According to the Talmud, the daily prayers were instituted by our fore-*fathers*. Abraham, who arose with the morning sun to perform God's will, established *shacharit* (morning prayers). Isaac, who went out to the field for meditation at the turning of day to evening, established *mincha* (afternoon prayers). Jacob, for whom the sun set to reveal the ladder connecting heaven and earth, fixed *ma'ariv* (evening prayers).[1]

The solar cycle creates the framework for Jewish daily prayers, but it is the lunar inflections that govern our festival celebrations. While living in exile from the sacred land, the rabbinic authorities developed the radical Jewish innovation of sanctifying historical time.[2] Whereas the biblical festivals had been rooted in the cycle of the harvest, the Rabbis infused them with new meaning by connecting them with formative events in the history of the Jewish people. For example, our sages associated the festival of Shavuot, which celebrates the conclusion of the barley harvest and the onset of the wheat harvest, with the giving of the Torah at Mount Sinai, though there is no explicit indication of this connection in the biblical text.[3] The celebration of the onset of spring and of the barley harvest, a time of eating unleavened bread, became the marker of the Exodus from Egypt.[4]

The Exodus story is a cornerstone of Jewish identity and social vision. The Rabbis emphasize the liberation aspect of the spring festival, focusing our attention on the birthlike drama of the Israelites attaining national autonomy and freedom.[5] While the spring harvest returns annually, the Exodus was a singular event. Linking the Exo-

---

Dr. Bonna Devora Haberman is resident scholar in women's studies and the founder and director of Mistabra: The Israel-Diaspora Institute for Jewish Textual Activism and director of education initiative at the New Jewish High School of Greater Boston. She holds a doctorate in philosophy from the University of London, England. She has taught at the Harvard University Divinity School, Brandeis University, and Hebrew College. Bonna founded Women of the Wall, an Israeli movement promoting the religious rights of women.

dus with the cyclical festival creates a yearly reenactment and affirmation of liberation. Reliving our historic experience of liberation extends it into our contemporary moment as we claim our place at the tables and barricades of feminist Jewish liberation.

Whence does the Passover night ritual of the seder derive, and who established it? In the analysis that follows, I propose that a close reading of a rabbinic midrash reveals that it was our foremother Rebecca who established the Passover seder. In discussing this anachronistic assertion, I will explore a complicated matrix of sacred place and time, ancestors and sages, written and oral transmission.

In the Book of Genesis, Rebecca and Isaac disagree about which of their twin sons is the rightful inheritor to their legacy. Isaac prefers Esau, a hunter and man of the field who tastes his prey in his mouth, while Rebecca favors Jacob, a simple man who dwells in tents.[6] No love was lost between the brothers themselves; the bartering of lentil soup for the birthright is well known. When Esau returns from a hunt tired and famished, Jacob tricks him into exchanging his birthright for a bowl of red lentils.

When Isaac is old and preparing to die, and his eyes have grown dim, he calls his eldest son Esau, following the norm of primogenitor.[7] Esau's response, *"hineini"*—"I am present!"—is reminiscent of the exchange between Abraham and Isaac during the sacrificial binding and foreshadows a portentous transaction. Isaac asks Esau to hunt and prepare a special feast so that he might bless his son before dying. Overhearing this exchange, Rebecca conspires with Jacob to thwart Isaac's plan and divert the blessing to Jacob. Jacob's wile is fulfilled as Isaac unwittingly bestows the firstborn blessing upon Jacob by means of an elaborate deception involving sheep's wool and a special meal. The following midrash creatively elaborates the scene:

> The eve of Passover arrived, and Yitzchak called to his eldest son Esau and said to him: "My son, this is the night that the whole world is singing *hallel,* and the treasure chests of dew open up this night. Prepare me special foods so that I will bless you while I am still alive." And the Holy Spirit answered saying: "Do not

eat the bread of one who has an evil eye" (Proverbs 23.6). He went to bring it, and was delayed there.

Rivka said to Jacob: "My son, on this night, the treasure chests of dew open up, the heavenly ones are singing *hallel*. On this night, your future children are destined to be redeemed from slavery; on this night, they are destined to sing the song (*hallel*/the Song at the Sea). Prepare special foods for your father so that he will bless you while he is still alive."

"And I shall bring upon myself a curse and not a blessing" (Genesis 27.12). Ya'akove was knowledgeable about the Torah, and he feared in his heart the curse of his father. His mother said to him: "My son, blessings will be for you and for your seed; and if there are curses, they are upon me and upon my soul." As it says, Upon me your curse my son (Genesis 27.13).[8, 9]

The midrash opens with a dramatic claim, which is the foundation for my proposal about Rebecca: the proposition that the blessing transpired on the eve of Pesach. Let us read the midrash closely. The interpreter's claim is rooted in the association of the biblical spring Passover festival with the onset of the Israeli season of dew. On the first day of Passover, we recite a prayer that serves as the liturgical transition from our prayers for rain to those for dew. In the biblical text, Isaac explains that he will bless Esau on the night when the heavenly dew chests open. Indeed, Isaac begins his final blessing with the gift of dew: "May God give you dew from heaven."[10] Furthermore, after the final crossing of the sea, the miraculous manna that sustained the Children of Israel during their wandering through the desert was delivered to the earth under a coating of dew:

> In the evening, quail appeared and covered the camp; in the morning there was a fall of dew about the camp. When the fall of dew lifted there, over the surface of the wilderness, lay a fine and flaky substance, as fine as frost on the ground.[11]

These connections between the Exodus story and the spring dew support my claim that the evening of the blessing meal is the incipient Passover eve.

In the midrash, Isaac says, "This is the night that the whole world is singing *hallel*." This mention of singing *hallel*, a compilation of psalms praising God, at night unmistakably rivets the blessing to the Passover seder, since Passover eve is the only time during the year when we sing *hallel* at night. Indeed, the special *hallel* of Passover eve, a hallmark of Jewish festivals, is called the Great *Hallel*. Yet, why would everyone be singing *hallel*, praises of thanksgiving, on account of dew? In the temperate climates of America, it is difficult to fathom blessing the dew. But in the Israeli seasonal cycle, there is total dryness between Passover and Sukkot, and the dew brings vital, life-sustaining moistness to the searing, deadly heat. Because it provides the minimal water required to sustain life and enable the crops to mature, the summer dew in Israel is cause for jubilation. The nighttime singing of *hallel* mentioned by Isaac, therefore, is an agrarian invocation and offering of gratitude for the blessing of dew.

Following the rabbinic bias against Esau, the midrash concludes by casting aspersions against him. The Holy Spirit colludes with Rebecca, detaining Esau at the hunt in order to allow for the deception. Indeed, though Isaac has predicted a scene of singing praise, Esau ends up being excluded from blessing. There is no rejoicing because of his pain: "Esau cried out a great and bitter cry."

Though the separate statements of Isaac and Rebecca to each of their two sons are very similar, there are some extremely significant differences. While Isaac connects the auspicious evening to dew and to the singing of *hallel*, Rebecca adds another dimension of meaning to the night of the blessing. Rebecca prophesies the redemption of the descendants of Jacob: "On this night, your future children are destined to be redeemed from slavery; on this night, they are destined to sing the song." Rebecca predicts the connection of dew—a subtle and delicate miracle of creation—with the dramatic miracles and wonders of Israelite liberation. Rebecca associates tiny droplets of moisture with the parting of the ancient Reed Sea into walls of passage.

Even more astoundingly, Rebecca prophesies the liberation from bondage and the eventual Passover celebration, at which, she predicts, Jacob's descendants will sing. The midrashic use of the term *shira* (song) implicitly refers both to the *hallel* and to the jubilant song sung at the sea after the crossing out of Egypt. The Song at the Sea is the first poem recorded in the Torah, a night-long communal celebratory response to the experience of redemption. It is referred to in rabbinic sources as simply "the Song."[12] Whereas the singing of *hallel* in Isaac's statement ends with the association of dew, Rebecca speaks to her son about slavery and redemption, and thereby performs the essential commandment of the eve of Passover: "and you shall tell your child the story of liberation on that night."[13] This statement is the equivalent of the *maggid*, the "telling" segment of the seder.

The intense symbolism of the seder food is also alluded to by the midrash. The contrast between the foods served by Jacob and Esau to their father strengthens the association between Rebecca and the seder. Isaac sends Esau to hunt; Rebecca sends Jacob to the flock. Rebecca's command to bring domestic animals foreshadows the Passover offering commanded in the Exodus story: "Take for yourselves a sheep for your families."[14] The careful preparation of the food hints at the laborious gastronomic effort we expend in preparing the seder feast. In the biblical text of the blessing that Isaac finally bestows upon Jacob, dew is mentioned first: "May God give you (blessing) from the dew of heaven, from the richness of the earth, plentiful grain, and the juice of grapes."[15] The dew is referred to first because it is necessary for sustenance from the earth, and for the wine and grain, the critical ingredients in the seder meal: the wine of the four cups, the flour for the matzah, the unleavened bread.

The midrash closes with Rebecca's expression of her unconditional willingness to shoulder the entire burden of risk involved in the deception. If Isaac curses, then Rebecca will accept his malediction upon herself, but she offers the blessing to Jacob without reservation. This brave posture of maternal commitment and caring is both expected and extraordinary. From where does Rebecca derive the moral stamina that allows her to act unflinchingly upon her deep conviction? Rebecca's ethical boldness, her humanity, are the foundation of liberation. Like the midwives standing in holy defiance of the earthly

Pharaoh, risking their lives for the sake of the continuity of Jewish life, Rebecca stands in defiance of the order of primogeniture, insisting on her determination of the future line of the Jewish people. Rebecca is willing to invest herself and take a risk in order to establish the Passover tradition. The annual seder compels us forever to arouse our children to experience the ongoing need for liberation.

Another powerful innovation of the midrash is to frame the seder with the passing of a blessing from one generation to the next. The reason for Isaac's request that special food be prepared and brought to him is the bestowing of a blessing. Food is meant to evoke a blessing for the Jewish people. Jacob stands before his father to have his lineage affirmed and blessed as the progenitor of the twelve tribes of Israel. The midrashic setting of the blessing from parent to child on Passover eve is poignantly relevant to our own time. By this midrash we are instructed that the driving force behind the form and method of the Passover seder must be our desire to convey our blessing to our children. This blessing is linked with the cycle of sustenance, the experience of sacredness in both time and place, in concept and body. Whether in biblical times—in the presence of disharmony and family tension—or at our own seder tables, liberation is at the center of our exchange. It is the message to our children, our gift, and our service to humanity.

In the final scene of this drama, Isaac trembles with terrible fear, and Esau cries out a tremendous and bitter cry. Rebecca's acts of liberation create disorder, undoing, deception, confusion, and even pain. Indeed, these are some of the characteristics of liberation. For how can the breakthrough, the release from bondage, be expressed in a smooth texture, orderly etiquette, assigned gestures, and rehearsed recitations? This is not an apology for the dysfunction of Rebecca's story but rather an admission of the complicated and difficult origins of our seder ritual. Rebecca first establishes the Passover seder in a troubling context and by problematic means. The rabbinic tradition formulated a tight and dense seder (literally, "order") to contain the chaotic Exodus in the wilderness and the miraculous transformations of the order of Creation through signs and wonders. Yet, upon closer inspection, the supposed "order" is neither linear nor conventional. The story told in the haggadah is layered and associative, riddled with questions, punctuated by drinking and eating, populated by personal anecdotes and fantastical interpretations. The seder beckons us to experience the liberation as if we ourselves had emerged from slavery to freedom. Rebecca establishes the Passover imperative: *"Sh'ma be'koli,"* "Heed my voice." Rebecca's command is to go, to prepare a night of blessing, a night for singing, a night for liberation. It is up to us to "fix" it!

If my theory of the establishment of the seder is meaningful to you, may I suggest that you add this midrashic process to your haggadah and bring it to your table. May we rejoice in Rebecca's prophecy, and pass on the blessing of her fervent desire and courage for liberation to our daughters and our sons forever.

≋

4

Telling Our Stories

What would happen if one woman told the truth about her life?

The world would split open. —MURIEL RUKEYSER

Between silence and speech, silence is the more dangerous: its very safety endangers the self…. It is for this reason that the Exodus, and the Passover festival that celebrates it, focuses so compellingly on telling and retelling the story. It is only by taking the real risks of language, by rupturing the autistic safety of silence, that the self can reclaim itself. To venture into words, narratives, is to venture everything for the sake of that "self before God."
—AVIVAH GOTTLIEB ZORNBERG, *THE PARTICULARS OF RAPTURE*

The commandment to tell is the fundamental obligation of our Passover observance. It is not enough for us to listen to others recounting the Israelites' liberation from slavery in Egypt; we are each responsible for relating this story aloud.

For Jewish women, whose voices have so often been repressed, dismissed, and obscured, sharing personal histories and experiences is particularly significant. As we tell the stories of our lives we begin to fill the void created over centuries of women's near invisibility in our history, literature, and sacred texts. Further, as many feminists have noted, personal stories provide a foundation for exploring new ways of thinking; they offer texts, ideas, and questions drawn from women's lives rather than from patriarchal culture.

Thus, at a women's seder, the importance of *maggid*—"the telling"—is emphasized and explored. Understanding that the collective story of our people is not complete without accounts of its women, participants not only tell stories of biblical and historical figures but also include contemporary personal tellings as a central feature of the ritual. Most often these stories draw connections between personal histories and the themes of the holiday; participants share their own experiences of wilderness, exile, oppression, and liberation. Indeed, drawing connections between one's personal history and the themes of the Passover holiday confirms the continuing relevance of the Passover texts and themes in our own time.

But because women's seders offer a rare forum for women to share their personal experiences, participants also take this opportunity to address other relevant topics. Personal "tellings" may center on issues of Jewish identity and spirituality or on critiques of our religious tradition. No matter what the topic, the experiences of telling one's story honestly, being heard, and listening to the stories of others can be transformative.

As women share and hear these stories, whether at a seder or as part of their broader observance of the holiday, they engage in an ever-deepening dialectic: bringing the texts and themes of the holiday to bear on our own personal experience enriches and adds meaning to our life stories. At the same time, informing our approach to these texts and themes with our experiences illuminates the holiday's meaning and imbues it with a sense of personal contemporary relevance.

The first authors in part 4 look at the metaphors of exile, Exodus, and the Promised Land through the lens of their personal experiences. Recounting an incredible range of physical and emotional journeys, these authors articulate the centrality and complexity of the Passover themes as they manifest in women's lives. In the opening reflection, poet and anthropologist Ruth Behar tells the story of her childhood seders in a Cuban Jewish family that is both Ashkenazic and Sephardic. "A Story for the Second Night of Passover" recounts her feeling of exile in Michigan as an adult and describes how celebrating the seder and telling her story have offered a healing sense of rootedness and homecoming.

Feminist activist Letty Cottin Pogrebin also examines the healing power of "exploring women's truths." In "Jephthah's Daughter: A Feminist Midrash," originally written to be shared at a women's seder, Pogrebin unearths the silenced story of Jephthah's Daughter, linking the fate of this biblical woman to that of an incest survivor in her community. Pogrebin raises bold questions about the ways in which Jewish texts and culture sanction abuse against women, forcing us to see that women remain in many ways exiled from positions of power in the Jewish community.

In "Memory and Revolution," Rabbi Dianne Cohler-Esses offers another important feminist critique of traditional Jewish communities. Cohler-Esses vividly describes her exodus from the close-knit, traditional Syrian Jewish community in which she was raised and her search for a balance between the values she grew up with and the liberal, feminist ideals she later developed.

Exploring a very different exile from traditional Jewish communities, observant feminist Chavi Karkowsky discusses women's *tefillah* prayer groups in "Leaving on Purpose: The Questions of Women's *Tefillah*." In her candid, astute analysis, Karkowsky examines the significance of these groups' "self-exile" from the wider community. She contemplates her journey to find a prayer group that allows her to unify her feminist values and her observance of Jewish law.

In "Of Nursing, in the Desert," scientist and women's seder organizer Janna Kaplan writes about her emigration from Soviet Russia and her journey to let go of the oppressive homeland that had become her personal *mitzrayim*. Focusing on her complicated relationship to the Russian language, this story sheds new light on the ways in which "Egypt" stays with us long after we have made the Exodus.

In "On Matzah, Questions, and Becoming a Nation," Leah Haber recounts an internal journey. Drawing closely on the Book of Exodus, Haber analyzes the relationship between the Israelites and God, probing her own evolving relationship with the Divine. Offering a unique spiritual wisdom, she provides an example of how women can explore their spirituality through an investigation of texts relevant to the seder.

Sharing a very different internal spiritual journey, author and spiritual counselor Kim Chernin imparts the lessons she learned during her three-decade quest to understand the feminine aspect of God. In "God's Bride on Pesach," Chernin explores Her exclusion from our communal story and suggests how we might reclaim and dwell with Her at the seder.

Émigré writer and teacher Jenya Zolot-Gassko's "The Matzah Set-Up" offers a moving reflection on anti-Semitism in the Soviet Union. This reflection, originally written for a women's seder, vividly communicates Zolot-Gassko's experiences of living without religious freedom, in exile from Jewish heritage and community. Her story then recounts the kindling of her Jewish identity during one Passover season.

The power of women's autobiography extends far beyond the experience of the individual woman giving expression to her own story. Judith Baskin, a professor of religious studies, probes the memoir of Bella Rosenfeld Chagall for insights that can help contemporary Jewish women understand the deeper roots of their own connections to the Passover holiday. "Women Re-creating the Passover Seder: Bella Rosenfeld Chagall and the Resonance of Female Memory" is not only a beautiful reflection on the untold story of an extraordinary woman; it is an eloquent testimony to the significance of personal storytelling as both a feminist and a religious act.

Each author in part 4 offers a unique example of how our personal stories can contribute to the seder. Each also demonstrates the power of women telling the truth about their own lives. Do they begin to illumine what Muriel Rukeyser meant when she wrote that if one woman told the truth about her life, "the world would split open"? Certainly, we are still learning what kind of truth Rukeyser had in mind. But perhaps we are also still finding out *how* to tell the kind of truth she envisioned. For Jewish women, who are searching not only for the truth of our lives but for our own ability to speak it, the act of gathering together each year to tell our stories holds a unique but as yet unsurmounted challenge.

A Story for the Second Night of Passover

RUTH BEHAR

I grew up having to explain my origins.

I am still explaining who I am. So I've had time to work on my routine.

I was born in Cuba, as were my parents. Spanish is my mother tongue, and I can cook black beans and flan.

"But you're Jewish too?"

Yes, it's one of those accidents of history. Let me try to make a long story short. You see, my grandparents left Europe with heads as cloudy as Columbus. All they knew was that they wanted to find America. They wanted to turn their backs on poverty, discrimination, and the growing nationalism in Eastern Europe and Turkey that excluded them. This was in the mid-1920s, when the United States was shutting its doors to Jewish immigrants. Cuba, they were told, was also America, and it was a country that accepted Jews. So they got on boats and went to Cuba. And stayed. Tucked away their woolen garments. Peddled blankets. Sold lace. Learned Spanish. Had children. Watched their

Dr. Ruth Behar is a professor of anthropology at the University of Michigan. She is also affiliated with University of Michigan programs in women's studies, Latina/Latino studies, and Latin American and Caribbean studies. She is the author of *The Vulnerable Observer: Anthropology That Breaks Your Heart* and the editor of *Women Writing Culture*.

children have children and hire black maids for next to nothing. Many of them prospered. Every Sunday they went to El Casino Deportivo, the beach club that was open to Jews. And they decided they were so happy in Cuba they'd stay forever.

Confident they would stay in Cuba for generations to come, they built two huge synagogues in the 1950s, one Ashkenazi and one Sephardi, not knowing that they were constructing monuments to mark their impending exile. Then Fidel Castro came in 1959 and took away their stores and the *shmattes* they peddled and their favorite beach club and scared them away. In the 1960s, most of the Jews of Cuba abandoned the island. That was how my Cuban family landed in the America that two generations earlier had been closed to them as Jews. I was a child and knew nothing, but they wept bitter tears as they departed from their beloved island. They were a people who had experienced diaspora upon diaspora. They knew what it meant to reduce their lives to one suitcase. They understood in their own flesh why their ancestors might have been in too much of a hurry to let the dough rise.

Now there's one more twist to the story. Most of the time I don't get to tell this part, because it's of little statistical value in diversity calculations in the United States, where they're always trying to figure out if I can count as "Hispanic." You see, I'm not simply both Cuban and Jewish. I'm also both an Ashkenazi and a Sephardi Jew. I was born of an Ashkenazi Cuban mother and a Sephardi Cuban father. My parents' marriage, in Havana of 1956, was viewed as a kind of intermarriage. Their families spoke different ancestral languages, Yiddish and Ladino; they ate different foods; and their lost European homelands— Christian, on the one hand, and Muslim, on the other—had given them different worldviews and sensibilities. I called my mother's parents *baba* and *zayde,* following Yiddish usage, and my father's parents were *abuela* and *abuelo,* acknowledging their link to the remembered Spanish world of *Sepharad,* which means "Spain" in Hebrew. I can claim roots in forgotten villages in Poland and Byelorussia, and in the town of Silivri, near Istanbul, which overlooks the turquoise sea. My mother's sister, with straight blond hair and green eyes, and my father's sisters, with incurably wavy hair and dark brown eyes, are equally my aunts. When I was growing up in New York, on the first night of Passover we ate gefilte fish, matzah ball soup, and boiled chicken; on the second night, we ate egg lemon soup, stuffed tomatoes, and *tish-pishti,* a holiday almond cake dripping with honey. And at the end of the eight days we'd go to El Rincón Criollo on Junction Boulevard for black beans, fried plantains, and *palomilla* steak with glistening onions.

Many, many years have passed since the Passover seders of my girl-hood spent with my four grandparents. They are now gone, and even in death they have returned to the earth separately, my Sephardi grand-parents to a cemetery in New Jersey, my Ashkenazi grandparents to a cemetery in Miami. Living in Michigan, equally far from Cuba and our immigrant home in New York, I look back with nostalgia and longing for those seders that each set of grandparents lovingly kept, year after year—seders so clearly born of two distinctly different Jew-ish worlds.

But it has also been years since I have been at a Passover seder with my parents and other Jewish-Cuban family members in New York. Oddly enough, my husband, my teenaged son, and I are more likely to go to New York these days for Thanksgiving, since we have the time off from work and school. Passover, like most of the Jewish holidays, tends to fall at an inconvenient time—at least from the perspective of the academic calendar, which is the one that I, as a professor, must fol-low. Typically, Passover comes near the end of the semester, during the crunch time of teaching, writing letters of recommendation, attending conferences, and preparing for final exams. And so we stay in Michigan and do Passover as best we can, not with family but with friends. Everything for the seder gets scrambled together at the last minute, in a hurry. But I know my ancestors have mercy; I know they forgive me.

During these fifteen years of living in Michigan, I have vividly felt myself to be an exile—an exile not simply from Cuba but from the unique Ashkenazi-Sephardi Cuban culture that my family re-created as immigrants in New York in the 1960s and 1970s. Growing up in a large extended family, where we only spoke Spanish, I came to feel the smallness and fragility of my little nuclear family, in which English dominated and the members consisted of a Papa Be(h)ar, a Mama Be(h)ar, and a Baby Be(h)ar. While achieving success in my academic career, I surprised myself as I struggled against unbearable periods of loneliness that struck suddenly in the middle of the afternoon, and weeping spells, when the tears fell to my lips and I could taste the salt. It would have been too easy to call what I was feeling depression. No, it was bigger than that. It was grief. Pure grief. The grief of the traveler who has no one to greet her when she returns from her journey. I was mourning everything I had lost and would never have again. Except—and it took me a while to see this—in the form of a story. If I could tell the story, it wouldn't disappear, that world I had known. It would exist, continue to exist, for as long as there were words, and books, and Passover tables to tell stories at. Once I came to this basic and fundamental understanding, happiness no longer eluded me. I embraced my exile; I set down roots in the sand of my own diaspora.

Passover is all about exile, and I am an exile in Michigan. My house is the house of an exiled woman. I am a daughter of so many places left behind—a daughter, too, of so many other places hesitantly claimed in a futile effort to remember the places I cannot. It is full of oak furniture from abandoned farms in Ohio and Michigan. On the walls I have drawings and paintings and tapestries I have brought from Cuba. I have ceramic pots that traveled from Mexico to Michigan in the backseat of our old car. On the floors I have rugs I brought from Turkey as well as rugs I purchased from a Persian lady in Michigan. And my pillowcases, in red and orange, come from the Arab market in Jerusalem. An elaborate mirror in the shape of a Star of David hangs at the entrance; it was a gift from a Catholic friend in Cuba. I have a second-floor deck off my writing room, with cedar fencing onto which my husband carved panels with the palm trees and mermaids I asked for. The facade of my house is painted eight colors, mostly in shades of blue, green, and lavender, with touches of yellow and pink for contrast, near the rooftop. These tropical colors are especially resplendent in the snow. For this house I left home. This is the house I open for Elijah on Passover.

Mine is the house of an exiled woman, but that doesn't mean it's a melancholy house. On the contrary, everyone who visits is impressed by the exuberance of my house, the sheer energy of the many beautiful things that exist side by side. In the years when I felt lonely, I didn't dare have guests over. I was afraid the house had absorbed my sadness and solitude. But now that I have come out of mourning, there is a constant flow of people coming in and out of the house. There are my own and my husband's friends, my son's friends, and lately one of my younger Jewish-Cuban cousins from New York, who is studying in Michigan and honors my house by adoring it and treating it as his second home and sanctuary.

In this house, I have chosen to always hold a seder on the second night of Passover. On the first night, we depend on our more organized friends to invite us over. But on the second night, when most Jewish people reheat leftovers from the first night of Passover if they celebrate the second night at all, I want to always have a glorious seder: one that has faith in the possibility of second chances and trust in the happiness that can come after long mourning. Friends come, Jewish and non-Jewish, and we set two large tables in the living room, the oak dining table and the kitchen picnic table that I painted pink. On every chair I place a pillow.

The second night of Passover is not something I could pass over. The second night in our immigrant family was the Sephardi night, the night that came after the big Ashkenazi night, the night when my mother would whisper to me, as we prepared to enter my Sephardi grandparents' house, not to eat too much of all those delicious foods swimming in olive oil and honey. But in my house I don't want to harbor resentment about the second-class status of the Sephardi seder during my girlhood. So the second night now brings together the memories and presence of both sets of grandparents. There is a Sephardi *charoset* made of raisins and dates, there is matzah ball soup (but served Sephardi style with lemon), there are stuffed tomatoes, there is chicken with prunes, there is *kugel,* and there is also rice (which the Sephardi Jews eat on Passover), and finally, there is *tishpishti* and the Spanish marzipan that I learned to make from a cookbook and shape into the same star, bird, and snake figures that my *baba* used to shape her sugar and cinnamon cookies.

Of course, before consuming all this food, we do read the story of Passover from a haggadah that my husband, a convert to Judaism, has prepared, with prayers and tales in English, Hebrew, and Spanish. In my head I hear the voices of *zayde* and *abuelo,* leading the seder in Spanish with their different Yiddish and Ladino inflections. My tongue recalls the taste of my *baba*'s fluffy matzah balls and my *abuela*'s so very sweet *tishpishti.* I look around my table and see that everyone is happy and relaxed. It is the second night of Passover, the night for a second chance to remake the world, to remake oneself, to invite in Elijah. I tell everyone at the table that before we hide the *afikomen* for the children to find later, we must do as my Sephardi grandparents did, and take turns carrying this *bultico,* this weight, on each of our shoulders as we tell the story of Passover and remember the exile of our ancestors.

The *afikomen* passes from shoulder to shoulder and eventually comes back to me. It returns like a suitcase, the one with which we left Cuba. It returns like a story, speaking to me in my dreams in the Yiddish and Ladino my grandparents spoke when they were young and their death was too far in the future for them to even imagine. It returns like a gift I'd forgotten about. It returns like someone dearly beloved, someone who was waiting for me at the port and I didn't see.

≈≈≈

Jephthah's Daughter:
A Feminist Midrash

LETTY COTTIN POGREBIN

At the Passover seder, we Jews are instructed to remember the past, to relive our enslavement and despair, so that we may never visit such treatment on others, never oppress "the stranger." Too often, though, the stranger is the Jewish woman; her oppression is rarely acknowledged, her spiritual and scholarly yearnings are unseen. In recent years, however, at the feminist seders that have been proliferating all over the country, women have begun to explore women's truths. Sometimes, changed and strengthened by the experience, we bring our stories, rituals, and reclaimed heroines to the seder tables of our families and communities.

Just as Judaism's ancient sages elaborated on sacred texts through rabbinic midrash,[1] over the past twenty-five years many of us have been elaborating on women's lives through feminist midrash. We have created these texts organically, passionately, sometimes sorrowfully, and recited them at our seders. By adding an evening of women's rituals, poetry, testimony, and blessings to the Pesach experience, we enrich and enhance the liberation narrative of the Jewish people and give voice to those who have traditionally been unseen and unheard.

Not long ago, at a New York feminist seder, in response to the evening's theme of "Omission, Absence, and Silence," I wrote a midrash to break the silence of Jephthah's daughter, one of the forty daughters in the Torah identified solely by her father's name. I brought J.D. into our seder circle by asking the kind of questions Judith Plaskow teaches us to ask as a strategy of reconstruction and remembrance: Where were the women and what were they doing? What was

---

Letty Cottin Pogrebin, a founding editor of *Ms.* magazine, is a noted feminist, and the author of nine books, including *Deborah, Golda, and Me: Being Female and Jewish in America,* and *Getting Over Getting Older.* Her first novel, *Three Daughters,* is about a Jewish family struggling with its secrets. Ms. Pogrebin, past president of the Authors Guild, lectures widely on feminism, Judaism, and the Israeli-Palestinian conflict.

their point of view? How did they feel about their lot? And what might their lives mean to us today?

In that light, the life and death of Jephthah's daughter has profound contemporary resonance. I see it as emblematic of women's suffering—a metaphor for the silencing and the sacrifice of women to the more commanding interests of men. I had J. D. on my mind because of a friend of mine who, like J. D., was a victim of her father's transgression. The man had sex with her—no, let me be precise: her father raped her—from the time she was three until she ran away from home at fifteen. She remembers cowering under the covers at the sound of his footsteps, the suffocating weight of him on her back, his heavy breathing, his hands twisting her small body into a position that pleased him. His threats if she didn't keep "our secret."

My friend is in her forties now, and, despite the ghosts crowding her marriage bed, she is trying, with intensive therapy, to achieve a healthy relationship with her husband. Meanwhile, her father—a big shot in the Jewish community, a VIP widely admired as a great guy and a generous philanthropist—denies everything. He won't save his daughter, even now. Won't admit what he did. Keeps calling her "crazy." Compared with his reputation, his daughter's torment means nothing to him. For twelve years, he sacrificed her flesh to his carnal appetites; now he sacrifices her sanity to his "honor."

As a plotline, sacrificing a daughter to fulfill her father's needs dates back to Jephthah, who, to protect his honor, kills his little girl. Her tragic tale begins, as do all biblical stories, with the story of a man.

Jephthah was the son of a prominent Gileadite and a woman identified only as a "prostitute" and "outsider."[2] When his brothers, the sons of his father's legitimate wife, came of age, they drove Jephthah away rather than let him share in their inheritance. Over the years, he became a famous warrior with a powerful private army,[3] and, when the Ammonites declared war on Israel, the elders of Gilead came to him and begged him to aid them in battle.[4] Jephthah agreed only after he had extracted from them the promise that, if victorious, he would become Israel's commander and chief.[5] Then, as if to cover his bets, he made this vow to God: "If you deliver the Ammonites into my hands, then whatever comes out of the door of my house to meet me on my safe return from the Ammonites shall be the Lord's and shall be offered by me as a burnt offering."[6]

Lo and behold, after routing the enemy, Jephthah went home and "there was his daughter coming out to meet him, with timbrel and dance! She was an only child; he had no other son or daughter. On seeing her, he rent his clothes and said, 'Alas daughter! You have brought me low; you have become my troubler! For I have uttered a vow to the Lord and I cannot retract.'"[7]

Though it was he who had made the lunatic vow, in classic blame-the-victim style, he declared his daughter at fault for appearing in the doorway of her own house ("She brought it on herself." "She asked for it." Sound familiar?)

And in keeping with age-old male fantasies of the feminine ideal, J.D. quietly accepted her fate.

"Father," she said, "you have uttered a vow to the Lord; do to me as you have vowed."[8] However, at her request, he postponed her execution for two months and allowed her to retreat into the hills with her friends to "there bewail my maidenhood."[9] Upon her return, Jephthah, true to his word, "did to her as he had vowed." Incinerated his only child on the pyre of masculine pride.

Ruefully, as if this were the essence of the tragedy, the text reminds us, "she had never known a man."[10]

I find it striking that during twelve years of Hebrew school and two years of yeshiva, I was never taught this story. We overlook, we ignore, we excuse by omission those events that embarrass us as a people or hurt our image. The silence that protects Jephthah is the silence that protects men like my friend's father from community judgment and the punishment they deserve. But today, as women wrestle with the biblical account of Jephthah's daughter and its modern parallels, our questions pierce the silence of the centuries, and the valley of time fills with our rage.

Our first questions are directed to God. As Jews have been asking in roars and whispers since the last ash rose from the Nazi ovens, we first ask, Where were You, Almighty One? How could You have allowed an innocent girl to be immolated in Your name? How could You have let Jephthah fulfill a madman's vow? You instructed us to choose life; You commanded us, "Thou shalt not kill," yet You allowed Jephthah to honor You with an act of murder, then promoted him to boot. You had the power and the will to help him defeat the Ammonites—twice we read, "And the Lord delivered them into his hands."[11] So why did You not stay those same hands from tossing his daughter to the flames?

You refused to let Abraham sacrifice his son to prove his faith, yet You let this man kill his daughter to serve a mindless vow. Abraham acted under a divine order; still You intervened and Isaac lived. Why save the son and let the daughter die? Was her survival of no consequence to our people? And why to this day have You turned your back on the daughters who are still being exploited, abandoned, neglected, abused, and violated—sacrificed on the altar of patriarchal power and male ambition by the men who are supposed to protect and love them? Dear God, if You don't save the daughters from the fire, who will?

Next, we have a question for those "companions"[12] who went up into the hills with J. D. As far as one can tell, you didn't lift a finger to help your doomed friend. Why didn't you try to save her?

As for the rest of the Israelites, we ask: Why did you let Jephthah commit this heinous act? You had to know what was happening; yet, you failed to protest. Worse yet, the Torah reports that, "Jephthah led Israel six years."[13] How could you have accepted this monster as your chief? There's not even a hint that his behavior troubled you. Are we to conclude that because you needed his army and his might, you willingly spent a half dozen years being ruled by a child murderer?

The questions raised by your inaction echo to this very day. Tell us, O Israel, where do you draw the line? Why is it that you tolerate horrific behavior in men as long as they promise security and win your wars? And why do Jews everywhere continue to accept as their leaders men who scorn the suffering of women?

Our harshest questions are reserved for Jephthah: What *were* you thinking when you made that gratuitous, ridiculous vow to sacrifice "whatever" came out of the door of your house? Did you imagine the portal might be opened by a dog or a goat? You must have realized a human being would pull the latch—probably a woman, quite possibly your unmentioned wife or unnamed daughter, who, presumably happy to see you return from battle alive, would rush out to welcome you home. When she danced through the door, shaking her timbrel as Miriam shook hers at the Reed Sea, your daughter was as overjoyed as any child would be to see her father. What adoring child doesn't fly into a father's arms after he's been away? Didn't it occur to you that she might be the one to burst from the house to greet you? Why were you willing to play Russian roulette with her life?

Even more astounding, Jephthah, is the fact that you, when faced with the dreadful consequences of your vow, did not throw yourself on God's mercy and beg for a reprieve. Most parents would readily give their lives to save their child; why didn't you offer to die in her place? Can it be that you loved power more? Were you afraid that God would rescind your victory and the Israelites would deny you the sovereignty you had bargained for, the throne that would show up those brothers who betrayed you? Could it be that you sacrificed your daughter not to keep your faith but to keep your job?

Or is the truth even more odious? Is it possible that you knew exactly who would come through the door and purposely killed the daughter who "had never known a man" to keep her from ever knowing a man? Or any man but you? Having heard my friend describe her father's proprietary sense of entitlement to her body, and knowing of the prevalence of child sexual abuse in all population groups, including among Jews, I can't help wondering whether Jephthah could have murdered his daughter to keep a future husband from discovering "our secret." Can it be that more than three thousand years before Freud and feminism, J. D. was an incest survivor who died for her father's sins?

Finally, to bring J. D.'s spirit into our midst at the seder, my midrash poses questions for Jephthah's daughter herself: Can the text be believed? Was it love or piety that made you so willing to give your

life to satisfy your father's vow, or was it fear and helplessness? Were
you really so meekly accepting of the fate your father decreed for you,
or has the account that's come down to us been prettified for posteri-
ty by a male narrator? Maybe the Bible's version of those ancient events
was intended to retroactively burnish the image of the man who was
to rule Israel for six years. Maybe you fought for your life. Maybe your
father lied about your willingness to die. We're told that you request-
ed and got a two-month stay of execution; maybe the truth is that you
begged for mercy and had to settle for sixty days. Maybe you ran to the
hills with your girlfriends in an attempt to escape and were caught by
your father's soldiers.

Another thing, J. D.: Where was your mother in all this? Did she try
to rescue you? Did she plead with her husband to spare your life, and
might a furious Jephthah have sent her away in anger for daring to
challenge him? Did he censor her with his fists? Or was she kept in the
dark, as Sarah was when Abraham trotted her beloved son, Isaac, off
to the slaughtering stone without so much as a farewell kiss for the
mother who had waited ninety years to have him? My hunch, J. D., is
that you were a motherless child. I think she was dead and you were
at the mercy of a father who was either inhuman, absent so much he
hardly knew you (and thus could bring himself to kill you), or your
abuser. Sounds extreme—but lacking your side of the story, dear
daughter, who knows?

All I know is, I find it hard to believe that all you had on your mind
as you submitted to the hot coals was your wasted virginity. You were
crying, I believe, not for your unclaimed maidenhood but for your
unlived life. Am I right?

Had the Torah been written or redacted by women, these questions
might be answered by the text, but without that perspective, we must
turn to one another. We must listen to the "crazy" daughters, heirs to
the nameless ones, whose stories have been squelched. My friend is one
of these women, but there are thousands more Jewish incest survivors
who must be encouraged to go public and seek redress, this time with
the guarantee that we Israelites will protect them and help them heal.

Had the Torah been written or redacted by women, our fore-mothers would not be invisible and nameless like Jephthah's daughter, and their lives would not elude us. But, lacking their voices, we are filling the gaps with scholarship and informed speculation. Many of us have felt ourselves standing in the shoes of J. D.—or Hannah or Vashti or Deborah or Zelophehad's daughters—and, ancient as they are, they fit. So we surmise and hypothesize. We break the silence and make new midrash and try to forge connections with those whose stories have been lost. We seek answers in one another. We find the missing Torah in our hearts.

Memory and Revolution
DIANNE COHLER-ESSES

Feminism saved my life, saved me from oppression by my very own people. It inspired my own exodus; it gave me strength and lifted me up. Yet, it was also feminism that alienated me from my people, cut me off from my history and ultimately from my very self. Exodus became exile. Now I am in search of reunion: a reunion of the identity I abandoned long ago for the sake of freedom with the identity that I developed in the name of liberation. Now I want integration, not rejection. I don't want to scorn, and I don't want to choose. I insist. It's both, not either/or. I want to embrace the traditional community I betrayed by leaving—and the rabbi I've become. I want to honor the mother I've left behind—and the mother I've become—without shame. I do not want an ideology that blocks me from the one who nurtured me or from the ones I nurture. I do not want an ideology that separates me from the people to whom I belong or from the people for whom I long.

Rabbi Dianne Cohler-Esses is the North American director of Bronfman Youth Fellowships in Israel and a rabbinic consultant to The Curriculum Initiative, which develops educational materials for ethics curricula.

Had I not left the traditional community I grew up in, I would have probably perished, if not physically then psychically. And so exodus was necessary, life-saving. And yet the exodus I chose cost too much. In my effort to leave everything behind, I left my very self somewhere out there in the past. I have been wandering through the desert, split and waiting to be freed, with half of me on my way to the Promised Land and another part left behind in Egypt. Waiting to embark on the journey as a whole.

No one leaves the tribe I come from. To do so, especially for females, is to transgress its most sacred taboo. As with the biblical Dinah leaving home to seek the daughters of the land, leaving means becoming sullied.[1] Virgin girls are at the heart of this community's centrifugal force, the very stickiness of its traditional web of extended families and interrelationships, its central symbol of purity and morality. A young woman who leaves the confines of the community threatens the very center of things and can never return. Exodus is betrayal.

My community consists of more than fifty thousand Jews from Syria residing in the heart of Flatbush, Brooklyn. They settled in this country after the turn of the previous century. The major immigration occurred between 1900 and 1924 to the Lower East Side of Manhattan, where dark-skinned Arabic-speaking Jews settled amidst a sea of lighter, Yiddish-speaking Jews.

In sharp contrast to other immigrant groups who arrived around the same time (most notably Eastern European Jews), Syrian Jews have remained a community of extended families tightly woven around traditions of food, music, liturgy, and ritual. Young women typically marry soon after high school (usually between the ages of seventeen and twenty-one) and settle within walking distance of their parents' home. Their primary role is to run a household, while young men most often enter their fathers' businesses and become wage earners for large and generally wealthy families.

I left. Alone. Forged my own adventure—determined a destiny that went far beyond the boundaries drawn for a young Syrian woman. I dared to be a self, a distinct individual forsaking my central role at the heart of the tribe. In my sophomore year of college I traveled far from home. Over the Brooklyn Bridge to Manhattan I went, to the dormitories of New York University in Greenwich Village (my parents thought Barnard too far from home).

But really I had left, psychically, long before. I was a preadolescent when I began to see that the model for a young Syrian girl was not for me. Like a too-small shoe, when I tried to force myself into its contours it became painful and inhibited growth.

The ethos of the tribe required girls' absolute obedience to family and community. Unlike many of my Ashkenazi classmates, teenage girls from the Syrian community were expected to be models of thinness and physical perfection (I remember looking through *Glamour* magazine at models in bikinis with my Syrian friends—the mere hint of roundness around the belly produced the authoritative declaration "she's fat"). We were expected to be beautiful and alluring—parading around the summer beach club on the Jersey shore in the skimpiest of bathing suits and high-heeled sandals, clinking a multitude of bangle bracelets and flashing rings—and at the same time to embody the community's ideal of purity. Sexy and obedient virgins we were to remain until marriage, flaunting our untouchable beauty. And despite the onset of marital sexuality, a certain innocence and even girlishness were to be maintained for the rest of a woman's life.

Even as a girl, I defined my very self by transgressing this model. My young life was full of rebellion, search for adventure, fascination with ideas, physical activity and sweat, a disdain for materialism, and an interest in sexuality. I was somewhat chubby (certainly by their standards) and habitually messy. My clothes were frequently stained, my hair a knotty mess, and my shoes scuffed and dirty—somehow I managed to wear them out within days. I almost always lost any jewelry given to me. Even when I tried, I could not quite achieve the script assigned to me. A beautiful innocence was not mine to be had.

Leaving home was simply the physical manifestation of a psychic abandonment I had long before visited upon my family. Feminism came into my life when I was a teenager in the 1970s. It arrived in the form of Ashkenazi friends I made in summer camp, friends who lived in Manhattan and attended Ramaz—a much cooler version of the Modern Orthodox yeshiva I attended, Brooklyn's Yeshivah of Flatbush. "Women's lib," as my father liked to call it, caught me, took hold, and soon catapulted me out of the community. In my mind I pushed the feminist "eject" button and landed in an alternative world, going straight from East to West in a day. It was as if the feminist foremothers had beamed me up to another galaxy.

In reality, the seeds of the West had been planted over time: at Ashkenazi summer camps, at an Ashkenazi day school, by a father who, despite his desperation to fit me into the Syrian world, himself established an alternative model by reading the *New York Times,* listening to Mozart, and constantly challenging me. The Syrian ideal was at once held out before my eyes and subverted: it beckoned and yet eluded me. Failure and subsequent alienation led me to seek a new world. The West was the answer to my failure. Feminism would supply the power for my powerlessness.

Like my Ashkenazi friends, I decided to go to college. Consciously, I was setting out to reject the life I was expected to live and adopt one scripted for my Western friends. I was switching tracks in the middle of my life's journey. I thought it was that easy, but my life has proved otherwise. The split was more powerful than I had been able to acknowledge. The repressed and rejected parts of my past have since returned with a vengeance.

To say the least, I was angry. Angry at my family and angry at the Syrian way of life. Angry at my community: why wasn't I accepted as I was? Why couldn't I achieve the model for the successful popular Syrian girl? Perhaps West really was second best. The prize for losers. Secretly, I think now, I really wanted East, but I couldn't have it. So I went to seek an alternative reality, on whose terms I could be a success. I felt rejected, abandoned, and misunderstood. To compensate, I set myself up as superior, smarter, more righteous. I saw the women of the Syrian community as inferior to me, ignorant and oppressed.

Feminism was the perfect ideology with which to reject and abandon. It took hold and jettisoned me out of there. My community was patriarchal, oppressive, materialistic. I also used terms like sexist, racist, conspicuous consumption, repressive, and superficial to describe my community of origin. With these words I thrust aside the people who spawned me and claimed me as their own.

At New York University, I found new words besides feminist to describe myself. I gave up on the word Jewish. "I was born Jewish," I would tell people, but now I called myself an atheist. Besides the word atheist, I added the words socialist, communist (I still don't really know the difference), and leftist. I had many words. All of them heralded a rebirth, a second genesis. With this newly acquired vocabulary, I rejected everything I had come from and everything I was. With these labels, I rejected my parents, my history, and my religion. Each word promised a new beginning, freedom, a messianic time in which I could leave the past utterly behind.

Soon after I left home, a thicker, darker, deeper depression than I had ever known came upon me—and I was no stranger to depression. I didn't complete any of my classes; I basically stopped functioning and became painfully self-destructive. I couldn't understand why I was so depressed if I had finally achieved liberation. What could possibly be wrong? I was living at NYU in a dormitory, unlike nearly all of my Syrian friends. I was taking courses like "The Meaning of Death" and "Atheism, Theism, and Existentialism," classes on English literature and political theory. I became a philosophy major. But just when I thought I was finally free, nothing made sense. My life did not match my newfound ideologies. In fact, it didn't even approach the words I had begun to use. Although I didn't realize it, I was like a severed limb—cut off from my people and history.

Part of what began to lift me from this complete depression was a return to my interest in religion and ultimately Judaism. I began to reattach myself to the tree. Looking back, I realize that a total break was just not possible. It is possible in theory, but not in reality, not in history, not in life. For we are not the only or the final authors of our lives; the hands of community, history, and God are partners in our creation. Ignore those hands and they choke you. I was choking on the lack of history in my life, the lack of relationship to my past. The sense of emptiness that I felt fueled my search for some kind of reconnection in the Jewish world.

About ten years after I left the Syrian community, I decided to become a rabbi. I am the first Syrian Jewish woman to become a rabbi. Moreover, I am the first Syrian Jew to become a non-Orthodox rabbi. For my parents, for my family, this was worse than leaving home. But for me, it was actually the beginning of an effort to come home. I was looking for a way back—a connection to my past that my own community could not offer me. I wanted history and I wanted God—I wanted fullness and I wanted liberation. I had begun to learn that disconnection was not, after all, the way forward.

I write now as a married woman, the mother of three. I write as someone who works part-time and whose primary work at this moment in her life is mothering. I write as someone whose life, painfully at times, does not match her ideology. I write as a woman whose husband has more than a full-time job, as a woman who manages her household. My life resembles my mother's more closely than I am comfortable with. Almost everything that I had rejected—living life as part of a family, as part of a community, as a traditional Jew—is back with a vengeance. But it is a sweet vengeance, for much of it I love. And yet I still yearn for the career-focused life not bound by gender that I thought would be mine.

Now I want a feminism that does not deem my current life powerless. I want a feminism that recognizes the power of birthing and mothering. I want a feminism that helps me integrate all that has nurtured me, and all that I now nurture. I want a feminism that can give me West and East—without sanctifying the sacrifice of one for the other, one that recognizes the power of history and the particularity of culture. I want a feminism that is life-giving, for all the forms that women's lives take.

Leaving on Purpose:
The Questions of Women's *Tefillah*
CHAVI KARKOWSKY

I attended my first women's Torah reading many years ago, in a small windowless room, far away from the larger congregation. The women at the *bimah* read—or tried to: their readings were atrocious, mixing up consonants and omitting vowels. As they chanted, the other women in the room cooed words of encouragement to the novice readers. It made me furious.

I felt as if I were back in junior high school, giggling pointlessly in the girls' bathroom, powerless, silly. Because, whether or not it is intended to be one, within the Orthodox community, a women's Torah reading is a political statement about what women are capable of. And I knew that women were capable of excellence; nothing less was acceptable. In a regular *minyan* (prayer service with a quorum of ten adult males), when mistakes are made, the *gabbai,* the organizer and supervisor of the prayer service, makes the reader go back and repeat until the verse is said correctly. People who can't read at the level required, don't. Treating the women as if this—this!—was the best that they could do was demeaning. I left.

I have since come to appreciate the small steps that these women were taking, steps that clearly required a tremendous amount of courage. Furthermore, women's *tefillah* (prayer) groups have vastly improved in recent years. For the most part, the ones that meet regularly are polished, organized, and competent. This is important, even essential, for feminists in the Modern Orthodox community, because if you're going to be a feminist and stay within the Modern Orthodox community, your only route to equality is, to contradict *Brown* v. *Board of Education,* segregation. A gathering of women to pray, learn, and read from the Torah—a women's *tefillah* group—is one of the only

---

Chavi Karkowsky is a fourth-year medical student at Mount Sinai School of Medicine, where she is a Percy M. Klingenstein Fellow. She graduated from Yale University in 1998.

opportunities Orthodox women have to lead public ritual in their lives. These groups have brought something valuable to the lives of many Orthodox (and non-Orthodox) women: the opportunity to descend from the balcony, tear down the *mechitzah,* and enter the world of prayer as a participant rather than as a spectator.

This solution is perceived as subversive and threatening by many rabbinical authorities; yet, at the same time, it is intentionally irreproachable in its deference to halakhah. After all, how does a women's *tefillah* group differ from a prayer service conducted by the ninth-grade class of the Bais Yaakov ultra-Orthodox school, where the girls are halakhically impeccable in their long skirts, thick stockings, and neat braids? Both groups are women only, both are led by women, both refuse to consider themselves a *minyan,* and thus, both are difficult to reprimand. The crucial difference lies in intent: women's *tefillah* groups intend to be radical, while (in theory, anyway[1]) Bais Yaakov girls just want to pray.

Therein lies the subversiveness of women's *tefillah* groups: almost purely through that difference in intent, women themselves have transformed what a group of women can mean. Instead of being sent to the edges of the synagogue, these women have absented themselves and, in so doing, have invented a new religious experience.

These women are all the more threatening to the status quo because of their bent-necked approach to halakhah. "We know that we are not a *minyan,*" they say, "and we are not trying to be one." Their painstaking observance of halakhah means that these women cannot entirely be ignored as non-Orthodox. Instead, they demand the begrudging acknowledgment that they do, in fact, respect traditional values, albeit in a nontraditional way.

And yet, women's *tefillah* groups are reprimanded heartily, and often as if they were indeed those fourteen-year-old Bais Yaakov girls in braids. They are castigated both for their trespasses of intent and for their creative—and occasionally questionable—ways of dealing with prayers. Most specifically, they are reviled for their negotiations with those prayers that are not traditionally said without a *minyan,* such as blessings over the Torah and the repetition of *shemonah esrai* (the central prayer of Jewish worship).

In fact, women's *tefillah* groups give up a tremendous amount in order to maintain their status as Orthodox. The manipulations that women's *tefillah* groups require their readers and leaders to undergo are very often foolish, often bordering on the childish. Do not say this blessing in your regular prayer so that you can say it over the Torah; do not say the traditional blessing over the Torah, but instead recite a verse that (surprise!) sounds very much like a blessing. None of these machinations is necessary in the general (that is to say, men's) Torah service or in egalitarian services. So it is possible to feel, well, silly: clearly, halakhah has left very little room for women to hold their own prayer service.

The results of our careful manipulations and attempts at molding the tradition into the form we wish it to hold can be almost comical. Why don't we just admit that this is not working, gather up the shreds of our self-respect, and consider ourselves a *minyan*, a gathering of adults? That would not be much farther from what the Orthodox rabbis had in mind than the ritual that we have so oddly constructed.

And yet, it is the very absurdity of the halakhic machinations women's *tefillah* groups have had to devise that makes them so valuable to the Jewish community. For, throughout Jewish history, isn't this how halakhic change always comes about—through a slow and unyielding argument of trivialities? And thus, the fact that these negotiations with detail are almost talmudic in nature is particularly significant. Precisely by ignoring the immovable halakhic view of women, by engaging the battle on a field of tiny banalities, that fundamental view is changed. Dr. Tamar Ross calls this "the death of a thousand silences": during an infinite number of insignificant debates, which entirely ignore the larger immutable concept, that immutable concept slowly tapers into a more negotiable form.

This is not to say that the process is an easy one. The segregation that the women achieve is, by definition, a marginalization. How does a women's *tefillah* group make its power felt within the larger community?

Do we liberate the women and not the men? By removing the women to a room of their own, don't we make dealing with issues of women's rights easy—perhaps too easy—for the rest of the community? A friend of mine told me once, "It's not enough for my daughters to see women in these ritual roles. I want my sons to see as well!" Perhaps removing women, and their complaints, from the larger Torah service impedes progress on these issues.

I would agree that all of these arguments are valid; marginalization is, in a way, a cop-out. But there is a subtle way in which taking yourself out of the larger community can be valuable, in which self-segregation can fuel a sense of subversiveness and, in that way, power. To some extent, it is that "naughtiness," the awareness of having placed oneself on the outermost fringe of acceptability, that protects us from falling into a sense of contentment and self-satisfaction.

Anyone who calls himself or herself a feminist today is well aware of how frustrating it is when people assume that we don't need such "radical" ideas any more, that the work is done, that it is all settled, when this is so obviously untrue. In essence, women's *tefillah* groups, by denying themselves acceptance, by militantly excluding themselves from the greater community, force everyone to recognize the continuing inequality. "Here we are, outside," they say. "It's not that we can't come in, but that we *won't*." In a similar vein, other separatist rituals such as women's seders send a message to the Jewish community. They act as reminders that the ritual opportunities we are offered as women may not be enough, that we need more, and that if we have to leave and invent new rituals to find this, we will.

This method is particularly effective within the Jewish community, which is exceedingly comfortable seeing itself as a minority, and feels great discomfort at being seen as the party in power or, worse yet, as oppressors. By identifying themselves as a minority group within this community, women remind not only themselves but also the rest of the congregation that equal rights have yet to be granted to half of the population—a disconcerting thought.

Women's *tefillah* groups, although imperfect, thus offer something of great value. For those who do not find the value of women's *tefillah* groups sufficient, the most popular alternative is an egalitarian service. In such a service, men and women pray together in a community, with leadership roles available to all, at least in theory. One Simchat Torah, on the morning when all adults (or all adult men, in an Orthodox service) are supposed to have an *aliyah* (the honor of being called to the Torah to recite a blessing), I attended a fully and stridently egalitarian service. During this foray into the wide world of mixed prayer, I felt relief. Contentment. Ease. There was no cooing, no feeling of childish naughtiness, no forced negotiations with the liturgy. I was an adult, I was there, and therefore I rose for an *aliyah*. The simplicity of it was marvelous. I laughed to myself and had to be led through the blessing that, despite my years of Jewish learning, I had never said aloud.

And yet, even in this service, populated almost equally by male and female rabbinical students, I have noticed that certain positions are assigned by gender. *Hagbah* (the lifting of the Torah before the community) is noticeably always left to a man. Granted, this could be justified as more a matter of muscle mass than regard—if it weren't for the fact that in women's *tefillah* women handle *hagbah* just fine, if only because there are no men to turn to. In women's *tefillah*, a woman lifts the Torah, gracefully or less so depending on her confidence, wrist strength, and how far that week's portion is from the middle of the scroll. Some women do what my friend uncharitably calls "chicken *hagbah*," clutching their elbows to their sides and lifting the scroll only inches from their heads, afraid of dropping the Torah. But some women proudly brandish the scroll, presenting it, bannerlike, to the congregation. The rest of us sing out, "And this is the Torah that was given by Moses before the Children of Israel, by word of God, in the hand of Moses." But what we mean is this: in the hand of Moses, but also in my hand. In my hands, as a daughter of Israel. I can raise the Torah; I can sing the Torah; I can learn the Torah. Do we learn this in egalitarian services? We can, but too often we don't.

Another advantage to women's *tefillah* that egalitarian services lack is, of course, sisterhood. When we first held a women's *tefillah* group at Yale Hillel, we set up twenty chairs, thinking that we were being wildly optimistic. Halfway through Kabbalat Shabbat (liturgy for welcoming the Sabbath), women were standing, lining the walls, coming in through the back stairway. Why did they come? Most of these women weren't Orthodox; our service offered them no unique opportunities. But when faced with the dizzying (and intimidating) task of choosing among Orthodox, Egalitarian, Reform, Reconstructionist, and Carlebach, it was a comfort to see a women's service, saying: Come on in. Welcome home. There, the women knew that they belonged; no test of praxis or dogma was required to join our community, only the shared experience of growing up female.

This advantage should not be taken lightly. One of my most hurtful experiences as a feminist occurred when a professor and Jewish leader whose intellect and passion I greatly admire told me that in order to be a feminist, I would have to relinquish my Orthodoxy and that if I chose to remain Orthodox, I should realize that de facto, I was giving up my identity as a feminist. I'm sure that she meant this only as the truth (and it isn't, in fact, entirely untrue), but her frank delivery destroyed me. What could I give up: my right arm or my left? If I wanted to remain in my community, did I have to become docile? Or did I have to leave entirely and exile myself from the essential substance of my life? I remember crying out, "But then you're leaving some of us behind, alone." She said, "There's nothing I can do if you do not choose to come."

And so, I ask whether women's *tefillah* has any value in and of itself, or if it is merely a stopgap measure on the rush toward equality within Orthodoxy, a dubiously attainable goal. I believe that it is both: it is eminently a stopgap measure, and yet, somehow, it also offers beauty and ritual that would not have been discovered otherwise. This advantage is one offered by other women-only rituals, most notably women's seders, at which participants come together as women to pray or celebrate at the center of a Jewish ritual. For many women, this is an entirely new experience. For some women it is, in fact, the only option, the only way they can feel comfortable coming with us, the only way they can keep both arms.

Between the immovable object that is Orthodoxy and the irresistible force that is egalitarian prayer, women's *tefillah* groups offer a third option: you leave, but you stay. You dig out a shadowy space, one where you have more opportunities but less status. Is it enough to be in that space? When we pray together there, are we merely throwing our lot in with the most oppressed among us? Are we fooling ourselves about what we really want, what we perhaps can never have: full equality within the Orthodox community? Are we relinquishing our ability to count in the whole community? The answer to all these questions is yes, but also no. The presence of separate women's religious rituals requires you to give up, but also to gain. Thus, they offer women a choice. The weighing of that choice is already something new, something that many Orthodox women would not have otherwise had. And isn't the presence of that choice the fullest expression of true feminism?

≈≈

Of Nursing, in the Desert
JANNA KAPLAN

I really do feel, every Passover, that I personally came out of Egypt. It is as if Exodus, the ancient Hebrews' liberation from Egypt, is a vivid and unforgettable memory from my own past, and I feel it deeply. The haggadah teaches us that it is a *mitzvah* to identify with the generation of Exodus, and for me this *mitzvah* is truly fulfilled.

Janna Kaplan is a research scientist at Brandeis University. She studies human adaptation to space flight conditions such as weightlessness and hypergravity. A former refugee from Leningrad (currently St. Petersburg), Russia, she came to the United States in 1982. For the past eight years Janna has been one of the organizers and leaders of the Boston Project Kesher Global Women's Seder, a community seder for American and Russian immigrant Jewish women.

My *mitzrayim* was Russia, the former Soviet Union, where I was born and grew up, discovered my Jewishness, and entered womanhood. Yet, as I look back on my life in Russia—childhood, youth, adulthood—I am overwhelmed by memories of suffering. Suffering from anti-Semitism, from humiliation and the vulgarity of everyday life, from lack of joy. Being Jewish in Russia was not exactly slavery; yet, it was an existence strictly controlled by the state. The intrusion of the state into all our personal and professional relationships was especially painful. Under pressure from the Soviet system, threatened with loss of a job or a benefit, or with harm to a loved one, a friend would denounce a friend who wanted to learn of her Jewish roots; a relative would disavow a relative who wanted to emigrate. When I became a *refusenik,*[1] so many of my Russian friends and colleagues broke off relations with me that I fell into profound isolation and deep emotional pain.

And yet, I loved Russia! The eternal beauty of my native Leningrad inspired me. I walked around the city for hours; especially during "white nights" in late June when the sun goes down to barely touch the horizon but never really sets. I enjoyed cold, snowy winters, golden autumns exploding with unbelievable colors, and early springs roaring with crashing noise when the violent waters of the Neva River break free from the ice.

I loved the powerful intensity of friendships so inherent in the Russian character. It was precisely because I treasured these friendships so much that losing them, as I eventually did, brought bitterness and a sense of void. I admired Russian literature and music, the arts, the language. I loved the Russian language passionately! It delighted me in its every form—spoken, written, versed, sung. I enjoyed thinking in Russian, sharing with friends, composing poems, and reading poetry to myself aloud or silently. When I immigrated to the United States from Russia at twenty-seven years of age, I had to leave behind everyone and everything I loved. The loss of the living language was, perhaps, my most profound and irreparable loss. Even now, twenty years later, I still feel it.

It took me a long time and much effort to rebuild my life after I came to the United States. I was able to find personal happiness and professional success, to repair relationships, and to forgive friends who had betrayed me. What never healed was my bond with the Russian language. Speaking Russian evoked in me an almost visceral reaction of discomfort and tension. Beautiful though it is, the language fundamentally reflects the darkest depths of the Russian people's painful history as well as the oppressive nature of every government they had ever had.

Transplanted to a culture where a person's privacy, pursuit of happiness, human and civil rights are real and undeniable, speakers of Russian like myself discovered the frustrating limitations of our native tongue. In Russian grammar, for example, past and future tenses are somewhat undeveloped in comparison with many other languages, reflecting fear and ignorance both of history and of what is yet to come. We lived in the present; truth about the past was denied to us for fear that those who knew their history would become empowered to shape their future. Control was only possible in the present; the past could not be changed, and the dreams we had of the future knew no boundaries. And so it came to be—for me—that in Russia, locked in the present, life felt like a dead-end road. Out of Russia, through years of wandering, my exodus would be about building the future.

Aside from the grammar, Russian lacks the vocabulary to express deeply personal, intimate issues, like sexuality or privacy. To talk about sex, for example, only two possibilities exist: an obscene jargon whose vocabulary is authentically Russian, or proper literary language, which evolved around the usage of Latin roots with, in some instances, Russian suffixes attached. In Latin-based languages, such words do not strike me as dissonant or artificial. But in Russian, they sound alien and unbecoming to intimacy.

English, even as a foreign language, helped me understand what was most precious in my new life, the personal, the intimate, the aspirations and values I struggled and sacrificed so much for. It gave me the voice and the words to express myself in the "desert" of my personal wanderings, and, as such, it was truly a blessing.

My separation from the Russian language was a long and agonizing process. Within months of my emigration I stopped writing poetry. Russian seemed inadequate; yet, no other language could transmit the poetic emotion I felt better than my mother tongue. I avoided other Soviet refugees so that I would not have to speak Russian and thus distanced myself from the only community that could have helped me preserve my bond with the language. The language spoken by this refugee community quickly became invaded by English words and expressions, as a result losing much of its unique harmony and intrinsic melody. Even so distorted, their Russian was, for me, heavily loaded with associations of my life in the Soviet Union.

Five or six years into my life in America, I realized that I had begun to think and dream in English. That awareness gave me a sense of lightness, a liberating feeling that does not usually come easily to me. Like many Russians, I always had trouble relaxing. So contrary was this private state of inner tranquility to the Russian way of life, to the constant deficit of personal space and time, that here, too, the Russian language never developed a word, nor evolved the vocabulary, to describe conditions of mind and body which we, here, know as relaxation.

When I married a wonderful American Jewish man, he decided to learn Russian, and I encouraged him with all my heart. Yet, more often than not, I would find excuses to avoid helping him in his study. I thought that when we had children, I would teach them Russian. On a rational level, I wanted them to know my native language. I also thought that if and when my parents left Russia and joined me, I would speak Russian with them, and they would help me teach it to my children. None of that happened. Although I would in time have children, and my parents would eventually leave Russia and come to live with me in America, the Russian language did not regain the place in my life that I hoped it would.

Interestingly, I never ceased to enjoy reading, watching movies, or listening to operas in Russian. My problem was with the spoken language and with writing, the most obvious means of self-expression. Using Russian began to feel forced and unnatural, as if something in my bond with it had broken irreparably. I did not forget the language, nor did I lose my fluency. The effect of this alienation was much more elusive: it was in the buildup of a subtle anxiety that seemed to hover in the background, causing constricting tensions somewhere deep within me. Where? I did not know. But I found out when my first child, my son, was born.

Nursing my baby, admiring and cuddling him, I was enjoying motherhood as I had never enjoyed anything else in my life. I felt that if for this alone—finding my beloved and having this child with him— all my sufferings were justified, for they had led me to these blessed moments of happiness. And yet, talking to my baby in Russian became a dreaded experience. I would feel the tension creeping inside of me. My son, with the unfailing intuition of an infant, would sense that anxiety and become restless, crying bitterly. Nursing became torture when I tried to speak to him in Russian. The tension within me would rise like a tidal wave, penetrating my whole being. I would feel painful constriction in my breasts, and my milk would stop flowing. I could not nurse in Russian! There, in my most female parts—in my nursing breasts—I was not free. I was still living in bondage.

A few months after the birth of my son, I gave up speaking Russian to him. When my daughter was born three years later, I never even started. Abandoning the effort altogether was like letting go of my *mitzrayim:* I finally left Egypt! Like the ancient Hebrews of Exodus, with mixed feelings but confident that I was doing the right thing, I left the country where I had a lifetime of experiences and memories, never to return, never to look back.

Two things connect the child to the mother. They cannot both work at the same time; one has to give way to the other. The umbilical cord to the mother culture was cut; the time had come to nurse. And I wonder, sometimes, in what tongue the Hebrew mothers nursed their babies in the desert. Did they sing to them in Egyptian? Or was it then that the Hebrew language became, in its divine beauty, the sustaining energy of my people Israel by freeing their women's milk to flow?

On Matzah, Questions, and Becoming a Nation

LEAH HABER

Living a Jewish life, I have learned to relate to God on numerous levels. The God whom I thank every morning for returning my individual soul is at the same time the God who created the world and orchestrated the Exodus from Egypt; God is present and personal yet also infinite and incomprehensible. It is a profound challenge to learn to relate to God as both a giving, loving father and an awe-inspiring king, a Lord with whom we exist in a contractual relationship based on the laws of Torah. As an Orthodox Jewish woman, a unique individual, a mother, and a wife, I continue to learn how to achieve a relationship with God that arises out of each of the disparate strains of my identity. Jewish texts often provide me with guidance about how to begin going about this task. In particular, the Exodus account of the Israelites' evolving relationship to God has offered me many lessons about how I can authentically relate to God.

The Bible and the haggadah both emphasize God's almost overpoweringly active role in the Exodus. In the Book of Exodus we read that God acted *"beyad chazakah uvizroa netuya"*—with a strong hand and an outstretched arm. The haggadah stresses that God performed the Exodus "not by the hands of an angel and not by the hands of a seraph, rather by God in His honor and Himself." Our texts make clear that a central purpose of the Exodus was to demonstrate God's glory and strength to the nations of the world and to the Jewish nation in particular.

Just as one might describe God's role in the Exodus as front and center, active and aggressive, we can characterize the Jewish people as passive, even reluctant to be liberated. Although they are grateful for

---

Leah Haber is currently completing graduate studies in clinical psychology. She is a graduate of Stern College, where she majored in Jewish studies. She has spent several years studying in Israel, at Michlalah Jerusalem College for Women and at Midreshet Moriah, where she also served as a mentor for precollege students.

Moses' initial efforts to intercede with the Egyptian monarch on their behalf, they soon become disenchanted with him when his message from God to "let my people go" causes Pharaoh to increase their workload. With the exception of those performed by Moses, who is directly instructed by God, we see few acts of initiative or leadership on the part of the Jewish nation.

Even after they have been liberated from Egypt, the people seem content to continue living as slaves, the only difference being that they follow God's instructions rather than those of Pharaoh. The Jewish people patently lack the excitement and enthusiastic participation one would expect the liberation from generations of brutal slavery to arouse. When reading their story, one can sense a certain numbness in the people, as though something prevents the Exodus experience from entering the collective consciousness of the Jewish nation. It has been said that it is easier to take the Jewish people out of Egypt than to take Egypt out of the Jewish people. But what precisely is "Egypt"? And why is it so difficult to remove?

As we learn from a midrash that is cited in many commentaries on the haggadah, the soon-to-be Jewish nation had descended so far into depravity in Egypt that they had entered the forty-ninth of the fifty gates of impurity. God had to redeem them quickly so that they would not descend all the way to the final and ultimate level of impurity. Thus, God liberated the Jewish people not simply from physical slavery but also from the spiritual wasteland of apathy in which they were existing.

God's active involvement does not end there. The Jews received the Torah forty-nine days after they left Egypt. This event is known as *matan Torah,* the giving of the Torah (by God). It is also called *kabbalat ha-torah,* the receiving of the Torah (by the Jewish people). Together, these two terms describe a relationship in which God assumes the active part, while the Jewish people accept the more passive, receptive role.

An intriguing passage in the Talmud brings this dynamic into sharper relief. We read, *"kafah aleihem har kegigit"*—when God was ready to bestow the Torah upon the Jewish people, God held Mount

Sinai over their heads until they agreed to accept it with the famous words *"naaseh venishma"*—we will do (meaning that we will agree to accept the Torah) and only then will we hear (what specific commitments acceptance of the Torah entails). Many commentators explain that these words reflect the mesmerized state of the Jewish people. After experiencing the great miracles that God had performed for them—the Exodus from Egypt, the splitting of the Reed Sea—it was as if they were incapable of making a *choice* to accept the Torah. Rather, it was the next step in a wondrous chain of events over which they had little control.

Thus, our first impression of the nascent Jewish nation is one of a young, immature entity. This inexperienced people leans heavily on the leadership of God and God's messenger, Moses. Lacking confidence in their own abilities to make wise decisions, they are more than happy to accept the structure and rules provided for them by their new master. However, as we follow the Jewish people through their forty-year sojourn in the desert, it becomes clear that something further is needed from them if they are to become the full-fledged nation that God would like them to be. Although they are initially compliant and docile, the Jews experience numerous trials and tribulations in the desert, many of which are a result of their *dis*obedience to God. The infant nation, which is "born" helpless at the time of the Exodus, undergoes a somewhat rocky adolescence during this desert journey. The Jewish people begin to question the authority of Moses and, by extension, that of God. They start to look out for their interests and make decisions for themselves. Their grateful and somewhat blind acceptance has given way to resentment, bitter questioning, and disobedience.

Like the Jewish people in Egypt, women are often regarded as taking a more passive, accepting, and supporting role in traditional Judaism. Indeed, God identified the very first woman as *ezer kenegdo*, a helpmate for Adam. Eve is called *isha* (woman) "for she was taken from man" *(ish)*. The Hebrew word for female is *nekevah*, which means hole, or opening, suggesting that a woman accepts or receives, rather than act-ing of her own initiative. In fact, many criticize the traditional Orthodox Jewish lifestyle as one in which a woman is not considered an individual in her own right but rather an accessory who exists for the sake of her husband and children.

In my mind, the position of the young Jewish nation strikingly resembles the quandary in which I find myself as an Orthodox Jewish woman. I accept the authority of the Scripture but at the same time do not wish to view myself as a passive recipient, either as a woman or as a Jew. Thus, I often ask myself whether our texts and traditions encourage us in some way to be passive and leave initiative up to others. Does God really want a nation that docilely follows the commandments without thinking through their meaning and value? If so, in what way can Passover be *z'man cheruteinu,* the time of our freedom?

Further, is not the idea of free choice, *bechirah chofshit,* central to Judaism? How can such bedrock events as the Exodus and the giving of the Torah be based on a relationship of de facto coercion rather than independent choice? Is it not true that lasting, genuine partnerships are based on some sort of mutuality?

It seems that the sages of the Talmud sensed the very same paradox. In response, they declared, *"ein lecha ben chorin ela mi she'osek baTorah"*—the only truly free person is one who busies himself with Torah. Somehow, the sages believed, it is possible—even preferable—that each person live with this contradiction: *that one be subjugated and free at the same time.*

I believe the key to this paradox lies in the matzah we eat at our seder tables. Matzah is known as *lechem oni,* which can be translated as "the bread of affliction" because it is a symbol of the Jews' life of oppression in Egypt. The slaves were so overworked and tightly controlled by their Egyptian overseers that they barely had time to make the bread they needed to subsist and could not wait for it to rise before they hurried it in and out of the ovens. Yet, at the same time, matzah is also a symbol of our liberation. The Bible recounts that the Jews were so rushed when they left Egypt that they could not wait for their bread to rise; it baked on their backs under the desert sun as they took flight

from Egypt. The question is obvious: how can the same object symbolize two utterly opposing states of being? The object itself does not
inherently contain either freedom or slavery; rather, it is the attitude
of the person engaged with that object that determines what the object
represents. When eaten by slaves, matzah is the epitome of oppression. When eaten by free people, it is transformed into a symbol of their
potential to assert control over their lives.

Another interpretation of the term *lechem oni* is *she'onim alav
devarim harbeh*—that many things are spoken about or answered
through it. The seder night is widely known as a night of questions.
Questions are so significant at the seder because our tradition views
them as the ultimate sign of freedom. A slave does what she is told
and does not enjoy the leisure or the mental freedom to explore her
attitude toward her life or her actions. Whether or not she wants to
do something is irrelevant—her job is simply to *do*. To ask would be
an expression of freedom; questioning would require that she break out
of her environment and look at it from the outside. To explore her
actions, she would have to engage and grapple with the larger concepts
and ideas underlying them. Thus, it is through asking and questioning that freedom is ultimately attained.

Too often, we interpret questions as a form of rejection. In this way
we misunderstand questioning; particularly at the seder, questioning
can be an act of embracing rather than rejecting. Only through questioning are we ultimately able to become active participants in our relationships—with God as well as with people and ideas. When the wicked
child is rebuked, he is not reprimanded for asking but for saying;[1] he
goes wrong not in questioning but in dismissing our practice without
engaging in a process of exploration.

When God physically liberated the Jewish people from Egypt, they
were only beginning the process of becoming emotionally and spiritually free. When they received the Torah, they were only embarking on
their journey toward a more authentic relationship with God—one
based on their own ability to question, choose, and make decisions for
themselves.

One can understand the Jews' passivity simply as a result of their immature state. Yet, one might also interpret this passivity as dangerous, leading to a disruption of their connection with God. In the long term, a coercive relationship is not viable because it inevitably creates bitter resentment and therefore rejection. Might this be one of the lessons that the Bible intended to teach us through the story of the Exodus? Perhaps the text suggests that passive acceptance in a relationship is not a sustainable way to maintain it. Indeed, feelings of dissatisfaction with such a relationship are the beginnings of a more mature way of approaching and understanding it. The key lies in whether we allow the difficult feelings to push us toward rejecting the relationship or use them as the motivation to investigate and engage further.

Every Passover, we perform the same rituals and conduct the same seder, which highlights the changes in our feelings, attitudes, and relationship with God from year to year. This process of assuming ownership over a part of our relationship, of taking an increasingly active and engaged role in our partnership with God, is a cyclical one. Over time we confront the same issues again and again. But each time we bring to these issues a new perspective, because we have learned and grown from our experiences. The enduring cycle of the Jewish year serves as a useful barometer for my own spiritual journey; it never fails to amaze me how each year, the same actions evoke such different meanings and realizations. Of course, they inspire new questions as well. For if there were no questions, how would the search progress? My relationship with God would be reduced to the one-dimensional realm of simple, obedient action, without the struggle and without the active engagement that is part of a *relationship* with God.

Just as the matzah looks the same while its meaning changes according to the attitude of the person who eats it, my religious practices remain the same, even as my attitudes toward them fluctuate and evolve. At times, I may feel enslaved or limited, but my faith that the laws of the Torah will bring me to a place where I feel actualized and free is firm, more so than if I had not had these strictures in the first place. For this reason, I am committed not to abandon my observance simply because it is difficult for me; instead, I grapple with and question it. Our texts commonly use the image of God as the bridegroom and Israel as the bride to depict the Jewish nation's relationship with God. Similarly, one can compare his or her individual relationship with God to a marriage: the relationship is ideally an absolutely committed one; as issues and difficulties come up, we work through them rather than finding in them a cause for rejection. Instead of seeing difficulties as obstacles or pitfalls, we can use times of doubt and friction to move the relationship to a more appropriate and fulfilling level. The goals are long-term rather than short-term.

The process of existing in—actively engaging in—a relationship with God is ultimately what gives my life meaning. As I travel along this quest, it may look from the outside as if I end up exactly where I started, but I possess greater understanding and greater love for God. In the haggadah we read, "In every generation, one must see himself as if he himself left Egypt." In our generation, it is our task to be fully engaged in our own personal exodus. I find meaning in the idea that the generation that emerged from Egypt never entered the Land of Israel. The conclusion of our search is ever elusive; it is the journey that is really the goal.

≈≈≈

God's Bride on Pesach

KIM CHERNIN

> How strange, god's
>   bride lives
>   in a cup
> of Pesach wine.

Kim Chernin is a spiritual counselor and the author of fourteen books, including a trilogy on hunger: *The Obsession: Reflections on the Tyranny of Slenderness*, *The Hungry Self: Women, Eating, and Identity*, and *Reinventing Eve: Modern Woman in Search of Herself*.

        Not visible
        perhaps,
     in the first
     sip, to be known
     at the breaking
        of bread
        by thoughts
     turning in ways you
        would not
     anticipate. This
     bitter herb: meant
     for those who seek
        Him/Who
        never can
     be known, they
     say, by sight or
     sense and so they
     give up on the world. This
     world, where
     every cry of a green
     newborn asks
     us urgently no
     longer to seek
     Her/Who
     has always abundantly
     here, been given.

I have to admit, the first time I met the Goddess she did not look Jewish. On the other hand, how should a Jewish Goddess look? Mine was
dancing. She had huge breasts that were lifting and flopping. She
picked up her knees, stretched out her arms, and bent from the torso in
a ponderous dance that was both sacred and ridiculous and seemed to
be taking place simultaneously at the center of my head, in my sinews
and veins, in the room around me, and nowhere at all.

        Although I had never met a Goddess before, I had no doubt about
her identity as she danced and disappeared and grew back into visibili-
ty again. I was wide awake, sitting at my desk. I felt that new life would

grow from her, that I myself, egged on by her image, would soon learn to perform this heavy, fleet-footed dance. Wherever she stepped and whatever she touched quickened and flowered; there was water where before there had been only rock. I was in the most extreme state of tranquility I had ever experienced, while at the same time I felt that my mind was moving fast around this still point of urgency where the Goddess was dancing. Some things puzzled me. On one hand, if there was a Goddess, why hadn't I met her before? And, on the other hand, a Jewish Goddess?

Looking back so many years later, it's hard to say when exactly I began to ponder this question. I had already been to Israel, lived on a kibbutz, come home again. This encounter with the dancing Goddess took place during a time when I was staying home, writing poetry, becoming aware of an inner world. That places this sacred dance sometime during my mid-thirties. After I met my Goddess I was not the same person I had been before. I'd been asking questions since I had begun to speak, but now my questions consumed me.

Why was I finding it so hard to think of this dancing figure as Jewish? She had breasts, a body, and dark, tangled hair, like so many of us. Jewish teaching tells us that God is invisible, all-knowing, omnipresent, unknowable. Pure spirit. A God without a body. This should imply that God is neither male nor female, neither old man with long hair dwelling in heaven nor big-breasted goddess dancing.

Yet somehow, in spite of the prophets' insistence upon the one God of whom there can be no likeness, we take it for granted that our God is masculine. I found myself asking: Why had a purely spiritual conception, with which, presumably, both women and men would feel equally at home, given way to a masculine image of God? Why didn't I inherit the concept of an ungendered, disembodied, spiritual God, the way the prophets had promised? It became clear to me that if our God were both male and female, if we, in this sense precisely, were made in God's image, it would be much harder to legislate against women touching the Torah or joining the male members of the congregation in prayer.

When I was in Israel, I discussed this subject with a young soldier interested in spiritual questions. He believed that our masculine conception of the Divine stemmed from grammar: because the two earliest names for God, *El* and *Yahweh,* as they are used in the Bible, are masculine (and appropriately accompanied by adjectives and verbs that take a masculine form), he reasoned, it was inevitable that for a Hebrew speaker God would be perceived as male.

I responded that in this tension between grammar and prophetic teaching, grammar had proved to be unexpectedly powerful in shaping our conception of God. In fact, it had overwhelmed all the instruction we had received about God's disembodied, nonphysical, unknowable, purely spiritual, ungendered nature. Moreover, while Hebrew grammar imposed some restraints, the language did have the capacity to let some nouns take either the masculine or feminine gender, leaving each speaker or writer the freedom to choose which form to use—a fact that, in some other context, he himself had told me. Therefore, I argued, this freedom of choice could presumably be exercised every time we evoke God by name. Depending on our mood, our need, our spiritual inclination of the moment, we could call upon the Divine by His masculine or by Her feminine name—at least so far as the possibilities of Hebrew grammar were concerned.

This argument may have had something to do with my visit from the Goddess several years later. Maybe She likes women who argue on Her behalf, even before they have come to know Her. It could be that the One with her big breasts had come, several years later, to remind me that it is indeed possible to name and rename the Divine and to locate missing aspects of It. She seemed to support my argument that there was probably more than grammar at work in this assignment of gender; and that, if we must after all have a gendered God, we might be missing the One who comes naked and dancing.

As an educated Jewish woman, I knew that the most natural thing to do upon meeting up with a Jewish Goddess would be to start reading. Eventually, of course, I did. Yet, at first, I felt there might be some other way of finding knowledge, a way more in keeping with this big-breasted, ponderous dance, which had arisen spontaneously out of nowhere. Many times the answers you are looking for have already been told and remembered and told to someone else, starting a chain that can stretch out over hundreds, even thousands of generations. I didn't think I should have to become a scholar to learn more about a Jewish Goddess. There are always traces—a hint here, a clue there—and no seeker after knowledge ever goes hungry. Where efforts have been made to efface, exile, or dismiss something that was once known, knowledge is likely to come in unconventional ways—showing up suddenly as a dancing figure or unexpectedly in stories.

Shortly after I had met my Goddess, I was introduced to a *falasha* at the home of a friend on Shabbat. Ruth was the first black Jew I had ever met, an Ethiopian woman whose people had been recognized as Jews very recently by the State of Israel. They were now regarded as the remnant of the Lost Tribe of Daniel, which had vanished from Jewish history twenty-seven hundred years earlier. Their tradition had been developed directly from the Hebrew Scriptures, prior to the Mishnah and the Talmud. Ruth told us that in *falasha* texts the Sabbath is personified as the daughter of God, a divine princess who intercedes with God on behalf of humankind, saves sinners from the torments of life after death,[1] judges the souls of the just, is called by God beloved, exquisite, guardian, radiant, revered. According to *falasha* tradition, her very name, Sabbath, means "I only am God."

I was excited. I wanted to know more, know everything I could find out. It was hard to imagine an ancient Jewish tradition in which the feminine aspect of God was named and celebrated. One day I went up to the library stacks at the University of California at Berkeley, forgot about breakfast and lunch, spent the entire day thumbing through the few relevant books I found. I learned that for the *falasha,* this exquisite being, Princess Sabbath, was one of God's earliest creations and paradoxically identical with God. She was God's compassionate, female aspect, before whom, the *falasha* say, even the angels tremble. My private, intimate, interior experience belonged to an ancient Jewish line.

The kabbalistic tradition offers a similar interpretation of the Sabbath, as I learned from a young woman I met at Berkeley who was studying Kabbalah. I told her about the way the *falasha* personified the Sabbath, and she replied that the *Zohar* offered a similar description, instructing to prepare for the Sabbath queen with embroidered cushions, covers, and festive garments, and a house full of lighted candles, as if we were receiving a bride. She explained that *Lekha Dodi* ("Oh Come My Beloved"), which we still sing in synagogue on Sabbath evenings, had been written by the sixteenth-century kabbalists from Safed. They went out into the fields surrounding the town to receive the Sabbath, once again understood as God's bride (or as we would say, God's feminine aspect), with whom God, as bridegroom, was to be united.

Again, I went searching for books, and within an hour or two I was walking out of a used book store heavily laden with books on Jewish mysticism, Kabbalah, messianic tradition in Judaism, and several different translations of the Hebrew Scriptures. I had gathered up anything, everything, that could help me follow the traces of this mysterious figure, the Sabbath, the feminine aspect of God, who did, indeed, in ways I had not known or suspected, belong to Jewish imagination and thought. How far back did this tradition run?

What is in exile seeks to return. The excluded comes back. The forgotten recalls itself. It is, truly, a question of traces. Perhaps it is not surprising, therefore, that I was able to follow these traces right back into the sacred pages of the Hebrew Scriptures.

This is what I have learned:

Our Bible was compiled by editors profoundly committed to monotheism, who did their best to eliminate all descriptions of Canaanite Goddess worship. Nevertheless, they named three Canaanite Goddesses: Asherah, Astarte, and the Queen of Heaven. They likewise made us aware, through their repeated references to abominations, of the popular religious tendencies they were attempting to eliminate. The worship of Asherahs, carved wooden figurines that depict a woman with large breasts, was one such abomination, as was the burning of incense beneath leafy trees on the high places, where the Goddess was worshipped. In these nude female figures and figurines, found everywhere in archeological digs throughout Israel and dating from every period of the Hebrew presence in Israel, we meet the fertile, fully embodied, large-breasted Goddess, similar indeed to the one who appeared to me.

Less well-known is the persistent, dedicated, stiff-necked devotion that was shown to the Goddess throughout the biblical period—and by our own people.[2] If our Bible sides with the prophets, judges, and kings in their struggle to suppress Goddess worship, that may mean it is still necessary, thousands of generations later, to revisit our sacred texts and no longer unthinkingly accept that suppression. The Goddesses are our history, and yet we scarcely know them; they are our past, and yet they have been almost entirely erased and excluded from our story. No wonder they have to show up abruptly, swinging their big breasts, dancing naked.

It is, of course, impossible to eliminate essential aspects of the Divine. The learned men, piecing together the Hebrew Scriptures, selecting, excising, transcribing, took great pains to keep traces of the Goddess religion from its pages. Traces remained. How could they not? The Goddess, the feminine, is an inevitable aspect of divinity, as real, as present in our imagination or perception as we allow Her to be.

In evolving the Talmud, the Rabbis were careful to avoid making God appear too anthropomorphic, since God was by definition beyond the reach of the senses. Consequently, they began to correct older biblical statements that described God as dwelling among the Children of Israel. They invented circumlocutions; they imagined intermediaries; they created nouns. For example, "Let them make me a Sanctuary that I may dwell among them" became "Let them make before me a Sanctuary that I may let my *Shekhinah* dwell among them."[3] Originally, it seems, it did not trouble the Rabbis that the noun *Shekhinah,* indicating this perceivable aspect of the deity, took a feminine ending.

On the other hand, we may by now appreciate the deeper meaning reflected in this progression from a feminine noun to a gendered presence to a personification. The use of a feminine name for an aspect of God called back the old, exiled conception of a female Goddess. A presence, a tangibility, a being-here-with-us, that had been denied the God of Israel, had now been restored. The *Shekhinah* came to be seen, by the Rabbis themselves, as the feminine aspect of God. The excised and forbidden Goddess mysteriously made her way back into Jewish lore, into the Talmud itself, through the intercession of grammar.

As *Shekhinah,* the Goddess comes with us into exile, comforts the ill and infirm, is present to those in need. In this ancient, almost lost conception of Her, She watches over sinners who repent, walks beside those who are brokenhearted, is the divine principle of compassion who intercedes with God on our behalf. She's ours, if we wish to reclaim her; She will dwell with us if we dare to venture outside the boundaries of the tradition we have been given. We can know her again as the Sabbath bride of the *falashas,* or as the sixteenth-century Sabbath Queen evoked by the kabbalists. How many old, rich, forgotten meanings return to us with Her. As contemporary women, gathering to form a women's seder, we may see her as earth itself, a deity of fruit-fulness. We may remember that the earth is our mother, pregnant with abundance. With this imagery the female body returns to a revered place in Jewish life. The senses become a source of celebration, for it is indeed possible to behold Her who is not beyond perception.

Now, some twenty-five years after I first met Her, I easily sense Her presence at the seder, way back behind the learned teachings and the familiar stories and the commentaries on the stories. I've glimpsed Her in the season itself, which marks the time of the early harvest in Israel. She is there in the *omer,* the sheaf of barley offered on the second day of the Passover. Present, if unrecognized, She lives in the cup of Pesach wine, just waiting to deliver her intoxicating stories. She is the wine; She is the herbs and the green of the field; She is the wheat, rye, oats, barley, and spelt from which the matzah can be made. She is the story behind the oldest story, the fertility and redemption our festive meal invokes.

I've caught glimpses of Her sitting comfortably in Elijah's place, sipping at his glass of wine. By the time he shows up the glass is full again. I've seen them wrangle when Elijah comes to claim his chair. These two have an old argument. It breaks out while the rest of us make our way through the haggadah. She's never forgiven him for dragging the prophets of Baal down from Mount Carmel and killing them in the River Kishon when they lost the rain-making competition.[4] He points out that no one laid a hand on the prophets of Asherah. By the end of the seder, whoever tips back in a chair or glances over a shoulder can see her with her hair set free, dancing about in the nude, around the seder table, around and around to sprinkle the entire company with ferment and wine.

≋

The Matzah Set-Up

JENYA ZOLOT-GASSKO

My grandpa Shmuel died just before I was born. He never had a chance to explain to me what it meant to be Jewish, not to mention what it meant to be Jewish in Soviet Russia. Thus, my grandma Sarah, the only observant person in our family, was the only one who could have taught me something about being Jewish. But she never did. Grandma was too sharp and sensible not to know where this "unnecessary" knowledge could get us—Jews living under the oppressive and anti-Semitic Soviet government—at that time. She didn't want us there.

Despite Grandma's sensible omission of the subject, I knew that she believed in God with all her ardent heart, and although she never talked about her faith, she didn't hide it, either. After Grandpa died,

Jenya Zolot-Gassko is an elementary school teacher in Boston, Massachusetts. For the past several years, she has been an active member of the planning committee of the Boston Project Kesher Global Women's Seder, which brings together over one hundred American and Russian new American Jewish women, as well as Jewish women from all around the world. Her personal stories, such as the one included here, have become highlights of the event.

she always stayed with one of her daughters' families—rarely with us though, so I couldn't often watch her observing her faith. Yet, once in a while, I would visit my aunt's house, where Grandma often lived, and see her praying. A small, still beautiful, impeccably neat old lady, she sat alone by the window, disunited from the whole world, holding in her tiny frail hands a very old book filled with strings of odd-looking letters. She was holding the book so gently that one could think this worn, black leather tome had been made of crystal or the finest porcelain and could easily shatter into innumerable pieces if not held with grand care.

I never saw it with my own eyes but heard from my mother that Grandma was sometimes fasting. This strange word "fasting," to my surprise, appeared to mean "starving"—a fact that struck me as absolutely unbelievable. Why would anyone voluntarily starve in Russia, where the constant shortage of food turned the very process of eating into a longed-for event? But I never asked my grandma about it; I probably wasn't that interested.

There is something else about my grandma that I can picture remarkably well at the time of Pesach. That queer word, "Pesach," always puzzled me. It didn't sound Russian. And how could it, being the name of a Jewish holiday? That much I knew: Pesach was the name of a holiday. But that was all I knew about it. I had no idea what this Pesach holiday was about and why my grandma was so fervently engaged in its celebration. Nonetheless, I did not even once ask her about it. However, it didn't slip from my teenage attention that every year during the holiday Grandma was eating red borscht, matzah, and gefilte fish. Of course, the borscht and gefilte fish she cooked herself. In Russia no one could even imagine that canned borscht and gefilte fish exist anywhere on this planet. But I never saw her baking matzah, and I certainly never saw matzah for sale in any food store. You had to be insane even to picture Jewish food in a Russian store at that time. So, once in a while I wondered where that matzah came from. But I never asked Grandma about it. Why would I care?

At that time in my life—I was fourteen—I tried to stay as far away from real life as possible. Two years before, in the summer of my sixth grade, a nasty anti-Semitic episode had split my life into the lighthearted, contented *before* and the silently tormenting *after*. The episode left an indelible wound in my fragile soul, which had been totally unprepared for the blow. The wound was still deep and bleeding, but I was diligently patching it with a thick layer of denial and neglect—the only healing technique I knew then was foolishly imagining that the trick was working.

I tried to avoid thinking of myself as Jewish: the thoughts led nowhere, except to the realm of helplessness and pain. I was convinced that—as we had been taught at school—in the Soviet Union all people were equal. My Jewish nationality didn't matter, so I should certainly forget the summer incident that had happened only because of that one mean girl and a few other girls who.... This feeble explanation didn't even abate the dull, ceaseless pain I felt every day and couldn't share with anyone.

But that enchanting, earth-smelling day in spring, I was in high spirits. We were visiting my aunt's family. They lived high up on the Vorobiev Hills, in the pale yellow two-story apartment building lurking among emerald-green poplar trees, my favorite place in Moscow.

The moment we arrived, I rushed through greeting the relatives with the mandatory "Hello" and immediately hurried to my aunt's library. I knew exactly which book I wanted to read, so in no time I sneaked to some quiet spot on the couch and curled up there with a sizable novel on my lap, tranquil and content. But right in the middle of the second page, I heard my grandma calling me to her room.

The minute I heard her solemn voice, I sensed trouble. Dragging myself toward her room, I rummaged through all the misdeeds I had been guilty of in the past few days. I knew that when I wasn't with a book, I sometimes did stupid things that made my adult relatives upset or even angry. What was it this time? I couldn't remember a thing, which was even scarier.

Tense and nervous, I shuffled into Grandma's room and tripped over her grave, concerned look.

"Jenya," she started in a somber tone. My heart throbbed in awe.
"Yes, Grandma?"

"Jenya, could you please do me a favor?"

I sighed with relief that she was not angry with me. I immediately agreed to her request for help, and Grandma continued, carefully weighing and measuring her every word. I realized from the tone of her voice that she had been almost certain that I would refuse.

"Pesach is coming, Jenya. Do you know that?" It was a rhetorical question. Of course I had no idea it was coming. Grandma then told me that she had ordered matzah for Pesach and asked if I would pick it up for her at the synagogue. My mother, she said, would be able to tell me how to get there.

When I realized what she was asking of me, I desperately sought the words to politely refuse. Why should I go and get this queer product no one eats in normal life anyway? I had heard the word "synagogue" not more than three times in my life. I didn't have the slightest idea where or what it was. Why on earth had Grandma chosen *me* to go there?

But while I was immersed in an industrious search for a polite way to reject this odd request, my alter ego, bold and impulsive, suddenly seized my thoughts and moved them along a completely unforeseen route. Why shouldn't I go? Was I doomed to hide in my book-refuge for the rest of my days? Why not do something "weird" for a change? This trip began to appeal to me as an adventure.

"Grandma, when shall I go? Now?"

"No, not now, darling. Tomorrow will be fine. And please ask your mother for something big to carry the matzah in. Matzah takes plenty of space."

"Do you mean I'll need a suitcase?"

"A big suitcase will do," said Grandma, tenderly smiling at me in a quite inexplicable way.

The next morning I got up at the crack of dawn, which utterly shocked my mother, who never saw me getting up on my own, not to mention so early.

"Mom, you didn't forget that I am going to the synagogue today? Could you please give me a suitcase for matzah?"

"We don't have a suitcase for matzah," Mom grinned. "We have only one suitcase, and it's a suitcase for everything." She dragged our huge blue-striped suitcase, one of a kind, from the closet and handed it to me.

To my surprise, the synagogue stood in the very heart of Moscow, right in the middle of Arkhipov Street. Its building, with neoclassical columns, somewhat resembled an opera theatre. But the minute I stepped inside I forgot the resemblance, forgot that I was in the center of Moscow, forgot that I had come for a purpose.

I walked right into the big room with rows of benches and a small stage. On both sides of the back wall, above the stage, there were some writings. The letters were big enough to be easily seen from the far end of the room. Some were Russian and some were the same strange-shaped letters I had seen in Grandma's book. The content was quite foreign to me, but I immediately realized that these were prayers. Never in my life had I seen any prayers. I began reading them—slowly and scrupulously, as if I had just learned how to read. I heard my heart pounding fast and loud. Suddenly someone tapped me on the shoulder. I turned around and saw an old man smiling at me.

"I am sorry, lady. The place for women is upstairs. This room is for men only. But you can have a peek."

For men only? I wondered if this strange old man knew that in our country men and women were equal. I assumed that he had probably gone to school before the Revolution and never learned that. But I didn't want to argue with him, so I went upstairs and looked at the prayers from there. Then I walked around the building and finally found the place where people were receiving matzah. I got in line. All the people in line were old, or at least they looked old to me. I was apparently the only teenager in the whole building, not to mention the only person with a suitcase. I bet everyone thought I had come to get the matzah all the way from Siberia. I saw their curious and admiring looks, but no one asked me a thing. The people were just talking quietly with each other, and whenever they caught my glance, they smiled at me graciously.

As a teenager, I felt comfortable only in familiar places and with people I knew. But here, although I was in a totally new place, surrounded by strangers, for some mysterious reason I felt at home—even in the room for men only.

Suddenly, unexpectedly, something inside me began to warm up like the burner of an old, electric stove that had just been turned on. The feeling was strange and inscrutable. What was that little thing inside me, gently pulsating and wordlessly talking to me? Was it possible that this little something was my Jewish soul, which from the day of my birth had been decidedly put to sleep by the demands of the Soviet regime and my parents' fears? Was that why I felt so right and so comfortable in this totally unfamiliar place? There was no answer. Why would I expect it? I didn't ask the question. I didn't know how to ask.

I could never have imagined then, at the age of fourteen, that ten years later I'd return to this synagogue for my first celebration of Rosh Hashanah and would stand upstairs, squeezed in the crowd of other Jewish people, mostly young ones, passionately singing *"Heyveynu sholom aleichem,"* seeing tears in their eyes, and feeling tears in mine. I wouldn't know any of those people around me. But feeling their shoulders touching mine and seeing their eyes sparkling with astonishing joy, for the first time in my life I would realize that the word "Jew" was not only a word that some vile people use to insult others.

On my way home, sitting in the subway with the blue-striped, filled-with-matzah suitcase guarded between my knees, I felt like a conspirator carrying a trunk full of underground literature from a secret meeting, thrilled and scared to death. The locks on the suitcase were so old and flimsy that I expected the suitcase to pop open any minute, to the amazement and delight of the Soviet subway audience. But to my great relief, it didn't.

The matzah was delivered to my aunt's house safe and sound. With pride spread all over my face, as if I had just performed a heroic deed worth recounting to my grandchildren, I handed the suitcase to

Grandma. She opened it; saw the matzah, with its wavy layers of the white and brownish goose bumps; patted it gently with her frail veined hand, still gazing at the matzah; and thanked me in a very casual manner, as if I had just brought her a glass of water from the kitchen. Then she slowly shifted her glance from the matzah to me and finally noticed my still-shining face, now a little perplexed by her unexcited response.

And then, once again, she sent me that same tender, inexplicable smile she had granted me the day before.

≋

Women Re-creating the Passover Seder: Bella Rosenfeld Chagall and the Resonance of Female Memory
JUDITH R. BASKIN

In her luminous memoir, *Burning Lights*,[1] Bella Rosenfeld Chagall arranges her childhood memories of growing up in a large and prosperous Chasidic family in early twentieth-century Vitebsk, White Russia, according to the holy days and festivals of the Jewish calendar. Chagall lived in a world dominated by distinct demarcations between Jews and gentiles; between struggling Jews of the rural *shtetl* and comfortable middle-class urban Jews; between religious Jews and those attracted by the secular world; and, not least, between women and men. Yet these boundaries were also permeable. Non-Jews shopped and worked in the Rosenfelds' store and provided numerous services to the family. Bella and her brothers were sent to Russian-speaking schools and universities, and none remained in the traditional com-

---

Dr. Judith R. Baskin is professor of religious studies and director of the Harold Schnitzer Family Program in Judaic Studies at the University of Oregon. Her books include *Midrashic Women: Formations of the Feminine in Rabbinic Literature* and the edited collections *Jewish Women in Historical Perspective* and *Women of the Word: Jewish Women and Jewish Writing*.

munity. Bella herself crossed social boundaries within the Jewish world when she married Marc Chagall, a young man from the *shtetl*. Jewish women and men, too, although separate in most aspects of the religious life that Chagall recalls, observed certain rituals together. The Sabbath evening meal is one preeminent example; so also is the Passover seder.

The women of her household played dominant roles in Chagall's recollections of this Jewish festival. As Judith Hauptman has observed,[2] despite some dissenting voices, talmudic legislation included women in traditional Passover obligations. Women were expected to participate in the Passover seder; to eat matzah,[3] the paschal lamb, and bitter herbs;[4] and to drink four cups of wine.[5] "Important" women might even recline at the seder table.[6] Scenes in medieval illuminated and early printed Passover haggadahs portray women and men sharing in festival preparations and sitting together at the holiday meal. In fact, a rather mordant visual pun in several medieval haggadahs is the illustration of a husband pointing to the wife sitting beside him as he recites *"Maror zeh"* ("This bitter herb").[7]

When Chagall's childhood self, Basha, turns the pages of her haggadah and finds an illustration of a family seated around a seder table just like her own, she feels deeply connected to a Jewish past filled with experiences and images of both men and women:

> I feel an ache in my heart. Here they are, our grandfathers, our dearest grandmothers. How weary, how dried up they are! I stroke them and turn page after page. I look for them everywhere. The piece of *matzoh* crumbles over my haggadah. It is as though the sand of the land of Egypt were grating under my feet. I murmur: "We were slaves—"[8]

Chagall's memoir reminds us that the new Passover practices that are being shaped by contemporary Jewish women are not a radical disjunction between past and present. They are an enhancement and transformation of women's continuous participation in reliving the Jewish journey to community and revelation.

Basha describes the mixed multitude of guests who gather for her family's seder, a true democracy of Jews, and she remembers her anxiety as she, the youngest child present, anticipates her recitation of the Four Questions:

> I sit in my accustomed place, squeezed in between Father and Mother. Because of Father's pillow, my corner is more cramped than usual. I feel hot and choked. But I know that soon, after a few phrases, Father will bend down toward me, as though the four questions were being addressed not by me to him, but by him to me. Now he is beckoning to me: "Come, the questions!"[9]

Although Chagall disparages the instruction in Hebrew and Bible that she and her brother received from a rather ineffectual tutor, it was sufficient to enable her to fulfill the role of the youngest participant at the seder service. Bella's rudimentary education in Hebrew was not unusual for daughters of learned and wealthy families, but the large majority of Eastern European Jewish women would not have been able to ask the Four Questions.

Most movingly, Basha accompanies her mother to fulfill the custom of opening the door for the prophet Elijah, the precursor of the messiah. This was apparently a traditional female role in the Rosenfelds' household. Basha is filled with awe and exultation:

> Each with an open haggadah in her hand—Mother holds the burning candle too—we go quietly out of the dining room. The men remain sitting at the table. No one budges. Each one looks at us, escorts us with his eyes, as though they were all blessing us, their envoys.[10]

Watching the reflection of a wandering candle in the house across the street, Basha wonders if there is a door opening now in other homes: "Is there in every doorway a mother with a little girl holding a candle in her hand?"[11] Facing the silent dark street, she listens to her mother reciting from the haggadah and ardently joins the family in their prayers that Elijah will hasten and commence the redemption of a long-suffering world:

> Having closed her haggadah, Mother makes a sign with her hands,

stroking the air—she might be bringing something down from heaven. Perhaps? Perhaps? She does not want to go away from the open door. She strokes the air for the last time—it is like a kiss—and she closes the door.[12]

The female involvement in the Passover seder that was so natural in the Rosenfeld family did not extend to all Jewish observances. The Judaism that could be such a source of richness for Basha also excluded her from many aspects of a religious world comfortably occupied by her father and brothers. Basha wondered what went on in the synagogue, a place to which she almost never went: "What does father do there, staying such a long time? He always comes back last."[13] On the holiday of Sukkot, only the males of the family are permitted to eat their meals in the *sukkah,* the temporary dwelling constructed to recall the wanderings of the ancient Israelites in the wilderness after the Exodus from Egypt. Their meals are served to them by the women through a little window. Basha feels saddened by her separation from her father and brothers; they seem to her like people from another world:

> In the apartment it is cold. It seems empty, and it feels as if there were no doors and windows. I sit with Mother and eat without zest.
>
> "Mother, why have we been left here with the servants, as though we too were servants? What kind of holiday is that, Mother?" I keep tormenting her. "Why do they eat apart from us?"
>
> "Ah, my little child, they're men," says Mother sadly, as she eats her piece of cold meat.[14]

Bella's exclusion from participation in this central Jewish observance is indicative of larger patterns of female marginalization in Judaism. As the absence of females from the Rosenfeld *sukkah* demonstrates, women were not obligated to participate in many of the communal rituals of traditional Judaism, including synagogue worship at set times, study of revealed texts, and recitation of the mourner's kaddish. This lack of obligation meant that in practice, most women simply did not take part in these defining and culturally esteemed Jewish activities. Thus, it is striking that a majority of rabbinic voices did insist that women are required to participate in the Passover seder. As we are told: "R. Joshua ben Levi also said: Women are obligated to drink four cups of wine because they too were included in that miracle [of redemption from slavery]."[15]

Why, if this is so, is it only recently that many women are enjoying a meaningful engagement with the seder and its rituals? One answer stems from past Jewish failures to educate daughters in their heritage. The traditional haggadah is written in Hebrew and Aramaic. Since very few girls or women were ever taught these literary Jewish languages of study and prayer, they were unaware of their equal obligation to relive annually the Jewish journey to spiritual peoplehood. Many felt alienated by lengthy haggadah recitations they could not understand. Bella Chagall came from a home where Hebrew literacy was valued for girls as well as boys; the competency she achieved was a consequence of her family's combined prosperity and piety, which allowed for the luxury of a resident *melammed* (teacher). Until the past forty or fifty years, few Jewish girls would have shared their ability to recite the Four Questions in the original language. The empowerment resulting from vastly improved Jewish education for girls in the course of the twentieth century, and the contemporary availability of haggadahs that combine thoughtful English renderings of the traditional text with a variety of inspiring readings, have encouraged attention and involvement from many of the women who formerly felt excluded from the heart of the seder experience.

The burden of labor placed on women to prepare for this holiday may also have soured its redemptive qualities for many. As Judith Hauptman has written, "The painstaking conversion of the kitchen from leaven-filled to leaven-free status has turned the Festival of Freedom into an intense period of domestic labor rather than a celebration of personal and national liberation."[16] In the Rosenfeld household of *Burning Lights,* where Bella's mother, Alta, works from early morning to evening running the family store, it is Hava, the Jewish maid, who assumes the heavy mantle of responsibility to prepare the house for Passover:

The first to be drawn into the Passover turmoil is Hava, our fat cook. Since the day after Purim she has been going about in a daze. The ordinary weekdays have died away for her. She has only one thought in her head—to have a kosher Passover.[17]

Of course, many Jewish women did not have the luxury of a maid to undertake the extensive Passover preparations for them. As a result, they were responsible for everyday household chores as well as the burden of readying the house for Passover.

The labor-saving devices of the modern world and a greater willingness on the part of some men to help in the holiday have improved this situation for many contemporary Jewish women. An interesting rationale for such male assistance can be found in the memoir of Pauline Wengeroff, recounting matzah making in Russia in the 1840s:

The baking took almost two whole days. My mother made tireless rounds to inspect the rolling pins of the women and scrape off the dough, which was considered to have become leavened and must not come in contact with the unleavened dough for *matzehs*. My brother and brothers-in-law helped [my mother] with this work, using bits of broken glass. The young men also helped prick the *matzeh*; it occurred to no one that this might not be "men's work." Anything to do with *Pesach*, and especially with *matzeh*, is sacred work.[18]

It may be only in the present that such arguments can find ready ears. Yet, women's intensive involvement in the domestic preparations for Passover and the Passover seder have given them a particularly intimate connection to this holiday. The Jewish feminist focus on Passover is grounded not only in Jewish legal tradition but in the centuries of women's work that made the celebration of this festival possible.

Further, the feminist focus on Passover has much to do with the fluid nature of the Passover seder and its liturgy, which encourage discussion, innovation, and inclusiveness. Since the haggadah is a book intended solely for domestic use, it is not affected by strictures that might prevent significant alterations and additions to the synagogue liturgy. Creative rewritings of the haggadah from a variety of ideological positions have been a feature of Jewish life for at least a century.[19] Similarly, the haggadah has never been subject to restrictions on decoration and illustration, which would certainly apply to the Torah scroll and to a lesser extent to other books used in synagogue worship. This adaptive quality of the haggadah text, as well as the very central place of the Passover seder in Jewish observance, have provided an opportunity for reconnection with a tradition of liberation in which many modern women have found echoes of their own particular struggles with Judaism and Jewish identity. What they have discovered, as well, is a tradition of female participation in Pesach that has deep roots in the Jewish past.

Bella Rosenfeld Chagall, like all the women in her childhood home, experienced the redemptive and spiritual qualities of the Passover seder as a full participant in the epic retelling of the Jewish journey from slavery to freedom. Strongly connected to generations past, as well as to the Jews of her own time, Chagall's incandescent memory of her childhood seders remains an inspiring and empowering vision for Jewish women today.

≈≈≈

5

Visions and Challenges
for the Future

*The future beckons us on with promise of wider, freer
life, unchecked growth and scope, broad, unhampered
human and spiritual fellowship. The past holds us with
invincible weight. "Deny me, and you deny yourself," it
says; "your very life is all that makes you what you are."*

—JOSEPHINE LAZARUS, *JUDAISM, OLD AND NEW*

*Just as men's study and commentary produced multiple
layers of Jewish literary tradition over the last fifteen
centuries, so women's interaction with Jewish learning
will inevitably affect and contribute to that corpus. In
this rapid and unwieldy period of expansion, a new
layer of tradition is evolving. Like many past innovations, it will ultimately be codified, made manageable,
and incorporated into tradition in ways we cannot
foretell.* —EMILY FEIGENSON, IN *LIFECYCLES, VOLUME 2*

Each year, when we return to the seder table, we listen to the same haggadah texts and Passover melodies; we taste the same foods and perhaps even see many of the same faces. And yet, we come to this familiar ritual as changed individuals, altered by another year of life experience. How do we—as women's seder participants, as feminists, as members of the Jewish community—ensure that we are truly moving forward, that we are coming to the seder table with a deeper understanding of the holiday each year? How can we—as individuals and as a community—take on the challenging task that Passover sets before us: the task of bringing about the redemption of the world?

In part 5, the authors help us articulate challenges and visions for the future—of women's seders, of Jewish feminism, and of the Jewish community as a whole. They enjoin us to respond more genuinely to the demands that the Passover holiday makes on us, to work even more vigorously for liberation. Focusing on topics ranging from the failures of the first women's seders to the contemporary violence in Israel, these authors challenge us to ask ourselves two essential questions: Have we left Egypt? And have we fulfilled our obligation to "love the stranger"?

The first three pieces in part 5 look specifically at women's seders, each posing distinct challenges for participants and organizers. In "Sanctified by Ritual," activist Phyllis Chesler reflects on nearly three decades of participation in feminist seders. Comparing the first women's seder organizers to the newly freed Hebrew slaves, Chesler argues that these early seders constituted only the first steps out of Egypt. She articulates several key challenges that must be surmounted by today's women's seders in order for these gatherings to help women continue their journeys out of Egypt and toward the Promised Land.

While Chesler stresses the need to evolve beyond the limitations of the earliest women's seders, filmmaker Lilly Rivlin, also a participant in these original women's seders, reminds us what made these events so significant. In "Reflections on the Feminist Seder as an Entry Point into Jewish Life," she advocates for women to keep seders intimate, participatory, and infused with discussions of political issues. Looking back on the political concerns that inspired the first women's seders, Rivlin urges today's women's seder participants to maintain this activist spirit.

"Placing Our Bettes: Keepin' it Real at the Seder Table" adds a young voice to this dialogue. Israeli-American writer Ophira Edut offers a provocative critique of the usual tone and content of women's seders. Exploring why contemporary women's seders have failed to engage some communities of Jewish feminists, Edut offers a new vision of Jewish women's gatherings that include "comedy as well as gravity" and acknowledge the accomplishments of contemporary Jewish women alongside those of biblical heroines.

While Edut imagines women's seders as gatherings of celebration, networking, and casual conversation, Martha Ackelsberg, professor of government and women's studies, suggests that we use women's seders to explore and celebrate the differences among us. In "Pluralism in Feminist Settings," she considers different strategies for reconciling the often conflicting needs and values of Jewish women. Drawing on her political science expertise and her own personal experiences in pluralist Jewish gatherings, she enjoins us to celebrate in solidarity with one another without compromising our political or religious values.

Ruth Kaplan focuses her attention on the fundamental conflicts between feminist values and Jewish tradition, arguing that all too often, women's seders encourage us to evade, rather than confront, these important tensions. Drawing on feminist and Jewish sources, Kaplan's "Conflict and Community: The Common Ground of Judaism and Feminism" articulates a model for facing this conflict through a long-term process of negotiation and communication and urges us to enter into this process at women's seders.

The challenges that Kaplan and Ackelsberg pose for women's seders also frame broader challenges for all Jewish feminists. Similarly, the next three pieces in part 5 extend their reach beyond women's seders, offering visions and challenges to the entire Jewish community. Each author charges us to apply the lessons of Exodus to our individual lives and our practices as a community. Rabbi Sharon Kleinbaum's "What Now? After the Exodus, the Wilderness" takes as its inspiration the Israelites' journey through the *midbar* (wilderness). Exploring the notion that "the way of the Lord is through the wilderness," Kleinbaum discusses the spiritual significance of our wilderness journeys, focusing on the liberation struggle of gay and lesbian Jews. For Kleinbaum, the central challenge is to create an identity based not on hating the Egyptians but on creating and living a life of Torah.

Kleinbaum describes the temptation we all face in our own journeys: the pull to turn back to Egypt. The struggle of the wilderness, the fear of the unknown, and the risks and responsibilities of liberation all push us to return to the safety of the familiar. Ela Thier's "Letting Pharaoh Go: A Biblical Study of Internalized Oppression" begins by looking at the biblical passage in which the Israelites do decide to turn back—just before reaching the Promised Land. For Thier, this decision is one of many manifestations of the Israelites' internalized oppression. Arguing that our liberation from slavery is not complete until we free ourselves from its internal effects, she challenges us to come to terms with, and heal from, the deepest effects of sexism, oppression, and slavery.

Thier focuses on the psychological impact of oppression. Rabbi and peace activist Lynn Gottlieb furthers this exploration, examining how Jews' history of oppression has shaped our contemporary perspectives on the situation in Israel. Focusing on the Exodus narrative's fundamental message of tolerance and compassion, "Reflections on Exodus in Light of Palestinian Suffering" asks us to look at the story of our own oppression in Egypt in relation to Israel's treatment of the Palestinian people. Gottlieb cautions that our Passover prayers for peace will remain hollow until we dedicate ourselves to working for the liberation of all.

For Merle Feld, author of "Walking the Way as Women," the oppression of women has left a legacy in every Jewish woman's life: by concentrating our attention and care on our families and friends, we have neglected to care for the self and to care for the world. Asking us to both "narrow and widen" the circle of our care, Feld explores going out of Egypt as a multifaceted and multilayered journey in which caring for ourselves, supporting other women, and actively engaging in the repair of the world are equally important, interconnected parts.

The power of women's seders lies, in part, in their ability to address these many layers of liberation and redemption. Each year, we give ourselves permission to recline and relax for one evening, serving ourselves rather than others. But we do not let ourselves forget our responsibility and capability as free women; we also rededicate ourselves to the work of repairing the world. A women's seder motivates us to nurture ourselves, inspire one another, and respond to those who are in need of our help on their journey to liberation. For women's seders to further the journeys of individual participants and the community, they must continue to evolve, confronting the new challenges posed by the reflections presented here in this part.

Sanctified by Ritual

PHYLLIS CHESLER

Passover teaches us that freedom is a miracle, but that with God's help this miracle is possible no matter what one's earthly, historical circumstances might be. Whether a Jew has just survived the ancient destruction of Jerusalem or a European or Arab pogrom, is imprisoned in an Iranian jail or in a Nazi concentration camp, she is still commanded to celebrate her freedom from slavery. Passover teaches us that there are many kinds of slavery and that earthly jails do not have the power to imprison our Jewish souls. Passover also teaches us that obtaining one's freedom is both immanent and transcendent, a part of the human historical process and outside it. The ongoing dialectic between slavery and liberation is, like the world, a work in progress. Once we achieve

---

Dr. Phyllis Chesler is an emerita professor of psychology and women's studies, a psychotherapist, and an expert courtroom witness. She is also a board member of the International Committee for Women of the Wall. She was a member of the original New York women's seders and is the author of eleven books, including *Women and Madness* and most recently *Woman's Inhumanity to Woman* and *Women of the Wall: Claiming Sacred Ground at Judaism's Holy Site* (Jewish Lights Publishing).

one level of freedom, it becomes the basis from which to struggle for the next level.

Is a story this monumental, a message this universal, meant for Jews of one gender only? Or even for Jews only? Can only religiously learned Jewish men officiate at a seder—or can any Jew, male or female, learned or not, also do so? Indeed, in what sense is Passover a holiday of women and slaves, an opportunity to wrest freedom from fundamentalist Judaism? Is freedom a Jewish religious value meant for all people, all faiths? If so, should Jews make it a point to invite non-Jews to seders? What will be lost in translation? Is it really possible to transmit what we have learned about slavery and freedom to children, strangers, and slaves, to those who dwell within our midst? This is precisely what we are commanded to do.

Over the years, I have learned many things about slavery and freedom from reading secular books and by leading, participating in, and observing the very earliest feminist seders. I have organized and attended seders that were run by and for women only, feminists only, lesbians only. I believe that such separatist, political, and secular seders have— or rather had—their place. They are the first steps out of the Egypt of patriarchy, but not, ultimately, the steps that will bring us into the Promised Land.

Leaving Egypt is hard to do. We must continue the journey every year—and by the long route, no less. The short route will not do; the vegetation must change; new people must be born and brought into our tradition. But it takes time for slaves to become free enough to enter the Promised Land; the first generation may have to die out first.

I have learned some important things from studying the Torah itself. For example, slavery shortens the human spirit and makes risk-taking and collective resistance difficult, perhaps impossible. It is precisely because the Israelites suffer from impatience and shortened vision that Moses seems dangerous to them. They fear and resent him. After Moses kills the taskmaster, it is the fearful, resentful Jews, not the Egyptians or the taskmaster's compatriots, who want to turn him in. This is why Moses flees Egypt. Being a liberator is dangerous work; one does not choose this honor/burden but is chosen. Understandably, Moses resists it, but he comes to accept God's will.

This is the reason that, although Moses—the liberator—is a central figure in the Passover story, he is not mentioned even once in the haggadah. Feminist seders often elevate Miriam, thus minimizing or missing entirely the haggadah's point, which is to emphasize God's centrality to the liberation. It is a form of paganism, it is religiously childlike, this hunger to see one's own gendered human image writ large. I once had this hunger, and I also insisted on satisfying it. In the beginning, after so many centuries of God-the-father, Jewish feminist women hungered for God-the-mother. We needed to wrestle her free into being; it was the beginning of our exodus from fundamentalist misogyny within Judaism.

In the beginning, women who had been rendered invisible to themselves demanded that a human being just like themselves occupy center stage: they did not want to share the space with any man (Moses, Elijah, the rabbis of B'nai Brak). Thus, the earliest women's seders were created In Our Own Image.

Although we were not slaves—all were educated, independent, women with professions, reputations, and ideals—the women in early feminist seders still resembled the just-freed Jewish slaves. For example, we were ambivalent about leaving Egypt: most still did our "real" seder with our biological families. The feminist seder was done on another night, suggesting that it was a social or political event or a luxury, not a necessity. Lesbian seders were more often done on a "real" seder night, suggesting a more serious break with persecutory and rejecting families and a greater need for new ritualized families.

Like the Jewish slaves who had left Egypt, some of the women at our seder behaved in spiritually bedraggled ways. They used no religious sources but instead relied on feminist critiques of monotheism, wonderful feminist poetry, odd bits of learning, political tracts. Many also talked about their own achievements a good deal. Some used the seder to make speeches about current events, not about the miracle of redemption or God's role.

I certainly understand the need to use the seders to discuss our political lives. In 1971, I first encountered anti-Semitism among leftists, progressives, and feminists. From that moment on, I devoted myself to raising consciousness about this. I formed pioneer organizations, spoke at countless conferences and rallies, wrote articles, visited (and brought others to) Israel. However, what I was doing was secular politics; what I was missing was Jewish religious nourishment for my soul.

In 1976, the first-ever feminist Passover seder in North America was held in my apartment. An extraordinary time was had by all. Afterwards, we were high for weeks. Over the next few years, we evolved into a core group, with high-profile politicians, writers, scholars, artists, media personalities, and feminist icons among our oft-returning guests. For a time, our greatest pleasure was to please and delight one another.

Looking back, I would characterize what we did as a combination of feminist consciousness-raising, group therapy, and a Broadway show—Judaism lite.

At the time, I thought of us as a small group of feminists who wanted to retain our connection to Judaism in a celebratory manner. We also wanted to create a World of Our Mothers, and a faith-oriented community. But our faith turned out to be more secular than religious; our unspoken "givens" were liberal, left, feminist principles. In the historical era of the first feminist seders, it was easy for us to explode into being an amorphous, joyful, spontaneous lot, who quickly came to be perceived as leaders and pioneers.

We began to evolve a counter-haggadah, one in which the previously hidden and silenced world of women—of our personal and collective mothers and grandmothers—became dominant. We devised a different, parallel, mirror universe of a haggadah and a seder—one filled with only mothers and daughters. At the time, what we did was absolutely necessary and the first step out of Egypt. But, in my view, too many feminist seders continued to repeat taking only the first step, year after year. As we shall see, they—and we—languished there.

One might argue that this *was* our tradition. Fair enough. But it is not enough. Of course what we did was important. We created the ritual of verbal matrilineage, and introducing ourselves this way was—and remains—psychologically powerful and liberating. We feminized rituals, reciting plagues that were specific to women, devising evocative and psychodramatic rituals. We discussed the civil disobedience and sisterhood-in-deed modeled by the women of the Exodus story.

Once, we were as silent as slaves at our own seders; now, we were as free as Jews at our own feminist seder. This is no small achievement. However, a madcap feminist secularity and zeal for political correctness often overtook our Judaism. And while there is nothing wrong with being primarily secular, political, and atheist, there is something very confusing about dressing up in religious garments and presenting oneself as rabbinical figures in order to do so. In my opinion, we were not transforming a patriarchal ritual. We were, instead, creating a minor cult of our own celebrity.

Some perfectly memorable, moving, feminist seders faced and sometimes failed at least five challenges: first, that of gender separatism versus gender integration. In 1978, I had given birth to my son Ariel. I needed and wanted to include him in my seders. I also felt it was important for Jewish boys as well as girls to have fond, firm memories of adult Jewish women officiating at seders. I tried reasoning. I also begged. It was like trying to reason with Orthodox Jewish men to include women in a *minyan*. Over an eighteen-year period, I was only allowed to bring Ariel once, to one seder, when he was about six or seven years old. My seder sisters, most of whom were (or had once been) heterosexual married women and who were mothers themselves, refused to include sons as well as daughters.

They were not wrong, but they were not right.

It is true that the psychological dynamics in an all-female group can change instantly, profoundly, with the introduction of even one perfectly nice man. Women do not behave in the same way toward each other when a man or men are present. Many women have a hard time developing leadership skills or feeling authoritative in a gender-integrated setting. The realities of male domination and of female collaboration with it make asserting one's opinion or taking charge harder for some women when men are present. Some women cannot bear to see their strong female friends simper and compete for male approval and attention, or withdraw their maternal gaze from women and transfer it to men.

I myself sometimes prefer to *pray* in a group of only women. Our energy is different; something changes when men join us. The Women of the Wall pray in a women-only group. We have no alternative, not if we want to include Orthodox women—and we do. But a feminist Passover that takes place in one's own home and follows new rules is another matter. It seemed to me that a group of strong feminist women might, after four or five years of journeying together, begin to invite *some* carefully selected men and male children.

Second, feminist seders have a responsibility to teach others about what we are doing so that they will continue our work. Each feminist haggadah that has been published has had this in mind. Some haggadahs include scholarly material; most do not. There is another way to pass on a legacy, namely by cultivating a "hands-on" connection to other similar grassroots groups around the country or around the world.

Many feminist seder groups preferred each other's company—this is our right—to the task of reaching out to serious newcomers who had made an express commitment to return to their own communities where they would initiate similar feminist seders. In my opinion, we were failing an important obligation.

The third challenge is that of size. Some people prefer a very large and public seder with charismatic leaders, *rebbes,* performers. Others prefer a more intimate seder so that every Jew, each woman, can be a participant, not a passive observer. Early on, some of us wanted to turn our feminist seder into a huge public event. I resisted doing so. Perhaps I was wrong. I certainly did not stop anyone from pursuing this, but the amount of time and money necessary was prohibitive for us. Most of us had to work hard to survive financially. Perhaps we were each temperamentally incapable of institutionalizing something, given our artistic and independent spirits.

Fourth, most feminist seder communities, including mine, did not collectively create an evolving haggadah, complete with specific rituals. We were so creative, so madcap, that each year we dared to have different rituals and focus on different themes. Nor did we collectively write down and attempt to share the many other life-cycle rituals that we had begun to celebrate, such as Jewish feminist Rosh Hashanah and Yom Kippur rituals, as well as rituals for giving birth, having a hysterectomy, and losing a loved one.

The fifth challenge is that of acknowledging, questioning, and refining one's own motivation and intentionality. Were we maintaining such seders in order to advance our own careers and reputations? In order to create secular communities? Were we doing any of this for the sake of Heaven, because as Jews we are commanded to do so?

As the years went on, I began to demand that we invite fewer people, fewer celebrities; that we invite sons, husbands, and male friends; and that we stop focusing so much on ourselves and on how important we are. We had guests whom we were obliged to serve. To lead these seders, I believe that we must serve God as well and that we have an obligation to be minimally learned in Judaism. For me, the thrill was gone. But, I stayed on. I did not disconnect. I dared not disconnect. These women represented *the* Jewish feminist world. If I left, I feared I would have nowhere else to go.

On December 1, 1988, that changed. On that day, I was among the women who prayed with a Torah at Jerusalem's Western Wall for the first time in history. I uncovered the Torah for us—an honor that will never be surpassed in my lifetime and that wedded me to the struggle for Jewish women's religious rights and to the study of Torah. Early in 1989, I helped form the Women of the Wall (WOW) and its International Committee (ICWOW). This group, and its important religious and political struggles, provided me with a new Jewish feminist world to immerse myself in.

Finally, after eighteen years, I left the seder group. Afterwards, others did too. Some returned, some did not, but it would never be the same. Over the years, I think we have each mourned the loss of "us":

our friendships, our love, our idealism, a headier moment in time.

Once, a lifetime ago, we were all laughing girls together, radiant with hope. I loved us all, I miss us still. One can forever miss Paradise before the Fall; one can also mourn one's exile from simpler times and from illusion itself.

≋

Reflections on the Feminist Seder as an Entry Point into Jewish Life
LILLY RIVLIN

Dear reader, where were you when you first participated in a feminist seder? By that, I mean what was your relationship to Judaism, to feminism, to your career, to your family, and what were the opportunities for women in the world around you?

It has been more than a quarter century since two secular women, Naomi Nimrod and Esther Broner, wrote a feminist version of the haggadah. In 1976 I was invited to the first feminist seder in the United States, which used this haggadah. In 1977 I officially became a "seder sister" along with Broner, Letty Cottin Pogrebin, Phyllis Chesler, and Bea Kreloff. This meant that for the next several decades, a few weeks before Pesach, I would be on the phone with these women, planning and brainstorming on the theme of the seder for that year.

Feminism was the wellspring from which our seder sprang. Who were we when we started the feminist seder? What was the need, and why did secular feminists give birth to the feminist seder? In Bob Dylan's words, the answer was blowing in the wind. It was a time when freedom was in the air. Civil rights. Freedom riders in the South. Demands for freedom in South Africa. The patriarchy was challenged,

---

Lilly Rivlin is an author, activist, and filmmaker. She was a member of the original New York women's seders, and is the coeditor of *Which Lilith?: Feminist Writers Recreate the World's First Woman.*

the distribution of power questioned. A nascent feminist movement provided us with concepts, a vocabulary, and the strength of numbers. In *The Telling,* Broner describes each one of the seder sisters individually, but I would like to characterize us as a sociological cohort: we were feminists—articulate, educated, secular Jewish women. We were writers, artists, and political beings. Most of us had developed our political consciousness in the protest movements of the 1960s. We had served as the coordinators or assistants of male captains, or had actually been in leadership roles ourselves, which meant that remaining silent was no longer an alternative for us.

When we finally turned our attention to our Jewish lives, we confronted a tradition that denied women a major voice and assigned us, for the most part, marginal roles. Most of us had been alienated from religious practice and from the synagogue. There were no women rabbis, no egalitarian services, no women in visible power positions, and certainly no oranges on seder plates. None of us had had a bat mitzvah. I was the only one who could read Hebrew, because it was my mother tongue, but I had never read from the Torah.

We came to the seder with many questions: Why are our mothers in the kitchen, cooking and serving the seder meal and not participating in the telling? Why are there only sons mentioned in the haggadah? Why are the women in the Exodus story forgotten or ignored? Why are women so invisible in our texts? Where are the great Jewish women commentators, record keepers, storytellers?

Had we been encumbered by tradition, we would not have made the feminist seder. Had we been daughters burdened by the self-censorship of orthodoxy, we would not have dared to create a new tradition. Had we been hindered by Orthodox naysayers—who remembers the accepted wisdom of those times: "Women cannot go up to the *bimah*"?—we would not have persisted. But we were hungry for community. It was the spirit of the times, and our desire to enter into the tent of the Jewish people, and not be excluded, that enabled us to make this journey.

Among us were women who felt a closer connection to Lilith and

Ishtar than to Sarah, Rebecca, Leah, and Rachel. Pagan verses whispered hints of ancient matriarchs and goddesses who preceded patriarchy. At first our themes were more feminist than Jewish—a mixture of the personal, the political, and the spiritual. We were concerned with both social and feminist liberation, and we hoped to create a new narrative in the framework of herstory. The Bible, the Kabbalah, the I Ching, and the Tibetan Book of the Dead were among our texts. We were eclectic, innovative, and unencumbered, thank God. We honored our mothers, women who had inspired us—labor leaders, union maids, heroines who fought for the Jewish people, mothers with disabled children, poets, artists, our political leader Bella Abzug (the first Jewish woman elected to Congress and a longtime member of our seder)—and we called them our Miriams.

And all the while we were building a community of women. We created a safe space where women could tell their stories, share their pain, have a sense of community, and reinterpret texts in the new tradition. One year, Pogrebin spoke of how difficult it was for women to accept leaders in their midst. We had to learn to share our power. We learned that we could be mother and daughter to one another; we learned how to mother ourselves; we accepted each other; we rejected each other; we reached out to other women and hoped the tradition would live.

In our ninth year, I filmed our seder and included it in my film *Miriam's Daughters Now*. After viewing the documentary, Moshe Shalvi, husband of leading Israeli feminist Alice Shalvi and a wonderful man in his own right, asked me, "Why do you say you are making a Jewish seder? Why can't you simply say you are creating a feminist ritual?" We could not. We had come together for thirteen years, building on the shoulders of the old tradition, interpreting the haggadah and our tradition so we could find our place within it. We wanted to be in the tent of the Jewish people, not outside of it.

For many of us, our experience of creating the feminist seder was a point of entry into greater participation in Jewish life. As the years passed, some of the original seder sisters became more active in Jewish life. Broner and Pogrebin began attending synagogue on a regular basis; both studied Hebrew, Jewish history, and Hebrew texts. Chesler, one of the founders of Women of the Wall, has become an ardent student of Torah. In 1999, I joined the Village Temple. For the first time in my life I became a member of a synagogue—and this one was headed by a woman, Rabbi Chava Koster.

I was asked to colead a feminist seder at the Village Temple with Rabbi Koster. Our text included the *The Women's Haggadah* by Esther Broner and Naomi Nimrod, which was published as a book in 1999. Except for the Ma'yan seder,[1] it was my first catered seder. There were other firsts: a first for a designer seder, a first for a belly dancer and musicians at the seder, and a first for sitting on chairs at tables and not on the floor. The feminist seder had come a long way.

The following year the planning committee, all members of the temple Rosh Chodesh group, chose Anita Diamant's book *The Red Tent* as the seder's theme. Even greater attention was paid to the design, and, truth to tell, it was like a theatre set. We sat at U-shaped tables covered with red, color-coordinated tablecloths and matching plates, napkins, and utensils, under four bolts of red cloth that hung from the ceiling in simulation of a tent. What would Bella have thought, I wondered.

The entry point of the participants was very different from that experienced by the sisters who had started a quarter century earlier. The Village Temple is led by a woman rabbi; the seder organizers were for the most part in their thirties and forties, working mothers, middle and upper class; some had even celebrated their bat mitzvahs. They were professionals, who did not have to struggle in the ways women of the previous generation did. The following year, the committee decided against using *The Women's Haggadah* because, they said, it was too angry a voice for them. The drama of the decor, the dancing, the music, the celebration, and the food—but most of all the sense of community they experienced—made for an unforgettable ritual. As Chesler said in *Miriam's Daughters Now,* "Ritual is like good theatre." Who can resist good theatre?

Even my bringing up the injustices befalling women in the world—the oppression of women by the Taliban regime, the increase of sexual enslavement—was barely addressed. Instead, it was the celebratory nature of the event that will be remembered. I can hear Bella Abzug saying, "Where have the politics gone? Where is the concern with worldly matters?"

What is it that then draws women to women's seders today? The entry point for these women is beauty, celebration, and—as we too felt twenty-five years ago—a hunger for community. But now I ask myself, what kind of community will evolve? Will we remember Bella's voice, urging us to address social and gender justice?

> We are here to speak on behalf of those who have not had an opportunity to go to school: the girl child.
> We are here to speak of the thousands of women who have been destroyed through war, who have been raped, battered, and butchered.
> We are here to speak of the violence against women done every single day in the family, in the home, on the street.
> We are here to speak for the women who have struggled in a life that may be different from that of many of us, but as the bell tolls for them, we must hear another sound.
> We must hear the sound of a whistle. We must hear the sound of a whistle blowing, demanding that freedom is our right, that liberation is our right.[2]

These are Bella's words. May her voice be the whistle, and may we remember, when we sit around the seder table, to speak of all these things.

Placing Our Bettes:
Keepin' It Real at the Seder Table

OPHIRA EDUT

A few years ago, I attended a famous feminist seder in New York. It was lovely, candlelit, and earnest. And I didn't quite know how to behave.

I arrived at the hostess's stately Upper West Side apartment and was ushered to a cushion-scattered living room floor, where I sat cross-legged and humbled in a circle of accomplished Jewish feminists. I joined hands with the swaying seder-goers, humming along uncomfortably as they crooned earnest hymns about Miriam and Ruth. All the touchy-feely trappings were there: A gender-inclusive haggadah. A woman rabbi. An orange in the center of the seder plate.

I soon found myself wishing that Bette Midler—my favorite saucy Jewess—would sashay through the door like a fallen messiah and kick up the tempo, Vegas style. Bette makes me proud to be a Jewish woman: she's tough, funny, brash, and irreverent. In the fine art of misbehaving, she is Picasso. Bette keeps it real.

It could have been a generational rift, but I wanted to loosen up the party. My idea of a feminist seder includes my little sister Leora and me, giddy from the requisite Manischewitz buzz, trying not to fall off our chairs laughing. There's comedy along with the gravity. This ceremony felt forced and formal, in spite of its well-meaning revisions.

With all due respect to my biblical sisters, I don't identify with them. At least, not to the degree that I relate to a modern-day example of their spirit, like Bette Midler. Partly, it's because Jewish feminism has idealized these women into icons. We've made them saints rather than the rule-busting badasses they probably were in their time. This

---

Ophira Edut has been an independent magazine publisher, writer, and website developer since 1992. She is the editor of *Body Outlaws: Young Women Write About Body Image and Identity,* a contributing editor to *Ms.,* and the founding publisher of *HUES* (Hear Us Emerging Sisters), an award-winning national magazine for young women of all cultures and sizes. A Detroit native and Israeli American, Ophira now lives in New York and spends her time speaking publicly, developing her Ophira.com website, writing, and consulting on online projects.

veneration has a quieting effect that I can't get with. I want to feel kinship, not worship. I feel stifled by the "oh-I-could-never-be-that-good" routine we Jewish women slip into so easily, constantly holding ourselves to some superwoman standard.

It's interesting: during Pesach there's talk of both past and future. We recall our ancestors' Exodus from Egypt. We sing *"L'shanah ha-ba'ah b'yerushalayim"* ("Next year in Jerusalem"). But what about now? In addition to celebrating the Jewish foremothers, what if we also mentioned the Semitic "It" girls of the moment—the Jewish women who made headlines, who changed the world, touched our lives, made us laugh, rant, gossip, rage, cry, or *kvell* this year? Whether these women were in *Entertainment Weekly* or our own homes, we can identify with them in a current context.

And what about taking time to revel in our own recent accomplishments while we're at it? If anywhere, a feminist seder seems just the place to do that. As a spicy, twenty-eight-year-old Jewess, I look for affirming reflections of myself every day. Why not spend some time celebrating what we've achieved in the year past, and then cheering each other on in our goals for the year to come? Seder time could include Jewish women's resource-sharing time: did you hear about this book, this band, this class, this job opportunity? It would be cool to break matzah, strategizing ways to help each other in the coming year's endeavors.

After all, the best thing that came out of the feminist seder for me was meeting an amazing Jewish feminist filmmaker who'd come of age in the 1960s and 1970s. We've since met for coffee, discussed our ambivalence toward the state of feminism today, and made plans to collaborate creatively on her website. We e-mail each other when we hear of opportunities that fit the other's goals. My circle of Jewish woman friends expands with each exchange.

Since the feminist seder, I've launched my own informal search for cool Jewish women's gatherings—hangouts that weave in a touch of tradition without forcing it. Even among my generation, I've found far too much hand-holding, hard-core ritual, and volunteer work for my palate. Where's the Midler-esque sauciness we Jewgirls are famed for? Not at these sugar-and-spice affairs. Instead of scoring a little Shabbat dinner before I hit the dance clubs, I've ended up feeling as if I were rushing a Modern Orthodox sorority.

Par example, a college friend recently e-mailed me this invitation to a *"midnight melevah malka"* (whatever that is) that read:

> I invite the weavings of music, storytelling, poetry, spoken word, dance, art, and just plain being together as we usher out Shabbat in ritual and party. Please bring beverage of your choice, instruments, teachings, favorite spice, art supply, song to share. The parsha is *Korach,* so think about the theme as we might embark on some creative midrash. Shabbat ends at 9:22...so the fun begins soon after.

Whoah. While I'm glad people are carrying Jewish texts into the twenty-first century, her cryptic invitation might as well have been to a Trekkie convention. I resented this friend's flaunting of exclusive Jewish knowledge, the way her presumptuous invitation left a mostly secular sister like me feeling sidelined.

So the question lingers: how to gather as young women without overdosing on the touchy-feelies? Last winter, unable to find a cool Jewgirl soiree, I hosted my own. It was an *Erev Shabbat* potluck that I dubbed the Jew Luck Club. Six or seven Jewish chicks, some Israeli confections, a vegetarian brisket (no joke) for the kosher sistas. We lit Shabbat candles—some of us giggling awkwardly over the *brachot,* the more knowledgeable leading us like pros—tore into the challah, and let the conversation flow.

The best part was the guest list: a motley, multiracial crew of converts and conventionals, pagans and princesses. The two most religious women sang the blessings and presided over a hand-washing ritual at my tiny kitchen sink. A couple of the secular guests were kind of weirded out by such close proximity to prayer, and they broke for the buffet the minute we said "Amen."

My vision of Jewish feminism has an open-door policy: if your identity is even loosely connected to Jewishness, come on over and have a plastic cup of Manischewitz. I'm not even sure that each woman at the Jew Luck Club considered herself a feminist. But these were definitely interesting women, each approaching her Jewish identity from a radically different angle. This diversity made me proud to call myself a Jewish woman. It also reassured me that honoring my Jewishness wouldn't pigeonhole me or eclipse other important, non-Jewish parts of my identity.

Over dinner, my guests and I talked about our Jewish backgrounds a bit, but not in a support-group way. Just part of the natural conversation, which also covered jobs, relationships, mutual friends, and movies. The obviously Jewish stuff constituted about 5 percent of the evening. Phone numbers were exchanged, and, after dessert, a few of us headed out to dance at a small neighborhood club. It seemed like an appropriate way to celebrate Shabbat: enjoying life, listening to pop music, unwinding on the dance floor. A few others retired home to observe Shabbat quietly, in the way that worked for them.

Is the Jew Luck Club a recipe for a Jewish women's gathering? Or just a half-baked attempt to "do Judaism," orchestrated by ambivalent gals with an identity crisis? I'm not sure. But to me, the point of religion is to connect people to the process of life. All our modern-world stress jars us out of that spiritual flow. Be it dancing or meditation, anything that helps us restore inner peace, blow off steam, and clear some space for philosophical thought seems like a good use of Jewish holiday time.

It may sound sacrilegious—or maybe I've lived in New York for too long—but why attend an event if you don't get something out of it? Sure, it's important to expose ourselves to unfamiliar situations. But it's equally vital to find spaces where our souls resonate.

I would never try to shut down the party for my observant sisters. If *havdallah* spices, peasant skirts, and panflutes are your thing, go forth and let your Judaism prosper. But if you prefer a lounge act like Bathhouse Betty—Midler's famous cabaret persona—then why not invoke her spirit instead? We can't truly honor our Jewish foremothers unless we're both naughty and nice.

I can't say I've found the magical balance between ritual and real-ness, even in my own efforts. But if anyone hopes to keep tentative Jews like me coming back for a second helping of cultural pride, let's not forget to put on our party hats and lean back, just as we're required to do on Pesach. To revise Jewish bad-girl Emma Goldman: if I can't laugh at this seder, then I ain't eatin' the matzah, baby. *Dayeinu*.

≋

Pluralism in Feminist Settings

MARTHA ACKELSBERG

These days, virtually everyone in progressive communities speaks favorably of "pluralism" and of the challenges of creating "truly plu-ralistic" communities. Indeed, the term "pluralism" was often intro-duced into these communities by feminists. But what does "pluralism" mean? What does it require of us in settings that bring together people with diverse perspectives, practices, and beliefs? What does it require of us in specifically feminist settings, such as a women's seder?

In our contemporary parlance, "pluralism" seems to go hand in hand with "diversity," the recognition that there may exist a vari-ety of *different and differing* perspectives on issues to which mem-bers of a larger community are committed. How do we recognize those differences—not try to wipe them out, or subordinate some to others, in the name of *shalom bayit*[1] or harmony—and, at the same time, develop ways to work with (including to *argue with*) one another?

Dr. Martha Ackelsberg is a professor of government and women's studies at Smith College. Her scholarship has focused on gender and public policy and feminist theo-ry, as well as on women in Jewish communities. She is the author of *Free Women of Spain: Anarchism and the Struggle for the Emancipation of Women* and is currently at work on *Making Democracy Work: (Re)Conceiving Politics through the Lens of Women's Activism*.

For me, one of the most dramatic confrontations with the complexities of creating and maintaining pluralistic Jewish communities came many years ago, at a gathering of the National Havurah Institute—an institution I have often described as a weeklong study and camp experience for adults and children. The institutes were created by people who lived their Jewish lives in *havurot* (informal Jewish communities) and wanted to make the experience of that informal, egalitarian, "do-it-yourself Judaism" more broadly available.[2] At this particular institute (held in the early 1980s), a group of Orthodox Jewish participants wanted to hold an Orthodox prayer service at the institute on Shabbat morning, complete with a *mechitzah* (a physical separation between men and women). They asked for the support of the institute coordinators, in the form of setting aside a room for the service and making a Torah scroll available. The coordinators were ready to agree to these requests in the name of pluralism, creating a welcoming community for all Jews. At the same time, however, a group of feminists (composed mostly of women, but including some men as well) argued that for the institute, which had always defined itself as an egalitarian community, to facilitate such a *minyan* would constitute a violation of one of its fundamental principles: the equality of women. The argument became quite heated. "Everything is negotiable," stated one of the organizers. "No, the humanity of women is *not* negotiable," replied the feminists.

The argument was bitter. In the end, it was settled with the understanding that, while the institute welcomes all who wish to come, its official programs are organized and run on egalitarian principles. If people want to organize a *minyan* with a *mechitzah,* they may do so in the privacy of their rooms but should not count on institute resources to make it happen. This was to become a defining moment for the institute and the movement associated with it.

The resolution to this conflict enacted an important principle: *pluralism* as a value—the goal of welcoming all Jews to experience the institute—would not be allowed to trump the value of *equality* between men and women: a value held to be foundational to the organization and essential to its continued functioning. I present this vignette here not to argue for the value of women's equality, which I take to be a given in feminist settings, but rather to highlight the possible tensions that may and do arise among the values we hold, in this case between equality and inclusiveness.

What does a commitment to pluralism demand of us, particularly in feminist contexts? Are there limits to what can or should be included? What should we do when deeply held values conflict, as they did—at least for some—at the Havurah Institute?

These questions are particularly difficult for feminists. They challenge our conventional ways of thinking about ourselves and our communities for several reasons, some having to do with feminist theory and practice and others having to do with our political context in the United States. First, since women traditionally play the role of facilitator, mediator, enabler, and negotiator of compromises, many of us tend to treat all conflict as a sign of failure and therefore to do anything and everything possible to avoid open disagreement. If, however, we blindly follow this impulse to suppress differences in the hopes of making everyone comfortable, we may run into other difficulties. We will probably create a situation in which no one feels her needs are being met, and, just as importantly, we will miss out on the opportunity to work *with* our differences, building real bridges through the search for new ways to address them.

Second, the call to hear women's voices was one of the very first, and most basic, feminist demands. Women have been silenced, we argued. It is wrong to claim that "the community" believes X, for example, when at least half of the members of that particular community—women—have been excluded from discussion and/or decision-making. How, then, one might ask, can feminists, when they are themselves in a position of relative power, take a stance that seems to silence others (by refusing support for a *mechitzah minyan,* for example)? What happens when a commitment to egalitarianism is experienced by some as a suppression of *their* dissenting, more traditionalist voices? Oftentimes the response to such situations is to attempt to "be

inclusive" by acceding to "the most Orthodox common denomina-
tor" on the assumption that, for example, for Orthodox women, having a *mechitzah,* or not recognizing ten women as constituting a
minyan, is a matter of halakhah and therefore not open to compromise.
But if we wish to try to hear *all* voices, then we must recognize that the
full equality of women before the law—including Jewish law—is an
equally fundamental *feminist* principle, one no less immune to compromise.

A third factor may influence our approach to dealing with differences within groups and communities. Within the broader context of
politics in the United States—a context that profoundly shapes the
ways we think about power, competition, compromise, and politics—
we have very little experience of dealing effectively with difference. As
both Lani Guinier and Iris Marion Young have written, our politics in
the United States tends to be of a winner-take-all variety: if you are
not the winner, you are the loser.[3] If a candidate wins an election in the
United States, no matter the margin of victory, he or she takes office
while his or her opponent receives nothing at all.[4]

While we speak of "pluralism," then, what that means, in practice,
is a system in which people organize themselves into groups to pressure
politicians to vote on behalf of one or another particular group.
Although a truly pluralist democracy is one in which no one group wins
every time,[5] there will, nevertheless, be winners and losers. But, as feminists and other dissidents have often pointed out, would-be participants come to the process with vastly differing resources that affect who
will win and who will lose. A simple commitment to pluralism, then,
cannot offer a sufficient guide to Jewish feminist practice, because pluralist practice does not necessarily address issues of structural (or other)
inequality. How, then, can we restructure our communities and our
decision-making processes, so that instead of creating winners and
losers, we devise methods that allow all to participate in developing policies that will creatively *reflect* our differences, rather than deny them?

Let me offer a vignette that describes one such creative solution. At
the first Jewish women's conference, held in New York City in 1973—

a conference that brought together women from Orthodox, Conservative, Reform, Reconstructionist, Havurah, and unaffiliated backgrounds—we held a single prayer service on Shabbat morning. What "rules" would we follow? The non-Orthodox women assumed that the hundreds of women gathered in the McAlpin Hotel would certainly constitute a *minyan*. For them, it was essential that the prayer service include those prayers which are normally said only with a *minyan*—including *barchu* (call to prayer), *kedushah* (a section of the *amidah* prayer), and kaddish (mourner's prayer). This meant that women would be called to the Torah for *aliyot* and say the full blessing when their turn came. For the Orthodox women, a *minyan* required ten men; they were uncomfortable saying *barchu*, kaddish, and *kedushah* or responding to others who did so. What would we do? Would the conference break down? After hours of painful discussion, we came to an agreement: the service would include all the prayers, but those who did not feel comfortable responding to *barchu*, kaddish, or *kedushah* would not do so, and those who wished to be called to the Torah without saying the full blessing would say only what they were comfortable saying. The result: we were able to pray together while acknowledging—and living with—the differences among us.

Although this particular resolution will not necessarily be appropriate in every circumstance, I offer it here because I think it provides an instructive possible model. First, neither group renounced its basic values in the name of some false "harmony" or community; we recognized that to do so would be to deny one of the most fundamental gains for which we were struggling as feminists. Second, despite the continuing (and deep) differences between us, we were able to be in solidarity with one another: to work (or pray) together where we shared common ground, without feeling that we had to compromise our principles. It is not always possible, as my examples have indicated, to agree on issues. In the absence of such agreement, our goal should be to find ways to do the work we do, or engage in the celebrations we enjoy, while allowing each of us to remain as true to our values as we can be.

What might all this mean in the context of a women's seder, given that there are—and will continue to be—significant differences among women? To what extent is it appropriate to change God language? May we question the actions of the various groups and individuals in the Exodus story? Is the seder a time to discuss women's oppression and liberation? Should a women's seder be a retelling of the traditional story from the point of view of women? In practice, women's gatherings often highlight those differences that do exist among women, often to the surprise of the participants.

Significantly, the seder offers a marvelously open-ended framework for discussion and debate. Haggadahs have varied greatly over time, and we are told that "whoever expands on the story of the going out from Egypt is to be praised." In other words, more discussion is better than less. Rather than dividing participants, then, some of the questions and differences among them might well be made a focus for group conversation: How does each of us feel about the God who sent the plagues to Egypt and hardened Pharaoh's heart? What might it mean to add additional voices to those we read in the traditional haggadah? What images of (or metaphors for) God does each of us find most meaningful? To the extent that the seder provides a framework for the discussion of such differences, it can become an important tool for bringing together diverse members of the community and serve as a model for a pluralism based on solidarity rather than on winning and losing.

≋

Conflict and Community: The Common Ground of Judaism and Feminism

RUTH KAPLAN

I have always been moved by women's seders, sometimes, I think, for the wrong reasons. It can be so pleasant to sit in a circle of women and go through a ritual together, to sing together and pray together. Yet, few of the women's seders I've attended have raised the difficult issue of the conflict between feminism and Judaism. The symbols that we've used—a cup for Miriam or an orange on the seder plate—were, for me, nice gestures, but not ones that forced me to confront the ways in which Judaism continues to be unjust to women. We have chosen to add rituals instead of facing the problems within our existing texts, practices, and communities.

Jewish women have more ritual and learning opportunities now than ever before. However, it is not entirely possible to integrate Judaism with feminism. While women are now able to read from the Torah in the synagogue, for example, the texts they chant before the congregation are often sexist. There are aspects of feminism and Judaism that seem simply antithetical, incapable of being resolved without loss on either side. Yet, like many other Jewish women, I am not prepared to give up either aspect of myself; instead, I seek a way to continue as a feminist and a Jew.

We attempt to reconcile Judaism and feminism—or act as if there is no friction between them—because the conflict is within us and between us, and it is painful. The more I learn about feminism and Judaism, however, the more crucial it seems to live with the conflict instead of trying to resolve or avoid it. Judaism and feminism both provide models for living with such a conflict—models embedded in their understandings of community.

***

Ruth Kaplan received her B.A. in English from Yale University in 2000. After spending a year studying and teaching in Germany, she returned to New York City, where she works as an editorial assistant at a publishing company.

In Judaism, community is a celebrated, fundamental value, but it does not require unity within a group. In fact, absolute unity is often perceived as dangerous when associated with human beings. A primary example of this is the statement in the Creation story that Adam was given a mate because "it is not good for man to be alone."[1] Rashi explains that this is "so that people should not say 'there are two powers; God is alone in the upper worlds, and has no partner, and this one is in the lower worlds, without a partner.'"[2] We can easily imagine the danger that such an analogy would pose: God, ruler of the heavens, is matched by Adam, ruler of earth. Absolute power without absolute understanding can be deadly and would necessarily be biased, since no one human can comprehend every side of an issue or problem. Therefore, the very possibility of that analogy must be eliminated.

Adam's partner is introduced to us as *ezer kenegdo,* as "a helper against him."[3] The challenge of interpreting that phrase has inspired much rabbinic commentary, but, for me, the key fact is that God gives Adam not simply another person, but a person who both helps him and is "against" him. Adam and Eve are deeply linked (as evidenced by Eve's physical creation from Adam's rib), but inherent in their connection is the idea of negotiation, or even confrontation. In order for humans to rule the earth, there must be difference of opinion among them. Perhaps we can infer that without the element of conflict suggested by the word "against," the problem of Adam's singleness would not have been solved no matter how many more people were created. Instead, there would have been singleness on a group level: total unity. In the story of the tower of Babel, God perceives collective human unity as problematic: "And the Lord said, 'behold, the people is one, and they have all one language...and now nothing will be restrained from them, which they have imagined to do."[4] The idea that a solitary human would be dangerously comparable to God in God's world is related to the idea that a unitary human race would be dangerously like God in its height and power. God is one; we must be many; to be many, we must at times be against each other, at times even unable to understand each other.

Feminism, as both a movement and an ideology, has also struggled to deal with difference among members of a community. As a
modern-day feminist I am aware that the accusations of racism and het-
erosexism leveled at feminist movements are often well deserved. The
question of slavery split the first American women's movement; the
founding mothers of 1960s feminism saw the participation of lesbians
as detrimental to their cause. But feminism has evolved precisely
because of those critiques. Iris Young, a contemporary feminist political philosopher, claims that:

> [T]he implications of group differences within a social group have
> been most systematically discussed in the women's movement.
> Feminist conferences and publications have generated particular-
> ly fruitful, though often emotionally wrenching, discussions of the
> …importance of attending to group difference among women.[5]

Such discussions have been informed by feminists' notion of difference as, in Audre Lorde's words, a "beneficial and dynamic human
force, and one which is enriching rather than threatening."[6]

The ability to see the expression of difference as "enriching rather
than threatening," to see contention as valuable in relationships, is
one area of common ground between Judaism and feminism. However, the modern world often presents us with powerful and competing
cultural ideals. Autonomy often seems, for example, to be valued more
highly than connectedness, complete union to be more desirable than
negotiated partnership. These alternative ideals are powerfully alluring
and exert their influences on us as we look for models to help us deal
with Jewish-feminist conflict.

In America, no model is so revered as that of the self-sufficient
man, from those of Emerson's or Thoreau's tracts to the strong silent
cowboys and 007s of Hollywood. The idea of solitude, of completeness
in oneself, has a strong and peculiar appeal. Certainly each of us has had
moments—especially during times of conflict with others—when we
have longed to live entirely according to our own needs, unburdened
by the demands of others. The teenager's rebellious desire to be free
of the family—a freedom that stands for freedom from authority and

from the influence of others—is a familiar manifestation of this drive toward individual autonomy.

In contrast to this romantic notion of complete solitude is our vision of love as a melding, a oneness, two parts joining to make a whole. The concept of coupledom as total unity is perceived as the ideal throughout our culture. Movies and books depict lovers not as companions but as people who seem to fit into each other—as Tom Cruise famously says to his girlfriend in *Jerry Maguire,* "You complete me." This contemporary idea echoes back to the words of Genesis that husband and wife "shall be one flesh."[7] A couple is thus not the meeting of counterparts but a single being. The flip side of total aloneness is our idealized image of total togetherness.

In A. S. Byatt's novel *Babel Tower,* a character named Frederica muses on love and a D. H. Lawrence passage on it. For Lawrence, love is a "consummation of my being and her being in a new one, a paradisal unit regained from the duality.... I have ceased to be and you have ceased to be: we are both caught up and transcended into a new oneness where everything is silent.... In the perfect One there is perfect silence of bliss."[8] In response, Frederica notes that in such a love "language is unnecessary and undefeated." Indeed, for human beings, the search for a "perfect silence of bliss" most often leads to silencing the other. Perhaps in union with God one can be silent; among people, silence is generally a sign of inequity. "Language fails man and woman trying to transcend it and themselves," Frederica decides.

The story of Babel examines this idea of unity among all of humanity. If we understand language as a metaphor for diverse perspectives, as does Frederica (after all, people who do not understand each other often feel as if they are speaking different languages), then we can see the people at Babel to be as Adam would have been had Eve not been created "against him." The people at Babel had one mind and one voice; we can imagine that the more people there were sharing the same language, the more intense their loneliness became. This, in turn, generated an intense need for togetherness, for union with another, different being. Perhaps it was not good for Adam to be alone because his loneliness might have prompted him to reach for God as a partner, ignoring—as did the people at Babel—the inequity of that partnership.

We therefore have the punishment, or perhaps the gift, that God gave us at Babel—diversity of thought and speech. We learn from Babel that instead of trying to "transcend" language and ourselves, our God-given exercise is to explore language and ourselves, to seek partnership on earth and not with heaven.

As we have seen, feminism and Judaism each present a model for such a partnership, anchored in their perspectives on community. As Judith Plaskow points out, "for the Jew, for the feminist, for the Jewish feminist, the individual is not an isolated unit who attains humanity through independence from others…rather, to be a person is to find oneself from the beginning in community or, as is often the case in the modern world, in multiple communities."[9] In this view, in order for teenagers to grow up, they do not "separate from their parents" (as pop psychology phrases it) but learn to negotiate with them. One creates oneself as an individual not by cutting off connections with others but by redefining those connections. Only when we negotiate and communicate with one another do we recognize others as different from ourselves, only then are we saved from the loneliness of Adam or the people at Babel, and only then will we finally cease our pursuit of transcendent union.

For we will not achieve a single, perfectly feminist Judaism with which we can reach up to God. Perhaps we are not meant to. In any case, that is not my goal. It is lovely to have symbols of women's inclusion at a women's seder; the orange and Miriam's cup are a step forward. But supplementary symbolism is not enough. Whether or not *chametz* is on the seder plate to represent the inclusion of lesbians is far less important to me than that the choice becomes a focus of discussion during the evening. We must not seek perfect unity at the expense of an honest discussion of the issues, nor should we see such discussions as evidence that it is impossible to be both a feminist and a Jew. In fact, we are both feminists and Jews precisely when we confront conflicts honestly *without* breaking away from either Judaism or feminism, when we live according to their shared concept of community and approach to internal opposition—an approach in which communication and negotiation are part of a long-term process that is valued for itself.

Young explains her feminism as "a mode of questioning, an orientation and set of commitments"[10] grounded in her focus on women's well-being in the world and her use of women's experiences and perspectives. At a women's seder we have the chance to focus that feminist approach on the Jewish world, to ask ourselves how "institutions, policies, and ideas"[11] affect Jewish women's lives, and to allow our experiences and perspectives to play a role in our seder. The seder is meant precisely for discussion and study. It instructs that we tell the story of the flight from Egypt, ask questions, and identify with the ancient community of slaves; in doing so, it ritualizes conversation and reinterpretation in the context of this identification with the community. If we use our women's seders as arenas for the exploration of the deep conflicts between feminism and Judaism, we express our deep allegiance to both.

≈

What Now?
After the Exodus, the Wilderness
SHARON KLEINBAUM

It is only when the Israelites come out of Egypt, when they abandon the comfort and security of their familiar—though oppressive—lives, that they begin to experience the abiding presence of God. Upon leaving Egypt, they become the sacred community that is God's dominion.[1] Pesach, the night of their liberation, marks the beginning, not the end, of their journey. It is a long journey, a journey of unremitting

---

Rabbi Sharon Kleinbaum is the senior rabbi of Congregation Beth Simchat Torah in New York, the world's largest gay and lesbian synagogue. She lives in Brooklyn with her partner, Rabbi Margaret Moers Wenig, and two daughters.

crisis, a journey that often seems to be nothing more than an aimless wandering, a new exile without end—no better and maybe even worse than their lives in Egypt. But it is also a spiritual journey, a journey of insight and understanding, of growth and revelation. The way of the Lord is through the wilderness. A scant seven weeks after leaving Egypt, the former slaves are at Sinai, and a new identity as a free people is born.

This experience of finding revelation in exile is a profoundly Jewish one. It is not in the Promised Land, the land of milk and honey,[2] that the Torah is given to the people. It is in exile, in *galut,* that our identity as individuals and as a people is formed. The escape from physical persecution and oppression is ultimately not enough to form a spiritual identity; the physical liberation must be coupled with a struggle for genuine identity that is not defined by the fight against an oppressor. It is a journey of cosmic significance for the Israelites leaving the familiarity of slavery; they risk the desolation of the *midbar* (wilderness) for the promise of physical freedom, only to discover that it is Sinai that awaits them.

For Jewish gays and lesbians today, coming out is also a spiritual journey, not unlike the coming out of our ancestors that we celebrate at Pesach. The closet is indeed a narrow place.[3] It is in the open, in the wilderness of family, friendship, work, community, religion—sometimes welcoming, sometimes indifferent, sometimes hostile—that we, individually and collectively, discover ourselves and our relationship to God.

In every generation, the haggadah tells us, we are bound to regard ourselves as if we personally had gone forth out of Egypt. The generation of the Exodus was not the first to experience the sequence of oppression, liberation, crisis, revelation, and growth; nor were they the last. We retell their story on Pesach not only to honor them with our remembrance but also because all of us—Orthodox, Conservative, Reform, Reconstructionist; learned, ignorant, observant, secular; women, men; lesbians, gays—have gone forth ourselves from so many Egypts and because so many more trials still wait for us in the wilderness.

As a Jew, a woman, a lesbian, and of course as a rabbi, I love the Jewish holidays and find them deeply meaningful. As an activist in

Jewish, feminist, lesbian/gay, and other causes, I find Pesach particularly special. I have known or witnessed many metaphorical Egypts and celebrated many moments of liberation. But I have learned that what at first seems to be the culminating act of liberation is always, in fact, just the beginning.

Nineteen eighty-five was one such beginning. In 1985, not one rabbinical student anywhere in the world was officially out to the faculty or administration of her or his seminary. Out rabbis were few and far between, and none of them were in pulpits. Then, in the spring of 1985, the Reconstructionist Rabbinical College adopted an admissions policy that stated simply, "RRC does not discriminate on the basis of sexual orientation."

The sense of relief was palpable. Faculty member Rabbi Linda Holtzman remembers it as "jubilation."[4] Only one problem remained: what now? What would this new freedom really mean in practice? Would lesbian and gay rabbis get jobs? Would donors to the RRC still donate? Would the college become a pariah? Would the movement itself suffer? What would we have to do now? Since no one knew, I formed a committee called "What Now?" to find out—and to help make sure that the liberation implicit in the new admissions policy did not remain on paper only.[5]

It did not. Lesbian and gay Jews have taken huge strides toward finding their place in Judaism. This didn't happen overnight, and it didn't happen in isolation. The gay synagogue movement—itself a product of the post-Stonewall[6] gay liberation movement—was crucial, as was the support of prominent members of the wider Jewish community.[7] Lesbian and gay synagogues have sprung up all over the world. Mainstream synagogues have outreach programs to lesbian and gay congregants, and strive to be "welcoming." Even the Orthodox community has an important—if necessarily still low-profile—lesbian and gay movement. The RRC is thriving. The Reform movement has voted to recognize lesbian and gay marriages. The Conservative movement's Jewish Theological Seminary now admits out lesbian and gay students into its academic programs.

And yet, we have a long way to go. At Congregation Beth Simchat Torah (CBST) we get a steady stream of telephone calls and e-mails pleading for help of all kinds: help with how to reconcile homosexuality with traditional Jewish law, help with coming out, help with how to find support in dealing with AIDS. The Jewish Theological Seminary still rejects out lesbians and gays as candidates for ordination as rabbis. Progressive congregations who don't mind having one out lesbian or gay assistant rabbi balk at having two or at having an out senior rabbi. And, of course, not all congregations are progressive. Gay and lesbian marriage is still not recognized legally (this is, of course, not only a Jewish problem). And hate crimes against gays and lesbians are still a tragic reality. Only last spring, the partner of a CBST member was brutally beaten on the street in a vicious "fag-bashing."

Many of my congregants at CBST are still not out at work or not out to their parents, or their children, or not out anywhere but at our synagogue. When one begins to take the risk of stepping outside the narrow place, the terror of the wilderness sinks in, and the pull to return to Egypt becomes almost irresistible. In the wilderness, the Israelite community grumbled against Moses and Aaron. The Israelites said to them, "If only we had died... in Egypt, when we sat by the fleshpots, at least we had our fill of bread! For you have brought us out into the wilderness to starve to death."[8]

This is not the only time the Israelites express their frustration. Later, they complain:

> Did you bring us out of Egypt to kill us and our children and our livestock? If only we had meat to eat! We remember the fish that we used to eat fresh in Egypt, the cucumbers, the melons, the leeks, the onions and the garlic. Now our gullets are shriveled. There is nothing at all! Nothing but this manna to look to![9]

When faced with the rigors of the wilderness and the uncertain promise of the Land, the people long to return to the comforts of familiar Egypt—even though it also means accepting oppression.

For gay people, the struggle to leave Egypt and enter the wilderness includes the perils of self-revelation and the consequent horrific risks. This journey comes with great pain and exacts an enormous personal toll. The invisibility offered by Egypt crushes the soul, but it does provide some measure of protection. At least in Egypt your job might be safe. At least your children might not be taken from you. At least in Egypt you might be a board member of your synagogue. At least in Egypt you can teach the stories of our people in a religious school. At least in Egypt you might not get beaten on the street or told you deserve AIDS, unlike the innocent victims out there. At least in Egypt there are leeks and onions.

The great tension of the experience of the wilderness is the tension between the impulse to go forward toward the Land and the pull back to Egypt. There is both a willingness and an unwillingness to put Egypt firmly behind us. Thus, the bulk of our Torah deals not with slavery nor with the Promised Land but rather with that trek, full of ambivalence and anxiety, through the wilderness. It is better to be out of Egypt even if we are not yet in the Land. But while parts of each of us, individually and collectively, are out of Egypt, others remain. And we are—all of us—still far from the Land. But *libi bamizrach,* the heart yearns for the East, the heart yearns to be in the East. The heart yearns for the Land. Despair is antithetical to Judaism, which teaches us that to imagine the Land while living in the vast emptiness of the wilderness is no less than a divine commandment. Hope is not a luxury. That struggle to hold onto a vision even while we wander in the wilderness has, for thousands of years, been the defining characteristic of an exiled people, homeless, always dreaming of coming home to the Land.

Moses' parting words to the Israelites forty years after the first Pesach are words of vision, words against despair. It is not an easy message to deliver from the edge of the wilderness. After all, as professor Arnold Eisen has pointed out:

> What has never been cannot be remembered and neither can it be described. All Moses has available is his language, and his own words will inevitably fall far short of the task assigned them because it is impossible to talk convincingly about a state of affairs which no one has ever experienced. What do wholeness and mean-

ing look like? What will it be like to be really completely at home?[10]

The Lurianic kabbalists, sixteenth-century mystics, took this a step further, teaching that the exile would end only when a complete repair of the broken world was achieved. Reaching the Land is not enough. The vision that Moses imparts even while he is dying is clear. Access to and tenure on the Land is conditional. We must do more than reach the Land: we must do it with justice, or else the "Land will spew forth its inhabitants."[11] We must construct a moral, ethical code that affirms, challenges, and even inconveniences us. It will not be enough to cross the physical River Jordan. We must really leave Egypt and its soul death behind. We must individually and collectively have the courage to live with a vision of Torah that both teaches us how to live in the wilderness and simultaneously pulls us further toward the Land. With such a vision we may even have the *zekhut*, the merit and privilege, to one day reach the Promised Land.

How do we get there? No matter where in the wilderness, no matter how close or how far we are from Egypt, we—all of us—must struggle to have a vision of the Land. If we don't have the Land to dream of, there is no hope, and the pull to return to Egypt will be overwhelming. That pull will suffocate the very breath of our souls that ache to be in the East. *Libi bamizrach.* The time in the wilderness must be one spent in creating and living a vision of Torah, not one consumed in hatred of the Egyptians. Such a focus will not ultimately form a living Judaism that will be spiritually sustaining for us, nor can it be our only bequest to the next generation—and not only the next generation of Jews, women, lesbians, and whoever else we count as "us." Pharaoh's last words to Moses and Aaron after telling them and the Israelites, finally, to be gone, are "And may you bring a blessing on me also!"[12]

Please God, may it be so.[13]

≋

Letting Pharaoh Go: A Biblical Study of Internalized Oppression

ELA THIER

Imagine several million slaves standing as a free people just miles away from the Promised Land. They have seen plagues that brought the world's most powerful despot to his knees. They have seen a sea split in two before their eyes and they have walked safely through it. They have seen an empire's army drown. They have been led by a pillar of cloud by day and a pillar of fire by night. They have watched food fall from the sky and water pour out of a rock for their sustenance. They have heard God speak at Sinai, revealing the most visionary law in human history. Now, after having lived through a year of miracles, with the Promised Land before them, the Children of Israel despair, cry out, decide to go back to Egypt, and turn to stone their own leaders.

This is what happens in Numbers, in the Torah portion of *Shlach*.[1] Before entering the Land, the Children of Israel send a delegate from each tribe to assess the situation. When the spies return, they report to the congregation that giants inhabit the Land, that they felt like grasshoppers, and that the people in the Land also saw them that way.[2] Two of the spies, Joshua and Caleb, plead for the people to maintain their faith, assuring them that they can and will inherit the Land. The debate escalates into chaos and despair, and the people turn against their leaders and decide to return to Egypt.

Yet, just as they threaten to stone Joshua and Caleb, God appears. Incensed by their lack of faith, God decides to wipe out the entire congregation and to lead Moses alone into Israel to begin a new nation. Moses pleads with God on behalf of the people, and God even-

---

Ela Thier is a graduate of the Scholars' Circle at the Drisha Institute for Jewish Education, where she studied Talmud and Jewish law, and taught Bible and Talmud. In addition to her work as a Jewish educator, Ela is a painter and award-winning screenwriter. Ela is also a teacher of Re-evaluation Co-Counseling, a grassroots organization that trains people to assist one another in healing from the emotional scars of oppression. She has recently completed her memoir, *My Twenties*, describing the spiritual journey of her young adult years.

tually relents. Instead, God determines that the Children of Israel will wander in the desert for forty years, until a new generation can enter the Land. Repentant, the Children of Israel decide to enter the Land after all. Moses pleads with them to cooperate with God's decree, but they ignore his protests. As they go up the mountain they are met by a hostile people who utterly defeat them.

Our people's story is not about the experience of slavery, nor is it about our liberation from it. In comparison to the wealth of stories that we have about the desert wanderings, we have hardly any information about the lives of the slaves in Egypt. Only a few chapters describe our Exodus from Egypt, while the rest of the Torah describes our desert experience. Instead, our story is about our liberation from the effects of slavery, from "slave mentality," as Nietzsche termed it. It took Ten Plagues before Pharaoh let us go, but it took us forty years to let go of Pharaoh. This liberation struggle, liberation from what we had internalized as slaves about ourselves and the world, would require more profound miracles than the splitting of the sea.

The spies return from the Land and say, "We were in our own sight as grasshoppers."[3] With these words, they tell us more about their lives in Egypt than any fact or description could explain. What must God's beloved endure to come to feel like a grasshopper? What brings a child of one such as Abraham to feel that powerless, insignificant, and defeated? "...and so we were in their eyes,"[4] the spies continue. Having internalized a sense of worthlessness, they presume that others see them as they see themselves, perpetuating, agreeing, and even instigating others' belittlement of them. This is internalized oppression, whereby people accept a misconception of who they are, act on this misconception, and cooperate with their own mistreatment, even to the point of "stoning to death" any attempts at liberation.

More than having been robbed of the fruits of their hard labor and of the pyramids they built, more than having been robbed of their male children, God's people have been robbed of their own will. They stand looking at the Promised Land, and they yearn for Egypt. Oppression has robbed these people of their hope and imagination. It has brought them to live in a Godless reality fraught with struggle and limitation, even when food falls from the sky and water pours out of a rock.[5] What a stark contrast to their passionate and adventurous ancestor, Abraham, who left both his father and his son to seek and discover God's mysteries.

The words *Shlach Lecha* echo *Lech Lecha*, the Genesis story in which God first speaks to Abraham, commanding him to leave his home and go "to the land that I will show you."[6] *Lech* means "go," and *shlach* means "send." These two stories are the bookends of our nation's story. *Lech Lecha* is the birth of our people's covenant with God. *Shlach Lecha* is the breach of the covenant. The Rabbis say that on this day all calamities have occurred, from the destruction of the Temple to the Spanish Inquisition. How are *Lech Lecha* and *Shlach Lecha* the antitheses of each other? In *Lech Lecha*, Abraham follows God's command to leave behind what he knows and go to a foreign land. How poignant that our own Jewish homeland had to be for us, at one point, a foreign land. *Lech Lecha* is the first chapter of our people's story because change is the heart of our tradition. *Lech Lecha* is another name for Judaism. It is the ultimate, and possibly only, workable attitude toward repairing a broken world. It is the act of total and complete separation from one's familiar assumptions and values in exchange for a hopeful future full of unknowable possibilities.[7]

At the other end of the spectrum is the mentality of a slave who has been beaten into paranoia and despair and perpetuates a vicious cycle of self-fulfilling prophecies. She is utterly unable to separate from the reality of the past. The Children of Israel send spies ahead for reassurance that the future is safe.[8] But their preparation, their search for a safe future is in itself the reliving of the past. They do not expect safety, and so they go to see Israel—but what they see is Egypt. They see a place where they are as grasshoppers, where they have no chance of victory and survival. They run ahead to see the future, and what they see, of course, is their past.

In response, God decides to wipe out the entire congregation and to send Moses alone to Israel. Echoing the story of *Lech Lecha*, God plans to start a new beginning and extends to Moses the original promise made to Abraham, using the same covenantal language: "I will make you into a great nation."[9] Moses follows the footsteps of his ancestor Abraham and argues with God. He challenges God by pointing out that killing all of Israel would lead other nations to believe that God could not protect and provide for the people.

When, compelled by Moses, God changes the decree and decides that the Children of Israel will wander in the desert for forty years, God ensures that the entire generation that had lived in Egypt would die in the wilderness, and a new generation would enter the land. If the Promised Land is a metaphor for godliness, for expansion and possibility, then a people who live in the past are a metaphor for the very thing that cannot exist in the Land.[10]

By the time the Children of Israel left Egypt, they no longer needed Pharaoh's taskmasters to live as slaves; they had become their own taskmasters. While they had no plans to stone Pharaoh, they were ready to stone their own leaders. This is the most tragic effect of oppression: When a people are attacked long enough, they eventually begin not only to cooperate in their mistreatment but also to attack themselves. Moses, who did not experience slavery, challenges God and insists on staying with his people. The people, who had endured slavery, later leave Moses behind in the camp.[11] Oppression confuses people's sense of unity and belonging. It strips people of their identity and of their connection to one another.[12]

But even when the Children of Israel mourn and repent, as they become aware of their irrational mistrust of God, they do not escape the effects of internalized oppression. The pendulum of despair swings from living in the past to denying the past altogether. In the story of the *maapilim*,[13] the Children of Israel decide to enter the Land despite God's decree. Strikingly, they leave Moses behind in the camp—a moving detail, given Moses' previous refusal to leave them behind. As the Children of Israel go up the mountain they are met by a hostile people and are defeated by them. Pretending that they do not feel like grasshoppers does not work. The story of the *maapilim* is a lesson about pretense, about the masks we all wear to cover our insecurities. The congregation could not enter the Land feeling and behaving like slaves. However, they also could not enter the Land by simply pretending they felt free.

There is a talmudic teaching that since the destruction of The Temple, the gates of prayer have been locked.[14] But the gates of tears, says Rabbi Eliezer, are never locked. Indeed, our crying was the first act that set our redemption in motion. In the Book of Exodus, God is absent through centuries of slavery and affliction. God first appears once we yell out: "and the Children of Israel groaned because of their work and they yelled, and their suffering rose up to God from the work. And God heard their crying and God remembered God's covenant with Abraham, with Isaac and with Jacob."[15] As we prepared to enter the Land, that very crying that set our liberation in motion also completed it. Perhaps our Exodus from Egypt had to have been initiated and concluded by our cries. Perhaps our crying and yelling in the desert was not our greatest calamity but, in fact, the final act of our redemption.[16]

Why did God bring us to Israel forty years before we were ready? Did God not know what would happen in our first attempt to enter Israel? I imagine that on the night of our first Passover, God watched the freed slaves leave Egypt, knowing they would not enter the Promised Land. Rather than have us wander in the desert numb and aimless, God first brought us to the Land to awaken us to our condition. The spies did not hurt us; the spies made us aware that we were hurt. Like a bruised child who cries only when the parent appears, we needed to see Israel before us; we needed to feel that much safety and hope, before the grief, rage, and despair of four hundred years of slavery could finally erupt.

Before his death, Moses speaks to the new generation as they prepare to enter the Land. He recounts the story of the spies and of the *maapilim,* saying, "You have circled this mountain long enough; turn northward."[17] Northward in Hebrew, *tzafona,* comes from the word *tzafun,* meaning "hidden." This hiddenness, the *tzafun,* is the only path out of walking in circles. The slave generation, the stiff-necked people who would die in the wilderness, are the real heroes of our people's story.[18] They have the task before them of parenting children who would not follow in their ways. It is upon the stiff and wounded people to heal from oppression and to raise a new generation that would leave Egypt behind and enter the unknown.

≋≋

Reflections on Exodus in Light of Palestinian Suffering
LYNN GOTTLIEB

Shadows flicker across an old woman's face. Serach bat Asher kindles the flame that carries us back to the beginning. "Remember? We were once slaves and chose another truth—the hand that loves over the hand that hurts. This is our first wisdom, the original Torah. 'Love the stranger as you love yourself, for you were once strangers in a foreign land.'"

Jewish legend tells the story of Serach, daughter of Asher, who journeyed to Egypt with her grandmother Leah's family. She endured the long centuries of forced labor, taught her people to survive by preserving their tribal language and names, and lived to see their redemption. As the entire nation of Israel hesitated before the Reed Sea, wondering how to go forward, Serach transformed herself into an eagle. Soaring heavenward, she sang her freedom song as a liberated being, and the waters parted as she beat her wings. Even babes in the womb clapped their hands. Since that time, Serach wanders the earth to see what the Children of Israel are doing, especially during Passover. Once she happened to arrive at a seder in ancient Jerusalem as the participants discussed the division of the sea. How did the waters appear? Serach

---

Rabbi Lynn Gottlieb was one of the first ten women in the world to be ordained as a rabbi. She is a storyteller, performer, and author of *She Who Dwells Within: A Feminist Vision of a Renewed Judaism.*

revealed herself and said, "This is what happened. As we rushed toward freedom we turned our heads to one side and saw all the generations that came before us reflected in the waves. Then, we turned our heads to the other side and saw all the generations to come, staring back at us from the sea. At that moment, in the mirror of the waters, we understood the true meaning of our liberation. Both the past and the future will be redeemed when we, the living, risk our lives for freedom."[1]

We Jews have resisted every effort to erase our names from the book of history. We have tied memory into stubborn knots of story and ceremony that bind the generations. The memory of our own suffering is the foundation for the Torah's central *mitzvah*, that of compassion. Jewish ceremony and sacred narrative teach us that loving-kindness is the antidote to the violence in the world. This is how we have managed to survive. Because we remember the suffering we once endured, we affirm that the true intent of Jewish ceremony and sacred narrative is to teach of loving-kindness.

Therefore, when we become aware that parts of our sacred narratives do not transform our fears into compassion but rather reinforce them, we must question their use. When ritual memories encourage our hatred of others instead of inspiring us to embrace humanity as a collective divine image, we must reevaluate their meaning and place in Jewish life.

The haggadah, like all the texts of our tradition, contains opposite points of view. The seder begins by inviting "all those who are oppressed [to] come celebrate Passover at our table." Yet, non-Jews are traditionally barred from attending. The haggadah reminds us that "In every generation there are those who want to rise up against us and kill us," and it expresses the collective entreaty to God, "Pour out Your wrath upon the nations that do not know You." On the other hand, as we recite the plagues that befell the Egyptians, we remove a drop of wine from our cups to diminish our joy in recognition that our enemies suffered. Some contemporary haggadahs also contain a midrash that God would not allow the angels to rejoice over the death of the Egyptian soldiers because God's "creatures are drowning in the sea." These contradictory impulses—to fear or curse our enemies and to struggle on behalf of the stranger or the oppressed—are both present in the text and conversation of Jewish life. Sometimes we are able to transform our fears into blessings. Sometimes, because of the tremendous burden of our suffering, our fears are distorted, hardened, and elevated. And sometimes our fears blind us to new realities that have replaced the old ones.

As we consider the contradictions of our collective memories we face yet another challenge to our future. We have survived the terrible horrors of the European *horban* (destruction) and lived to see the establishment of the State of Israel on our ancestral land. We hold the world accountable for our suffering and castigate those who stood idly by while we died. In our desire to live again, we have empowered ourselves with a state, an army, and a preeminent concern for our security. However, in the process of building a new nation, we have entered a conflict with another people, living in the same place, who now suffer mightily under the burden of our rule. As we reflect upon the meaning of Exodus, how do we respond to Palestinian suffering?

The Exodus myth seeks to delineate the pathway to liberation. It begins by giving voice to the everyday hardships and humiliation of oppression. Exodus rejects the use of state power over vulnerable people exploited for their labor. Exodus gives honor to people robbed of their dignity and endows them with priestly status. Exodus challenges the narrative of those who dominate by force and brings to the center the truth of the oppressed. Exodus demands that the military and economic institutions of the privileged give way to the needs of those who suffer under their enormous weight. Finally, the Exodus story becomes the foundation for a new law that attempts to bring justice to the relations between rich and poor, male and female, freeborn and slave, citizen and stranger.

We have always seen ourselves as the victims in the story, seeking relief from those who oppress us. Are we able to reverse our identification with the weak and see ourselves as wielders of state power over a stateless and exploited people? Can we comprehend that history has given us a new task? To let another people go?

The haggadah gives voice to the lament of the oppressed. How can we know what to change if we don't know what hurts? The impulse to recount our own suffering has been part of our healing process. However, can we also hear the lament of Palestinians? It is painful to hear Palestinian stories; the list of wrongs against the Palestinians is profoundly disturbing. For me, the real turning point came as I listened to several Palestinians—including my friends George, Hishem, and Lucy—talk about their experience of being tortured in Israeli prisons. I began to evaluate Palestinian experiences from the context of my own tradition's demands for ethical conduct. "Let all who are oppressed, share the freedom meal." The message of the haggadah obliges us to respond to Palestinian cries for justice.

Our response to Palestinian suffering must include questioning our assumptions about the recent history of Israel, our exclusive right to the Land, and our treatment of Palestinians in Israel and in the territories. However, because questioning Israel often provokes deep hostility within the Jewish community, many Jews have felt uncomfortable speaking up.

The haggadah narrative initiates Jewish children into the tradition of critical thinking. It invites our questions and interpretations. We read in the haggadah, "Everyone who adds their interpretation of the story is worthy of praise." We are told that the meaning of the four children is to offer instruction according to the level of understanding of each individual. Yet, the skeptic of the bunch is condemned. The haggadah understands her question "What does this mean to you?" as a rejection of the common discourse and communal assumptions. Because she refuses to embrace traditional meanings, the second child is perceived as distancing herself from the community. The haggadah marginalizes her questions and her place in the community by labeling her the "wicked child."

As women have awakened to their own oppression within patriarchal societies, we have learned to question, for example, the traditional commentary's view of women in order to make space for our own observations. Feminists have learned that power, not truth, is often the driving force behind the way we tell history and understand the present. We know that the bold questioning perceived here as "wickedness" often constitutes the first step towards freedom. As women sitting at the Passover table we need to be open to the idea that the Palestinians also have a truth in their story, which has been repressed.

We have to prepare ourselves to hear what our history has meant to the Palestinian nation. While we might be uncomfortable with their experience of our historical struggle, we cannot move forward until we face the actual impact of our history on their lives. The haggadah condemns Pharaoh because he hardened his heart. He always found another excuse to delay liberation. And his own children paid the price.

To the Palestinians, we are the hard-hearted taskmasters. They have witnessed generations of their children condemned to resistance. Since 1967, over eight hundred thousand Palestinians have been arrested, out of a population of three and a half million. Thousands have been tortured, beaten, and maimed. Thousands have become stateless refugees. Thousands have been made homeless. Thousands have lost their livelihood and their land. Thousands of acres of land have been confiscated. Thousands of trees have been uprooted, orchards destroyed, and homes demolished. Thousands of bones have been broken. Thousands of children have wet their beds as soldiers burst into their houses at night. Thousands have become traumatized for life without any hope for a productive future. Thousands have no medical services. Thousands have learned to hate us.

And the price we pay? Thousands of people have been killed in ongoing wars and as the result of the Palestinian use of violence as a political tool. Thousands of our children have grown up learning how to kill. The militarism we have hated in others has become our way of life. Thousands have fled Israel to avoid a lifetime of army duty. Israeli middle-school children have the seventh highest incidence of classroom violence in the world. Thousands of women suffer the consequences of militarism in the high rates of domestic violence. And we too have learned to hate.

When will the cycles of violence end? When we gaze into the waters of the parting sea and behold the children of both peoples reflected in the waters of liberation. When we understand that everyone is invited to feast at the freedom table, Jew and Palestinian alike. Otherwise, those who are oppressed will continue to resist, and the way of violence will overcome all our prayers for peace.

≈≈≈

Walking the Way as Women
MERLE FELD

I. Can I See Myself as Someone Precious?

When we got in the car, the four of us, sometimes headed for the air-port and a faraway adventure, sometimes only driving the five hours to Boston for the weekend, I would ask, "*Tefillat haderech*[1]—who wants to start?" The children would express their hopes and fears for the trip ahead, mostly hopes really, because young children resting comfortably in the safe protection provided by their parents are free to exult in unknown cheerful possibilities. Then usually Eddie would take his turn, and finally me. I waited for last probably because I carried the family fears, my prayers for the road were a kind of umbrella with which I sought to protect us all. I'd listen carefully to Lisa, to Uri, to Eddie, noting all the conceivable loopholes, then closing them with a final "We should all go safely and in health, and come back home safe-ly and in health." The mother, especially the superstitious mother (are there many mothers who aren't superstitious mothers?) sees herself as the last line of defense against the evil eye.

All these years later, as Eddie and I head out on trips together dur-ing our first "empty nest" year, I've realized with a start that we're already en route before I remember to call out *"Tefillat haderech,"*

Merle Feld is an award-winning playwright, poet, educator, and activist. She is the author, most recently, of *A Spiritual Life: A Jewish Feminist Journey*.

and we both remark that rituals we set in place when we were parents of small children need renewed attention now that we're again two adults traveling unencumbered in the world. And suddenly I recognize another truth: when I'm traveling alone, I never think to say *tefillat haderech*.

Since the publication of my book *A Spiritual Life,* I've done an enormous amount of solo traveling, crisscrossing the country, speaking and teaching at synagogues, retreat centers, study institutes, and college campuses. I've learned so much on these journeys: about the hunger we all have—women and men, young and older—for meaning, for connection, the ache to talk about the real stuff of our lives, to make sense of childhood, of family, to articulate our stories and have them heard.

What else have I learned; what skills have I acquired? I've met many extraordinary people, and first and foremost, I've learned how to listen. I don't mean to imply that that's a skill I didn't have and that now I've acquired it, rather, that I was a good listener for a long time and I am now engaged in a lifelong process of deepening that skill. It's exactly the opposite of riding a bike—every day, every hour, you need to concentrate yet again to remember how to do it.

The value of becoming a careful listener cannot be overstated, both because listening helps develop empathy and connection to others and also because we so desperately need to learn to hear ourselves. Slowly, slowly, I am practicing listening and so learning about myself. Learning: how to breathe, how to stay focused on what's important, how to eat, remembering to drink a lot of water. I am finally able to live more and more in the moment, to be present in the moment. Increasingly I am attuned to life's details—that is, after all, much of what I am teaching and speaking about! As I travel and teach, using a slim volume of my own stories and poems as my teaching tool, my words refracted through others and returned back to me are pointing to the very lessons I have most needed to learn in my life. And the hardest lesson of all to learn is how to take care of myself.

I took an informal survey this winter of half a dozen of my closest women friends, each of them intelligent, full of life and love, fifty-something, in long-term committed relationships, mothers, active and accomplished in their professions and in the important fights that need to be fought in our wounded world. And I asked each of them, "How do you care for yourself?" I started a computer file of their responses, because I was so struck by the common thread that I thought it would make the beginnings of a truly important book. None of them could answer the question to her satisfaction; most responded sadly if not with despair, "I don't know how to care for myself."

Like Shifra and Puah, like Miriam and Yocheved, like Pharaoh's daughter, we are outer-directed, we channel our energies to the care of Moses. I don't say that out of hostility toward the golden-haired brother, the favorite son—I've done my time on that road, the "you love him more than you love me" road, the "his piece is bigger than mine" road—it gets old, more to the point, it's a distraction from the real question: whether those around me have blessed me or not, how do I finally marshal my resources to bless myself? Certainly by midlife, it's time, and if the younger sisters reading these words can do it in their teens, their twenties, their thirties, their forties, Halleluyah! That's my idea of going out of Egypt: learning to be sweet and gentle with myself; finding what is precious, what is sacred within; then nourishing, affirming that sacred self.

What does all this have to do with God and with women celebrating seder together? I see God as that precious core of self, that holy core of self, not just in the others I meet on the way but in myself as well. And failing to see the sacred in the other or in the self renders us unfit to leave behind the dead confines of enslavement and move to the broad plains of possibility and joy. We learn to be slave/caretakers from our mothers, who learned it from their mothers, who learned it from their mothers, and I think the only way of breaking the cycle of self-inflicted pain and harm and diminution is to model for one another the love of women, of daughter, sister, mother, to encourage new behavior toward the woman/self. To share with one another openly and frankly the struggles and failures in attempting to care for ourselves, the advice and the triumphs and the mutual dedication to this new women's learning. It can begin with something as simple as initiating *tefillat haderech,* not only when I am the mother of small children, not only when my partner and I set out on a journey, but for myself, alone, when I travel on the road.

II. What Is My Share of *Tikkun Olam* in the World?

As difficult as it is to locate one's inner sacred core and then to cherish and care for it, that's only half the task at hand. To be holy, we must engage in a serious way in the repair of the world. (I smile with the realization that once again, as always, I've been rediscovering the wheel: "If I am not for myself, who will be for me; if I am only for myself, what am I?") Recently I had occasion to see a haggadah created especially for a local women's seder, and was saddened and disturbed that, although it was beautifully written, it seemed to exist in a world of its own, a world of personal pain and personal liberation, celebrating Passover as if with the blinds drawn. I found myself feeling pointedly grateful for the work of the Jewish Women's Archive, whose general retrieval of our historic foremothers, and whose specific poster projects that highlight a few particularly illustrious Jewish women each year, have provided substance for women's *haggadot* to celebrate women who have modeled lives of purpose and achievement.

I don't believe that women who are politically or socially inactive are selfish or oblivious to the suffering of others. I think we all possess the ability to be empathetic, the problem is that we feel overwhelmed by the pain in the world around us, and so we feel impotent to be change makers. Last year the Jewish Women's Archive honored several women in the Boston area where the organization is based at an evening celebrating "Women Who Dared"—ordinary women who in a wide range of efforts reached out into the world to do some social justice work—registering black Southern voters in the 1960s, rescuing Ethiopian Jews, working for civil rights in El Salvador, protesting the nuclear arms race. I felt honored to be included in this evening, cited for my work in organizing and facilitating dialogue between Israeli and Palestinian women on the West Bank during the first *intifada*. When, as part of this program, I was asked how to encourage women to engage in the repair of the world, I answered:

> I believe two qualities are necessary for engaging in *tikkun olam*: One, that you have the ability to see the other, to see a problem, to see pain, to see injustice—not the theory of it, but the actual face of it, to see the face of the other. And secondly, that you are able to see yourself as a person capable of creating change, that you see yourself as intelligent enough to think about a problem, that you have the courage to ask even what seem like stupid questions, to keep at those questions over and over until the answers make some minimal sense to you, to see yourself as a person of fundamental worth whose ideas have some merit and who therefore deserves to be heard. Another way to put that: find your voice, then practice speaking up. If you develop these two qualities—seeing the other and respecting yourself—then you will deepen your heart and become a powerful force in the world. There are other important aspects too—find yourself mentors, become a mentor, build a community with whom you can work— but the first two qualities I mention come before all else.

And how do we find those pieces of "repair work" that have our name on them? Just this week I sat on my porch in the sunlight, listening to an undergraduate who had heard me lecture and who had e-mailed me with her own questions: Is it more important to be loved or to give love to others? How do I figure out how to be of service in the world? I had advised her in a long e-mail response and then when I came to the end of the e-mail, realized that e-mail wasn't adequate for this depth of conversation, so I offered her a face-to-face meeting to pursue the questions further.

As we sat together enjoying the mild spring breeze after a too-long winter, I talked about my dialogue efforts on the West Bank. I talked about the years I spent in New York working for Beyond Shelter, a unique coalition of synagogues on Manhattan's West Side that does advocacy and fundraising for New York's low-income householders. And then I spoke about my deep commitment to Project Kesher, an international Jewish women's organization based in Chicago, that on the shortest shoestring I've ever seen supports and encourages the Jewish renaissance in the former Soviet Union, providing leadership training and partnership to women there and fostering the skills needed to create communities where Judaism, feminism, and democracy can thrive. I detailed for this undergraduate how these projects used my particular talents, how she needed to do some investigating to find the causes that excite her passion and authentic concern, and to avoid projects that may be worthy but for whatever reason taste "medicinal" to her. In order to find those pieces of *tikkun olam* that have your name on them, I told her, you need to move toward what genuinely excites you.

What does it all mean in the end? I realize, rereading these words, that I was brought up a child of the 1950s to care for the small circle of my immediate family—the husband and children I was supposed to have. And what have I come to realize as an adult woman? That I also need to care for myself and need to care for the stranger—in other words, I need to both narrow the focus of my care and widen the focus of my care.

In the *amidah* (a standing prayer read silently during the worship service), we address our prayers to the "great, mighty, awesome, transcendent God," and sometimes when I encounter such words in quiet devotional moments, I become restless. I think, doesn't God grow weary of this endless inflated flattery? But just recently I came upon a stunning commentary[2] that, by referring back to the full context from which the phrase in the *amidah* is drawn, puts the matter in a new light:

> For Adonai your God is above all gods, the supreme power, *the great, mighty, awesome, transcendent God,* who shows no favor and takes no bribe, but upholds the cause of the fatherless and the widow, and befriends the stranger, providing him with food and clothing. You too must befriend the stranger, for you were strangers in the land of Egypt.[3]

The full context serves to remind us of *why* God is praised, and in doing so, reminds us that we are enjoined to imitate God. When we were unable to care for ourselves, when we were enslaved and suffering in Egypt, God befriended us, God cared for us. And now, we come

together to celebrate, to affirm—that we are free women, joyful, powerful, ready to care for ourselves, ready to care for the stranger. This,
as I see it, is the call to women as we sit together at the seder table,
preparing to go forth into freedom.

≋

Notes

Preface

1. Lillian Hellman, *An Unfinished Woman: A Memoir* (Boston: Little, Brown, 1969).

Introduction

1. William Cutter and Yaffa Weisman, eds., *And We Were All There: A Feminist Passover Haggadah* (Los Angeles: American Jewish Congress Feminist Center, 1996), i.
2. Maida E. Solomon, "Claiming Our Questions: Feminism and Judaism in Women's Haggadot" in *Talking Back: Images of Jewish Women in American Culture,* Brandeis Series in American Jewish History, Culture, and Life, ed. Joyce Antler (Hanover: Brandeis University Press, 1997), 239.
3. Ibid., 224.

Part 1: Why Women's Seders?

For Women Only

1. We use the translation "Reed Sea" throughout this book because it is more faithful to the meaning of the original Hebrew than the translation "Red Sea," which may be more familiar to some readers.

Creating the Ma'yan Women's Seder: Balancing Comfort, Challenge, and Community

1. This idea for the *brachot* was originally used by Rabbi Sue Levi Elwell in a haggadah she edited for the Los Angeles Jewish Feminist Center. Rabbi Elwell served as the rabbinic director of Ma'yan from 1994 to 1996 and was instrumental in creating the Ma'yan haggadah and seders.
2. The piece, which plays on the repeated use of the same Hebrew word for oppression used in both stories, grew out of a powerful study session I

attended, cotaught by biblical scholars and feminist theologians Phyllis Trible and Tikvah Frymer-Kensky.

3. For a fuller explanation, see "Power and Parity: The Roles of Women and Men on the Boards of Major American Jewish Organizations," a study by Bethamie Horowitz, Ph.D., Pearl Beck, Ph.D., and Charles Kadushin, Ph.D. (New York: Ma'yan: The Jewish Women's Project of the Jewish Community Center of the Upper West Side, 1997), June 1997.

4. Marilyn Frye, "Some Reflections on Separatism and Power," in *Lesbian Culture: An Anthology,* ed. Julia Penelope and Susan Wolfe (Freedom, Calif.: The Crossing Press, 1993), 443–450.

Miriam and Our Dance of Freedom: Seder in Prison

1. Judith Clark is serving three life sentences for her role in the 1981 robbery of a Brinks truck by radicals in which three people were killed. While initially avowing her actions, she has long since repudiated them and publicly apologized to the victims. She notes, "The study and rituals of Judaism helped me to confront the toll of my actions on others and to rebuild my moral and spiritual grounding."

Every Voice Matters: Community and Dialogue at a Women's Seder

1. Elaine Moise and Rebecca Schwartz, *The Dancing with Miriam Haggadah: A Jewish Women's Celebration of Passover* (Palo Alto, Calif.: Rikudei Miriam Press, 1997) labels her the irreverent daughter. *Jewish Women's Seder 1999* (Mandell L. Berman Center for University of Michigan Hillel) labels her the uninvolved daughter. Lynn Hazan, *Project Kesher Haggadah,* 1998 labels her the angry daughter. *San Diego Women's Haggadah,* 2nd ed., Jane Sprague Zones, ed. (San Diego: Women's Institute for Continuing Jewish Education, 1986) labels her the bitter daughter. *The Journey Continues: The Ma'yan Passover Haggadah,* Tamara R. Cohen, ed. (New York: Ma'yan: The Jewish Women's Project of the JCC on the Upper West Side, 2000) labels her the daughter who wishes to erase her difference.

2. *The Yale Women's Haggadah,* Joseph Slifka Center for Jewish Life at Yale (1999).

3. The *shehecheyanu* is a blessing of renewal. Traditionally it is said only to mark our reaching an important, repeated occasion (such as eating the first fruit of a new season) or on a holiday.

God's Redemption: Memory and Gender on Passover

1. It is strange to note that despite Passover's popularity, it does not seem to displace this American fixation on a synagogue-based Judaism.

2. For many reasons, I am saddened by the necessity for the community seder that takes place in a synagogue setting.

3. We can find this search in homes and schools, in academia, and in communal celebrations. It is a search for female ancestors as authentic models for contemporary women as leaders of the community.
4. Deuteronomy 29:14.
5. Exodus 12–15, Numbers 20:15–16, Deuteronomy 5:15, 26:5–9.
6. Deuteronomy 26:7–8.
7. Deuteronomy 7:12–24.
8. Deuteronomy 7:22.
9. BT *Sotah* 11b.

An Embrace of Tradition

1. E. M. Broner, *The Telling* (San Francisco: HarperSanFrancisco, 1992), 197.
2. Ibid., 72.
3. Ibid., 197.

Part 2: Reclaiming and Re-creating Passover Rituals for Women

1. Two rituals proposed by Rabbi Sasso are available in *The Women's Seder Sourcebook: Rituals and Readings for Use at the Seder,* the companion volume to this anthology.

Thoughts on Cleaning for Pesach

1. Judith Lorber, *Night to His Day: The Social Construction of Gender* (New Haven: Yale University Press, 1994), 33.
2. *Zohar* 182a.
3. *The Carlebach Haggadah: Seder Night with Reb Shlomo* (Jerusalem: Urim Publications, 2001), 10.

We Can't Be Free Until All Women Are Important

1. This analysis has been informed and inspired by the following sources: Shlomo Yossef Zevine, et al., eds., "Hassiba" [Reclining], *Entziklopedia Talmudit* [Encyclopedia of the Talmud] 9 (1959), 529–536. Rachel Adler, "The Jew Who Wasn't There: Halacha and the Jewish Woman," *Davka* 1, no. 4 (summer 1971), 6–11. Sylvia Barack Fishman, *A Breath of Life: Feminism in the American Jewish Community* (New York: The Free Press, 1993), 174–176 and notes 62–68, 290. Avi'ad haKohen, "'Nashim Atzlaniyot Hen'?! 'Nashim Hashuvot Hen'!" [Women Are Lazy?! Women Are Important!], *Alon Shvut Bogrim* [Yeshivat Har Etzion Alumni Journal] 11 (1998), 63–82. Har'eli Mizrahi and Ktura Kaydar, "Hiyuv Nashim beMitzvat Hassiba" [Obligating Women in the Mitzvah of Reclining], *Hassibat Nashim* [in this context: A Women's Symposium!], an anthology of comments on the 10th chapter of Tractate Pesahim, written and edited

by twelfth graders, Neve Hana Yeshiva High School for Girls (1998), 8–12. Grossman, Grossman, *Hassidot uMordot, Nashim Yehudiyot beEiropa biYmei haBeinayim* [Pious and Rebellious, Jewish Women in Medieval Europe] (2001), 326–328.

2. The Mishnah's final editing was circa 200 C.E. The Babylonian Talmud's final editing was circa 500 C.E.

3. *Mishnah Pesahim* 10:1.

4. BT *Pesahim* 108a.

5. Esther 7:8. Esther is depicted throughout as one sexual object among many, albeit the most treasured one, elevated to the status of queen. When she realizes that her people are scheduled for genocide, and that her unique position in the king's palace may give her some influence on his policies, she schemes to engineer a circumstance that will give her a strategic advantage in that sexist context. First, she puts on her regal robe and takes the risk of seeking an interview with the king. This succeeds—the king likes her looks and is prepared to grant her wish. She invites the king to a private feast with his prime minister, Haman. This feast is also a success, so she uses the good mood to ask for a second, similar feast the same day. In the course of this second feast, she finally expresses her request: to spare her people. The king, completely taken up in her charms by this point, loses his temper and demands to know who dared upset his beloved queen by this preposterous plan. When Esther points at Haman, the king is so overwhelmed that he leaves the feast room to take a walk in the garden. Haman, left alone with the queen, falls on the bed on which she is lounging—to beg for his life—and is caught in this posture by the maddened king, who returns into the room, screaming, "On top of it all, you are intent on conquering the queen in my own home?!" Esther's plan proves foolproof: Haman is doomed, and the tables of the regal policies are overturned.

I included this reference in this essay for two reasons: first, because Esther's bravery can be appreciated only if we take into account the fact that she oversteps her assigned role as a sex object, and second, she succeeds precisely because she understands that in this context the only power she has is sexual, and she uses this power to achieve her goal.

6. For example, see Maimonides, *Mishneh Torah,* Laws of Chametz and Matzah 7:7–8.

7. The time between the twelfth and sixteenth centuries was the formative period of Ashkenazi halakhah, including on this issue. The examples from art that I have included are from all periods up to the present day, because the image of woman runs through the ages in Western culture.

8. Rema's additional notes to the Shulhan Arukh, *Orah Hayim,* 472:4.

9. Note that this is the classical logic of liberal feminism: women are allowed to participate in the public sphere as long as everyone agrees on the issues that are tucked away in the private sphere.

10. One particularly interesting example is by Rabbi Chaim Karlinsky (1981), "Nashim beDin Hassiba" [Women in the Law of Reclining], *HaDarom* [Halachic Journal of the Rabbinical Council of America], no. 51, April, 12–18. The question was presented to him by an Orthodox doctor in New York who attended a group seder in a big hotel and was "greatly impressed" by the arrangements made for women also to recline—a practice he had not seen before. He wanted to know whether this practice was allowed. Karlinsky goes to great lengths to prove that the true reason for excluding women from this practice in the past stemmed only from the recognition that most women were not used to reclining, and that nowadays, when all our women are important and even rule over their husbands at home, they should recline. He even suggests that we may need to exclude men from reclining for the same reason that women were excluded in the past.

However, Karlinsky warns that this line of reasoning is only theoretical, engaged in only for the purpose of reward for Torah study. Halakhists whom he follows have already said, at the end of this very reasoning, that women do not recline, which he takes to mean that when something is not done it is actually forbidden to do it. Karlinsky concludes his responsum as follows:

> When the issue is a woman who maintains "the honor of the King's daughter is all inside," and she celebrates the seder in her home with her family, our great halakhic decisors instructed that a woman is not allowed to undertake the extra requirement to recline; how much more so when the issue is a woman participating in a public seder, in one room and even at the same table with men and women from many families. Women reclining is liable to lead to lightheadedness, and infringe upon the ways of modesty, especially when it comes to the last cups, "when wine goes in...." This is strengthened by the fact that the question was presented by a man whose writing is proof of his Torah scholarship and his loyalty to tradition, and he testifies that the impression made by the women reclining was great. If women's reclining increased the impression of the holiness of the Holiday of Redemption, even slightly, then care should be taken to avoid this reclining, just as minute quantities of *chametz* during Passover are avoided. It is clear that in such a seder a woman is not allowed to practice the extra *mitzvah* of reclining in public. Certainly "this displeases the sages." Such things can come under the recommendation of "better sit and do nothing" [omit rather than commit].

This intricate text may throw light on the origins of the orange on the seder plate. As documented by Rabbi Rebecca Alpert in her book, *Like Bread on the Seder Plate,* an ultra-Orthodox woman responded to the probability of accepting lesbian Jews by comparing this idea to bread on a seder plate. I suggest that the expression "like *chametz* on Pesach" is a traditional idiom that connotes "far-fetched, absurd, imaginary, impossible, totally illogical" rather than "sinful," since it was coined in a world that could not imagine the existence of Jews who do not observe Pesach halakhically. Karlinsky thinks that women who overstep their customary boundaries fall into this category and disturb the social order, and therefore, for him, the fact that they do this out of extra piety is completely irrelevant.

Setting a Cup for Miriam

1. Penina Adelman, *Miriam's Well: Rituals for Jewish Women Around the Year* (New York, Biblio Press, 1990).
2. Ibid., 6–8.
3. Penina Adelman, "A Drink from Miriam's Cup: The Invention of Tradition among Jewish Women," in *Active Voices: Women in Jewish Culture,* ed. Maurie Sacks (Urbana and Chicago: University of Illinois Press, 1995), 114.
4. Erwin R. Goodenough, *Jewish Symbols in the Greco-Roman Period,* ed. and abridged by Jacob Neusner (Princeton: Princeton University Press, 1988), 19.
5. Eric Hobsbawm, "Introduction: Inventing Traditions" in *The Invention of Tradition,* ed. Eric Hobsbawm and Terence Ranger (Cambridge: Cambridge University Press, 1983), 1, 6, 7.

The Celebration of Challenge: Reclaiming the Four Children

1. This midrash was informed in part by *ReVisions: Seeing Torah through a Feminist Lens,* by Rabbi Elyse Goldstein (Jewish Lights Publishing: Woodstock, Vt., 1998). The author would also like to thank her mother, who inspired her in the writing of this piece through her ideas and by being a woman who questions and challenges.
2. Translation adapted from the *Passover Haggadah* by Rabbi Nathan Goldberg, (Hoboken, N.J.: KTAV, 1993), 10.
3. Deuteronomy 6:20.
4. Exodus 1:15–20.
5. Exodus 12:26.
6. Numbers 27:1–11.
7. Exodus 13:14.
8. Exodus 13:13.
9. Genesis 1:27.
10. Rabbi Nathan Goldberg, *Passover Haggadah* (Hoboken, N.J.: KTAV, 1993), 10.

Orange on the Seder Plate

1. Mary Daly, *Beyond God the Father: Toward a Philosophy of Women's Liberation* (Boston: Beacon Press, 1973).

2. Adrienne Rich, "Compulsory Heterosexuality and Lesbian Existence," *Signs* 5:4 (1980).
3. Genesis 1:28.

The Open Door: The Tale of Idit and the Passover Paradox

1. *Pirkei d'Rabbi Eliezer* 25.
2. *Pirkei d'Rabbi Eliezer* 25 and Nachmanides on Genesis 19:17.
3. *Sanhedrin* 109a–b; also Louis Ginzberg, *The Legends of the Jews* (Philadelphia: Jewish Publication Society, 1968), 245, 249 (a compilation of sources based on Yashar Bayera 35b–38a).
4. *Bereshit Rabbah* 50:9 says that Lot had two married and two betrothed daughters.
5. *Bereshit Rabbah* 50:4.
6. *Bereshit Rabbah* 50:5.
7. Nachmanides on Genesis 19:17, *Pirkei d'Rabbi Eliezer* 25.
8. Ibid. The only other person in the Torah who saw the back of the Divine was Moses.
9. *Bereshit Rabbah* 5.
10. The name "Idit," meaning "choicest," contains the Hebrew letters *ayin, dalet,* which spell the word that means "witness."
11. From the Passover Haggadah, Psalm 79:6–7; Psalm 69:25; Lamentations 3:6.
12. I am grateful to my Bible study partners, Anne Jones (Episcopalian) and Shirley Gilson (Catholic) for their helpful vision in developing this image.

A New Song for a Different Night: Sephardic Women's Musical Repertoire

1. Originating from the Babylonian Talmud.
2. Exodus 15:20–21.
3. Menendez Pidal, quoting from *Historia de los Reyes Católicos,* in *"El romancero Sefardi: Su extraorinario caracter conservador." The Sephardi Heritage,* Richard Barnett, ed. (New York: KTAV, 1959).
4. I use the term "Sephardim" to represent the Jews whose ancestry came from Spain and Portugal.
5. Judeo-Spanish is the medieval Castilian Spanish spoken by the Jews of Spain at the time of the expulsion.
6. These captivating melodies inspired the 1978 creation of Voice of the Turtle, Inc., a performing group whose mission is to perform, record, and disseminate this repertoire. Our performance and research are informed by the work of Dr. Susana Weich-Shahak, Professor Edwin Seroussi, and Dr. Judith Cohen.
7. Sung by Cantor Aviva Rosenblum.

8. *Chants Judeo-Espagnols,* Isaac Levy, ed. (London: World Sephardi Foundation, 1959).

9. *Chants Sephardis,* collected by Leon Algazi (Publication of the Fédération Séphardite Mondiale, Département Culturel, 1956). Introduction by Ovadiah Camhy, Secretary General of the federation.

10. Through the generosity of the National Sound Archives at Hebrew University in Jerusalem, and particularly of Dr. Susana Weich-Shahak, I was able to listen to interviews on field recordings and was introduced to women who were prolific informants.

11. Susana Weich-Shahak, *Un Vergel Vedre.* Flores del Repertoiro Sefardí. Iber-Caja and Alberto Hemsi, *Cancionero sefardí,* Edwin Seroussi, ed. (Jewish Music Research Center, Hebrew University of Jerusalem, 1995).

12. Collected by Dr. Weich-Shahak with information from the prolific informant Mazal-Tov Lazar from Bulgaria.

13. Sung by informant Alicia Ben Dayan, from Tetuán.

14. This song was found in the Levy collection, volume 3, with no attribution of informant.

15. These versions of the songs are informed by original field recordings from the National Sound Archives at Hebrew University, or from versions that appeared with musical notation in the *Antologia de Liturgia Judeo-Espanola,* collected and edited by Isaac Levy. All songs (with the exception of *"Pesah a la mano"*) appear on recordings of Voice of the Turtle. Available at http://www.voiceoftheturtle.com.

16. Flory Jagoda, composer, performer, artist, and one of the winners of the 2002 National Heritage Fellowship by The National Endowment for the Arts, is one of three family survivors of the massacres of the Jews that occurred in Bosnia in 1942. The power of her music—her voice reemerging after a silence dictated by the pain of memory—has encouraged people to look at their own traditions, to remember them, to document them, and to build on them with new creations. She has performed internationally—in Yugoslavia, Bosnia, and Croatia—to audiences who are grateful for her presence not only as a performer of music they share but also for the statement of healing that her concerts signify.

17. From the field recordings of Susana Weich-Shahak, at the National Sound Archives at Hebrew University, Jerusalem. The source of this song is the prolific informant Mazal-Tov Lazar of Bulgaria. The spelling of the Judeo-Spanish texts reflects the pronunciation used by the informants and varies depending on the informant's regional pronunciation style.

18. Ibid. The source is Esther Rofe BenShimol of Morocco.

19. Ibid. The source is Alicia Ben Dayan.

20. Levy, op. cit.

21. Ibid.

22. Ibid.

23. *The Flory Jagoda Songbook: Memories of Sarajevo* (Owings Mills, Md.: Tara Publications, 1993), available at http://www.jewishmusic.com; recordings available at Altarasa Records, 6307 Beachway Drive, Falls Church, Va. 22044.

I Will Be with You: The Divine Presence on Passover

1. Exodus 15:21.
2. Exodus 20:2.
3. Job 42:5.
4. *Pirke Avot* 3:3.
5. Psalms 34:9.
6. Deuteronomy 29:4–5.
7. Deuteronomy 30:14.
8. Exodus 3:12.

Part 3: Women of Exodus

1. Avivah Gottlieb Zornberg, *The Particulars of Rapture: Reflections on Exodus* (New York: Doubleday, 2001), 5.
2. A famous talmudic passage refers to "the seventy faces of Torah." This phrase is often interpreted to signify that there are a multiplicity of meanings to each word of Torah, which can be understood from many different perspectives and on many different levels.

Shiru l'Adonai: Widening the Circle of Memory and History

1. Joseph was a Hebrew slave who interpreted Pharaoh's dream, saved Egypt from famine, and became Pharaoh's key adviser. After Joseph's death, a new Pharaoh took the throne, who, according to Exodus 1:8, "didn't know Joseph."
2. Exodus 1:17.
3. Exodus 1:20.
4. Exodus 2:3.
5. Exodus 15:21.
6. Exodus 15:1.

Miriam's Leadership: A Reconstruction

1. Exodus 15:21.
2. *Exodus Rabbah* to Exodus 15:20.
3. *Exodus Rabbah* to Exodus 1:13.
4. Ellen Frankel, *The Five Books of Miriam: A Women's Commentary on the Torah* (New York: Putnam, 1996), 113.

5. Numbers 12:2.
6. Just as Lot's wife turns to salt (Genesis 19:26) and the body of the anonymous wife/concubine in Judges 19 is cut into twelve pieces—an apparent symbol of the fragmented body politic—Miriam's leprosy is a sign, and her body is the site of representation.
7. Numbers 12:13.
8. Numbers 12:14.
9. Numbers 20:22–29.
10. Numbers 20:1.
11. Numbers 20:1.
12. Numbers 20:2.
13. Babylonian Talmud, *Ta'anit* 9a.
14. Numbers 20:8.
15. Ilana Pardes, *Countertraditions in the Bible: A Feminist Approach* (Cambridge: Harvard University Press, 1992). I intend by "countertradition" what Pardes describes when she writes that one of her goals is "to explore the tense dialogue between the dominant patriarchal discourses of the Bible and counter female voices which attempt to put forth other truths" (p. 4). This reconstruction of Miriam is also indebted to a conversation with Judith Plaskow, Martha Ackelsberg, and Alicia Ostriker that took place at a National Havurah Institute.
16. Rivkah M. Walton, "The Rock: A Midrash on Numbers 20:1–13," *Living Text: The Journal of Contemporary Midrash*, no. 1 (July 1997), 21–22.

Their Lives a Page Plucked from a Holy Book

1. "Their Lives a Page Plucked from a Holy Book" from "Women Songs," a poem by Kadya Molodowsky. You can find Adrienne Rich's translation of this poem in *A Treasury of Yiddish Poetry,* edited by Irving Howe and Eliezer Greenberg (Austin, Tex.: Holt, Rinehart, & Winston, 1969). This piece was first published as a sermon in Jana Childers, ed., *Birthing the Sermon: Women Preachers on the Creative Process* (St. Louis: Chalice Press, 2001).
2. This midrash appears in several different versions: in one Sarah dies upon hearing from Satan the news that Abraham had killed their son. In another, Sarah's soul departs in a sigh of joy upon hearing that Isaac was still alive. See *Tanchuma Vayera* 23 or *The Legends of the Jews,* by Louis Ginzberg, translated by Henrietta Szold (Philadelphia: Jewish Publication Society, 1937), vol. 1, 286–287.
3. *Genesis Rabbah* LVI:11.
4. I am deeply grateful to Dr. Marianne Ultmann and Gerson Goodman, members of Beth Am, The People's Temple, for listening to an earlier draft of this sermon and offering valuable criticism. It was they who insisted that I precede the sermon with a brief discussion of the techniques of midrash. I am also grateful to Rabbi Danny Zemel and the members of Temple

Micah for inviting me to serve as their scholar-in-residence. I wrote this sermon for my visit to their congregation. Finally, I am grateful to my partner,
Rabbi Sharon Kleinbaum, who is without question a student of Miriam.

5. Exodus 1:15–21.
6. Exodus 2:1–9. At first, Moses' mother is referred to only as "bat Levi"
   (a/the daughter of Levi). Later, in verse 6:20, she is called Yocheved.
7. Exodus 2:4, 7, 8.
8. Exodus 2:5–10.
9. Exodus 2:15–22, 4:18–26. Only one of Moses' sons is mentioned here by
   name, Gershon (2:22). Nachmanides says that Tziporah was pregnant with
   Elazar when they returned to Egypt. (See note in the Soncino Chumash,
   p. 339.)
10. Exodus 6:23.
11. *Parshat Shemot* encompasses Exodus 1:1–6:1.
12. Pharaoh's daughter certainly saved the life of a son of her "enemy." Those
    who believe that the midwives were Egyptians would say that they too saved
    the lives of the sons of their enemies.
13. Exodus 2:4.
14. Exodus 7:20–21.
15. Exodus 12:1–13.
16. Genesis 18:23.
17. Why was Pharaoh so stubborn? One of the most troubling aspects of this
    story is the repeated statement *"Veyitchazek Adonai et lev Paroh,"* God
    hardened Pharaoh's heart. On the face of it, this strikes most readers as
    unjust: God hardened Pharaoh's heart and then punished Pharaoh and all
    of Egypt for his hard-heartedness. Not fair! Moreover, for those who
    believe in the free will of the individual, the very notion that God hard-
    ened Pharaoh's heart is outrageous. God does not, insists Maimonides,
    deny an individual his or her free will. So how can we understand the state-
    ment *"Veyitchazek Adonai et lev Paroh"*? Twenty times the text tells us that
    Pharaoh's heart was hardened against the appeal of Moses. But the Hebrew
    words expressing that notion vary tremendously. Sometimes the verb is
    chazak (strong, stubborn), sometimes it is *kaved* (heavy, swelled, weighed
    down, puffed up), sometimes *kashe* (hard, insensitive). Sometimes the verb
    is intransitive, and Pharaoh's heart is the subject. Sometimes Pharaoh's
    heart is the object of a transitive verb, and Pharaoh (not God) is the subject.
    Only in half of the cases is God the subject of the verb. Immediately before
    the first five plagues, God is not the subject of the verb "to harden" (Exo-
    dus 7:13, 7:14, 7:22, 8:11, 8:15, 8:28, 9:7). On a closer look, then, Pharaoh
    apparently hardened his own heart, or the heart of Pharaoh was not moved.
    With the sixth plague, however, the text actually says, as God earlier fore-
    warned Moses (4:21, 7:3), that *God* hardened Pharaoh's heart (9:12). What
    is the text trying to say by attributing to God this hardening of Pharaoh's

heart? A Mishnah in *Pirke Avot* teaches: *"Mitzvah goreret mitzvah, averah goreret averah."* One *mitzvah* leads to another. One sin leads to another.

Perhaps we can understand Pharaoh's stubbornness this way: Initially, Pharaoh sinned of his own free will, over and over again. Pharaoh's arrogance, or Pharaoh's lack of responsiveness to reason, or Pharaoh's lack of compassion, or—as I suggest in this midrash—Pharaoh's enslavement to his own political right wing, ultimately defined him. His intransigence became habitual. His character became his destiny. Attributing to God Pharaoh's hardness of heart, in the latter five plagues, is a way of saying that Pharaoh dug himself in so deep that he ultimately lost the ability to dig himself out.

18. Exodus 12:35.
19. Exodus 12:36.
20. Genesis 39:20 gives us evidence of a Pharaoh's use of a prison.
21. Moses' mother, Yocheved, and Aaron's wife, Elisheva, are never again mentioned in a biblical story. (Yocheved appears only in a genealogy in Numbers 26:59. Elisheva's name never reappears.) Particularly noticeable is the absence of any mention of Aaron's wife at the time their two sons, Nadav and Avihu, are killed.
22. Exodus 12:29.
23. *-ot* is typically the feminine plural noun ending. It is true that in the Torah and in rabbinic literature, the feminine-looking plural *bechorot* is sometimes used as the plural of the masculine noun *bechor*. Nonetheless, given that the more expected masculine plural *bechorim* or *b'chorei mitzrayim*, as used in Psalm 135:8, was also an option available to the biblical author, it is in good rabbinic tradition to assume that the use of the feminine ending here instead of the masculine ending was not an accident but was intended to convey some meaning.
24. Exodus 15:1–4.
25. Exodus 15:20–21.
26. From "Tattered Kaddish" by Adrienne Rich, in *An Atlas of the Difficult World: Poems 1988–1991* (New York: Norton, 1991), 45.
27. Even in the face of his sons' deaths, Aaron is silent/emotionless. See Leviticus 10:3.
28. From "Natural Resources" by Adrienne Rich, in *The Dream of a Common Language: Poems 1974–1977* (New York: Norton, 1974), 67.
29. The Torah gives no explanation for Nadav and Avihu's unauthorized offering of incense and strange fire (Leviticus 10:1). I think their independent spirits came from their mother, Elisheva, and their aunt, Miriam.
30. Following the Exodus the only references to Miriam are in Numbers 12:1, 12:4, 12:5, 12:10, 12:15, 20:1 (her death), 26:59, Deuteronomy 24:9, I Chronicles 4:17 and 5:29, and Micah 6:4.

31. "To be of use" by Marge Piercy, in *Circles on the Water* (New York: Random House, 1982). Used here with permission.
32. Exodus 18:2.
33. Exodus 18:1–7.
34. While Moses' sons, Gerson and Elazar, are mentioned later in genealogies or lists of tribes, it is Joshua, not either of Moses' own sons, who succeeds him.
35. From "Women Songs" by Kadya Molodowsky, translated by Adrienne Rich in *A Treasury of Yiddish Poetry,* ed. Howe and Greenberg (Austin, Tex.: Holt, Rinehart, & Winston, 1969), 284.
36. Ibid.
37. Proverbs 31:10–31, traditionally recited at the table every Friday night by a husband to his wife.
38. This ending occurred to me when I saw the following book title: *A Price Below Rubies: Jewish Women as Rebels and Radicals,* by Naomi Shepherd (Cambridge, Mass.: Harvard University Press, 1993).

With Strong Hands and Outstretched Arms

1. Deuteronomy 26:8.
2. My own thinking on the significance of this human cry, and the meaning of the Divine response, has been greatly influenced and enriched by Avivah Zornberg's discussion of this subject in her book *The Particulars of Rapture: Reflections on Exodus.* See especially chapter 1, *Shemoth,* 30–48 ("Pain and Empathy: The Fate of the Individual"). I am also profoundly indebted to my friends and colleagues Rabbis Dianne Cohler-Esses, Susan Fendrick, and Sharon Kleinbaum for many hours of conversation and *hevruta* (shared study) on the themes that I explore in this reflection.
3. Exodus 2:23–25.
4. *Pirke d'Rabbi Eliezer* 48, as cited in Avivah Gottlieb Zornberg, *The Particulars of Rapture: Reflections on Exodus* (New York: Doubleday, 2001).
5. *Song of Songs Rabbah* 2:15, as cited in *The Book of Legends, Sefer Ha'aggadah,* edited by Hayim Nahman Bialik and Yehoshua Hana Ravnitzky, translated by William G. Braude (New York: Schocken Books, 1992), 59.
6. Sefat Emeth, *Shemot,* p. 18, cited in Zornberg.
7. Exodus 3:4.
8. This distinguishes the call to Moses from every other instance in which God calls out to a human being by name, with this kind of emphatic repetition. See, for example, Genesis 22:11 and Genesis 46:2. There and elsewhere, the two occurrences of the name are separated by a *pasek,* a vertical line in the text.
9. *Exodus Rabbah* 2:6.

10. Exodus 14:11–12.
11. Exodus 14:13–14.
12. Exodus 14:15–16.
13. BT *Megillah* 15b.
14. Exodus 15:2.
15. *Shemot Rabbah* 23:8.

The Secret of Redemption: A Tale of Mirrors

1. BT *Sotah* 11b.
2. This reflection is excerpted from *The Particulars of Rapture: Reflections on Exodus* (New York: Doubleday, 2001).
3. *Tanchuma Pikudei* 9.
4. Rashi 38:8.
5. Compare the commentary of Ibn Ezra (38:8), which makes just this ascetic suggestion.
6. See, e.g., 1:6: "Don't stare at me because I am swarthy, because the sun has gazed upon me." The aesthetics of blackness—and of tanned skin—here clearly appeal to convention, to the imagery of a laboring and sun-exposed slave class, and to a submerged association with moral taint.
7. Rambam 38:8.
8. The use of the ewer for the *Sotah* (the wife suspected of adultery who is put through a ritual involving water: see Numbers 5:11–31) ordeal is of central importance; it does not, however, enter my main area of discourse in this chapter. Thematically, of course, there are clear connections between the subject of this chapter and the problem of misarticulated sexuality, suggested by the *Sotah*.
9. See *Torah Shelemah, Vayakhel-Pikudei,* appendix 6.
10. The polished copper mirrors of Masada come to mind.

"Fixing" Liberation, or How Rebecca Initiates the Passover Seder

1. *Brakhot* 26b.
2. Abraham Joshua Heschel extols this innovation in his famous essay *The Shabbat* (New York: Farrar, Straus & Giroux, 1951).
3. Exodus 34:22.
4. Deuteronomy 16:9.
5. For a full analysis of the Exodus as birth, see my chapter "Blood and Ink: Birthing Liberation," in my forthcoming book tentatively entitled *Beyond the Wall: From Text to Action.*
6. Genesis 25:27–8.
7. Genesis 26:35.
8. My translation/rendering.

9. *Pirke d'Rebbe Eliezer* 33.
10. Genesis 27:28.
11. Exodus 16:13–14.
12. Exodus 15:1–22.
13. Exodus 13:8.
14. Exodus 12:21.
15. Genesis 27:28.

Part 4: Telling Our Stories

Jephthah's Daughter: A Feminist Midrash

1. Judith Plaskow, author of *Standing Again at Sinai: Judaism from a Feminist Perspective* (New York: HarperCollins, 1990), defines midrash as "imaginative exegesis and literary amplification."
2. Judges 11:1–2.
3. Judges 11:3.
4. Judges 11:4–6.
5. Judges 11:7–11.
6. Judges 11:30.
7. Judges 11:34–35.
8. Judges 11:36.
9. Judges 11:37.
10. Judges 11:39.
11. Judges 11:32, 12:3.
12. Judges 11:37.
13. Judges 12:7.

Memory and Revolution

1. Genesis 34:1.

Leaving on Purpose: The Questions of Women's *Tefillah*

1. I do think that something more provocative is going on at Bais Yaakov—not only with those girls who lead prayer, but also by those girls who instead, sit in back and discuss the latest issue of *Teen Beat* magazine: they exercise (or rather, invent) their option not to pray—a major radicalism in that community.

Of Nursing, in the Desert

1. *Refuseniks* in the Soviet Union were Jews who declared their desire to emigrate to Israel but were denied permission to leave by the state. Consequently, they were treated as enemies and deprived of jobs, sources of livelihood, and basic human rights. Severe persecutions affected adults and

children alike. *Refuseniks* created a vibrant underground Jewish culture in the Soviet Union in the late 1960s, 1970s, and 1980s, which included an elaborate system of Jewish education, religious education and practices, arts, literature, music, and community life. Most of the *refuseniks* were finally given permission to emigrate in the early 1990s.

On Matzah, Questions, and Becoming a Nation

1. *Shemot* 12:26.

God's Bride on Pesach

1. Sheol.
2. Raphael Patai, *The Hebrew Goddess* (Hoboken, N.J.: KTAV, 1967); Gershom Scholem, *Major Trends in Jewish Mysticism* (New York: Schocken, 1961).
3. Ibid.
4. This often overlooked detail is quite clear and explicit in I Kings 18:40.

Women Re-creating the Passover Seder:
Bella Rosenfeld Chagall and the Resonance of Female Memory

1. Bella Chagall, *Burning Lights,* translated from the Yiddish by Norbert Guterman (New York: Schocken Books, 1946; reprint New York: Biblio Press, 1996).
2. Judith Hauptman, "Pesah: A Liberating Experience for Women," *Masoret* 2 (Winter 1993). On women's halakhic mandates to perform specific positive time-bound commandments from which they would otherwise be exempt, see Judith Hauptman, *Rereading the Rabbis: A Woman's Voice* (Boulder, Colo.: Westview Press, 1998), 230–231. She demonstrates how talmudic legislation included women in "observance of the key rituals of Pesach, Chanukah, Purim, and to a large extent, the Sabbath." In the case of Pesach, Chanukah, and Purim, the rabbinic justifications are that women, too, were part of the miracles of deliverance commemorated by these festivals; their obligation regarding the Sabbath is linked to their responsibility to pray.
3. BT *Pesachim* 43b.
4. Ibid., 91b.
5. Ibid., 108a.
6. Ibid.
7. For examples of this scene, see Bezalel Narkiss, *Hebrew Illuminated Manuscripts* (Jerusalem: Keter, 1969), 69, from a fourteenth-century Spanish haggadah, the "Brother" to the Rylands Spanish Haggadah, now in the British Museum in London; and Thérèse and Mendel Metzger, *Jewish Life in the Middle Ages: Illuminated Hebrew Manuscripts of the Thirteenth to Sixteenth Centuries* (New York: Alpine Fine Arts Collection, 1982), 225, illustration 338, from a fifteenth-century Italian haggadah contained within

the Rothschild Miscellany, now in the Israel Museum in Jerusalem. For a study of the medieval illustrated haggadah, see Mendel Metzger, *La Haggada enluminée* (Leiden: Brill, 1973).

8. Chagall, 232.
9. Ibid., 230.
10. Ibid., 235.
11. Ibid., 238.
12. Ibid., 240.
13. Ibid., 52.
14. Ibid., 103.
15. BT *Pesachim* 108 a–b.
16. Judith Hauptman, "Pesah: A Liberating Experience for Women," *Masoret* 2 (Winter 1993).
17. Chagall, 205.
18. Pauline Wengeroff, *Rememberings: The World of a Russian-Jewish Woman in the Nineteenth Century,* translated from the German by Henny Wenkart (Bethesda, Md.: University Press of Maryland, 2000), 37.
19. On "visions and revisions" of the haggadah in modern times, see Yosef Hayim Yerushalmi, *Haggadah and History: A Panorama in Facsimile of Five Centuries of the Printed Haggadah from the Collections of Harvard University and the Jewish Theological Seminary of America* (Philadelphia: Jewish Publication Society, 1975), especially 66–85. For a classic feminist haggadah, see E. M. Broner and Naomi Nimrod, *The Women's Haggadah* (San Francisco: HarperSanFrancisco, 1993).

Part 5: Visions and Challenges for the Future

Reflections on the Feminist Seder as an Entry Point into Jewish Life

1. Ma'yan: The Jewish Women's Project of the JCC of the Upper West Side hosts women's seders in Manhattan each year, drawing approximately five hundred participants on each of four nights.
2. Remarks from Bella Abzug at the 42nd Session of the United Nations Commission on the Status of Women, 1998.

Pluralism in Feminist Settings

1. Literally, "peace in the home."
2. They have been taking place every summer since 1980, at different locations around the country, though mostly on the East Coast.
3. Lani Guinier, "Lift Every Voice," 273–311; and "The Task Ahead," 251–272, both in *Lift Every Voice: Turning a Civil Rights Setback into a New Vision of Social Justice* (New York: Simon & Schuster, 1998); and

Guinier, "The Tyranny of the Majority," in *The Tyranny of the Majority: Fundamental Fairness in Representative Democracy* (New York: The Free Press, 1994), 1–20. Iris Marion Young, "Communication and the Other," in *Democracy and Difference: Contesting the Boundaries of the Political*, ed. Seyla Benhabib (Princeton: Princeton University Press, 1996), 120–135; "Polity and Group Difference," *Ethics* 99, no. 2 (January 1989); 535–550; and "The Ideal of Community and the Politics of Difference," *Social Theory and Practice* 12, no. 1 (spring 1986); 1–26.

4. As opposed, for example, to a parliamentary system of multimember districts, where candidates are elected to parliament roughly in proportion to the votes cast. In such a system, the "losing" party will hold fewer seats but will not necessarily be totally shut out of office-holding.

5. The best-known advocate of this position is Robert Dahl, most notably in his classic *Who Governs?* (New Haven: Yale University Press, 1961). See also his *A Preface to Democratic Theory* (Chicago: University of Chicago Press, 1956) and *On Democracy* (New Haven: Yale University Press, 1998).

Conflict and Community: The Common Ground of Judaism and Feminism

1. Genesis 2:18.
2. Rashi commentary ad loc. Genesis 2:18.
3. Genesis 2:18.
4. Genesis 11:6.
5. Iris Marion Young, *Justice and the Politics of Difference* (Princeton: Princeton University Press, 1990), 162.
6. Audre Lorde, "Scratching the Surface: Some Notes on Barriers to Women and Loving," *The Black Scholar* (April 1978), 31.
7. Genesis 2:24.
8. A. S. Byatt, *Babel Tower* (New York: Vintage Books, 1997), 315.
9. Judith Plaskow, *Standing Again at Sinai: Judaism from a Feminist Perspective* (New York: HarperCollins, 1990), 77.
10. Iris Marion Young, *Intersecting Voices: Dilemmas of Gender, Political Philosophy, and Policy* (Princeton: Princeton University Press, 1997), introduction.
11. Ibid.

What Now? After the Exodus, the Wilderness

1. Psalm 114.
2. Deuteronomy 11:9.
3. The Hebrew name for Egypt, *mitzrayim*, means "narrow places."
4. Linda Holtzman, *Struggle, Change, and Celebration in Lesbian Rabbis: The First Generation* (New Brunswick, N.J.: Rutgers University Press, 2001), 45.

5. The committee included Rabbi Rebecca Alpert, Rabbi Jacob Staub, Rabbi Linda Holtzman, Rabbi Sharon Cohen Anisfeld (then a student), Rabbi Dan Kamesar (then a student), and myself (also then a student).

6. Stonewall is the name of a bar at which the gay patrons resisted police attempts to arrest them in June 1969. It is seen as the beginning of the modern gay liberation movement.

7. Most prominently, Rabbi Hershel Matt *z"l*, Rabbi Alexander Schindler *z"l*, and Rabbi Arthur Green.

8. Exodus 16:3.

9. Numbers 11:5–6.

10. Arnold Eisen, *Galut: Modern Jewish Reflection on Homelessness and Homecoming* (Bloomington Ind.: Indiana University Press, 1986), 21.

11. Leviticus 18:25.

12. Exodus 12:32.

13. This reflection is an adaptation of the keynote sermon given at the 12th International Conference of Gay and Lesbian Jews in San Francisco, May 24, 1991. I could not have written this without the wisdom of Rabbis Sharon Cohen Anisfeld, Yoel Kahn, and Margaret Moers Wenig. Rabbi Wenig's reactions to early drafts were insightful and helpful. Sections of this piece were first worked through in an extraordinary seminar taught by Rabbi Nancy Fuchs-Kreimer at the Reconstructionist Rabbinical College in the spring of 1990. I would also like to thank Andrew Goldfarb and David Rosen, Religious Action Center legislative assistants, for their help.

Letting Pharaoh Go: A Biblical Study of Internalized Oppression

1. Numbers 13–15.

2. This and the event described in the following paragraph take place in Numbers 13 and 14.

3. Numbers 13:33.

4. Ibid.

5. According to the *Midrash Rabbah,* the desert wanderers had a traveling well, clothes and shoes that grew on the children's bodies as they grew, hills and valleys that flattened themselves as the Children of Israel traveled, and bowels that needed no emptying for the entire forty years. The Rabbis used their imagination to create the benign reality in which the Children of Israel lived, thus emphasizing the irrationality of their fears and complaints. So radical was the Rabbis' sense of possibility that one midrash claims that had the Children of Israel not sent spies to the land, they would have been granted physical immortality. Fittingly, *Parshat Shlach* includes the story of the man who gathers wood on Shabbat. Like the spies, the wood gatherer has no sense of hope. Shabbat is a trust game that we play

with God. Eternally, God offers us this dare to spend a day each week, living as if the world is perfect, safe, and abundant.

6. Genesis 12:1.

7. The word "Hebrew," *Ivri*, comes from the word *ever*, which means "to cross over, to transform."

8. While the plain meaning of the text is that God commanded Moses to send the spies, the traditional rabbinic understanding of the text explains that the Children of Israel asked to have spies sent.

9. Numbers 14:12.

10. Moses cannot enter the land for the same reason. When, in the Book of Numbers, God tells Moses to speak to the rock, Moses hits the rock as he did forty years before in the Book of Exodus. Like the people of his generation, he is caught in reliving the past.

11. Numbers 14:44.

12. The hostility and divisions between different Jewish communities, such as the secular and religious communities, is an example of internalized oppression, whereby Jews target one another with the hatred, intolerance, and violence that we ourselves have endured in recent history.

13. Numbers 14:39–45.

14. BT *Bava Metzia* 59a.

15. Exodus 2:23–24.

16. It may be interesting to review the stories of Moses drawing water from the rock as metaphors for weeping.

17. Deuteronomy 2:3.

18. The Children of Israel are described by God as a "stiff-necked people" several times in the Torah, in reference to their not following God. It is in line with my thesis that turning away from God is connected to being rigid and set in one's ways. The word "healing" in Hebrew, *refuah*, is connected to the word *refui*, which means "loose" or "lax."

Reflections on Exodus in Light of Palestinian Suffering

1. *Pesikta de Rab Kahana* 11:13.

Walking the Way as Women

1. *Tefillat haderech* is a traditional prayer one says before embarking on a journey, asking for protection from the dangers of the road. Our version was extemporaneous rather than formulaic.

2. I've been giving a little bit of editorial assistance to an ambitious multiyear project to create a new High Holy Day prayerbook for the Conservative movement: I found this beautiful insight in a marginal note to the Yom Kippur *ma'ariv amidah*.

3. Deuteronomy 10:17–19.

Glossary

Adonai A commonly used Hebrew name for God, often translated as "Lord." "Adonai" is a pronounceable substitute for the tetragrammatron, the four-letter Name of God, written YHVH.

afikomen Lit. "dessert" (Greek). Half of the middle matzah at the seder, which is set aside to be eaten at the conclusion of the meal. It is customary for young children to hide the *afikomen* in the hope that the leader of the seder will reward them with a gift if they return it.

agunah Lit. "a chained woman" (Hebrew). A woman whose marriage has ended and who has not been given a *get* (divorce) from her husband. Traditionally, only a man can initiate a Jewish divorce. Plural: *agunot*.

aliyah Lit. "ascent" (Hebrew). 1. The act of moving to Israel. 2. The honor of being called up to the Torah to recite a blessing during a prayer service. 3. One of the seven sections into which each *parsha* of the Torah is divided.

amidah Lit. "standing" (Hebrew). A prayer consisting of a series of fixed blessings that is included, with some variation, in all major prayer services and forms the backbone of the traditional liturgy.

Arov Locusts; the fourth plague with which God struck Egypt (Exodus 8:16–28).

Ashkenaz The Hebrew word for Germany; term used to refer to Jews whose families come from France, Germany, and Eastern Europe. Plural: Ashkenazim.

avodah zarah Lit. "strange worship" (Hebrew). The worship of idols and other gods, prohibited by the Torah.

Barad Hail; the seventh plague with which God struck Egypt (Exodus 9:13–35).

bat Daughter of (Hebrew).

bat mitzvah Lit. "daughter of the commandment" (Hebrew). 1. A girl who has reached the age of twelve or thirteen and is consequently considered

283

an adult according to Jewish law and obligated to observe all the commandments. 2. The ceremony marking this milestone.

bimah Lit. "pulpit" (Hebrew). The raised platform in a synagogue from which the rabbi or leader conducts the prayer service.

borchu Lit. "blessed be" (Hebrew). The first word of the liturgical call to prayer recited during the morning and evening services, and when a person is called up to the Torah.

bracha Blessing (Hebrew). Plural: *brachot.*

bubbe Grandmother (Yiddish).

Chad Gadya A well-known and entertaining Passover song, which is also interpreted as an allegory representing Israel's trials throughout history.

challah An eggy bread, usually braided, that is eaten on the Sabbath and holidays.

chametz Lit. "leaven" (Hebrew). A grain product that has risen for eighteen minutes or more and is consequently prohibited on Passover.

charoset A ritual food, often made of some combination of apples, dates, nuts, wine, and spices placed on the seder plate and eaten on Passover as a symbol of the mortar that the Israelites used to make bricks in Egypt.

Chasid An adherent of Chassidism, a movement of Orthodox Judaism initiated in White Russia by the Baal Shem Tov (1698–1760).

chazaka Strong (Hebrew). Term used in the Bible (Deuteronomy 26:8) to describe the strong hand with which God redeemed the Israelites from Egypt.

conversos Lit. "converts" (Spanish). Jews who converted to Christianity to save their lives or livelihoods during the Spanish Inquisition, beginning in the fifteenth century.

Dam Blood; the first plague with which God struck Egypt (Exodus 8:14–25).

Dayeinu Lit. "it is enough for us" (Hebrew). Title of a Passover song chronicling God's beneficent actions on behalf of the Israelites, beginning with the Exodus from Egypt and culminating in the still-awaited-for rebuilding of the Temple in Jerusalem.

Dever Cattle disease; the fifth plague with which God struck Egypt (Exodus 9:1–7).

ezer kenegdo Lit. "a help in opposition to him" (Hebrew). Most commonly translated as "helpmeet," this term is used in Genesis 2:18 to refer to Eve, the first woman, who is created by God from Adam's rib.

falasha Lit. "stranger" (Amharic). The black Jews of Ethiopia, who call themselves Beth Israel ("the house of Israel"). By 1993, most had been brought to Israel through a special rescue operation.

gabbai Lit. "warden" (Hebrew). A respected community official. In today's synagogues, the *gabbai* is the lay person who allocates the honors associated with the opening of the ark and the Torah reading.

gazar Decreed (Hebrew).

genizah From *ginzakh,* lit. "treasury" (Persian). The *genizah* functioned as a repository for documents that contained the name of God and that could not be destroyed, as well as for community documents. The famous Cairo Genizah, hidden from at least 750 C.E., was located in the attic attached to the women's section of the synagogue.

gezerah Lit. "decree" (Hebrew). What must be, existing order.

Ha lachma anya Lit. "This is the bread of affliction" (Aramaic). Opening line of a paragraph recited at the beginning of the *maggid* section of the haggadah, in which the seder participants invite those who are hungry or needy to partake of the food on the table.

haggadah Lit. "saga" or "tale." The haggadah is the text of the Passover seder and tells the story of the Exodus from Egypt. It is a collection of passages from the Bible, Mishnah, and rabbinic midrash as well as prayers, hymns, and blessings. It was likely compiled during the time of the Second Temple, but the earliest surviving complete haggadah is from tenth-century Babylonia.

halakhah Lit. "way" or "path" (Hebrew). Jewish law, established by rabbinic authority.

Hallel Lit. "praise" (Hebrew). A group of Psalms praising God, remembering the Exodus, and expressing hope in God's salvation. Hallel is recited on festivals and new moon days, and it is included in the haggadah as the thirteenth step of the seder.

havdallah Lit. "separation" (Hebrew). Ceremony using wine, spices, and candles, performed on Saturday night to mark the conclusion of the Sabbath and the start of the work week.

havurah Lit. "fellowship" or "companionship" (Hebrew). A small prayer group, usually egalitarian, led by individuals rather than a rabbi. Many American Jews formed such groups in the late 1980s because of their discontent with organized Jewish life.

hineini Lit. "Here I am" (Hebrew). This word is Moses' response when God calls out to him at the Burning Bush (Exodus 3:2–3).

horban Lit. "destruction" (Hebrew). Term used to refer to the destruction of the Temple in Jerusalem, first by the Babylonians in 586 B.C.E., and then, after it was rebuilt, by the Romans in 70 C.E.

Hoshech Darkness; the ninth plague with which God struck Egypt (Exodus 10:21–29).

ish Man (Hebrew).

isha Woman (Hebrew).

Kabbalah Lit. "receiving" (Hebrew). Jewish mysticism, which first emerged in southern France and Spain in the thirteenth century.

Kabbalat Ha-Torah Lit. "the receiving of the Torah" (Hebrew). The Jewish people's experience of receiving the Torah at Sinai, as recounted in Exodus 19–20.

Kabbalat Shabbat Lit. "the receiving of the Sabbath" (Hebrew). The liturgy for welcoming the Sabbath, recited on Friday evenings before sunset.

kaddish Lit. "holy" (Aramaic). Prayer extolling the greatness of God, recited by the cantor to mark the end of a section of liturgy, and by mourners following the death of a relative.

karpas Leafy green vegetable, usually parsley or celery, placed on the seder plate and eaten at the seder to symbolize the freshness of spring. In the third of the fourteen parts of the seder, the *karpas* is dipped in salt water and eaten.

kedushah Lit. "holiness" (Hebrew). A section of the *amidah* proclaiming God's holiness and describing the heavenly angels engaged in Divine worship.

kiddush Lit. "sanctification" (Hebrew). Prayer of sanctification recited over a cup of wine on the Sabbath and festivals. The recitation of the *kiddush* is the first of the fourteen steps of the seder.

Kinim Lice; the third plague with which God struck Egypt (Exodus 8:12–15).

Kos Miriam Miriam's Cup (Hebrew). A recent Passover custom of placing an additional goblet filled with water next to Elijah's Cup on the seder table to honor the talmudic story of Miriam's well, which brought water as the Israelites traveled through the desert, just as Moses' sister Miriam nurtured the people throughout their journey.

kugel A dish resembling a pudding or casserole, often eaten on the Sabbath and holidays. Most commonly a sweet noodle pudding, a *kugel* may also be made with matzah, shredded potato, or *farfel*.

kvell To beam with pride or pleasure (Yiddish).

lechem oni Lit. "bread of affliction" (Hebrew). Term used in the Bible (Deuteronomy 16:3) and the haggadah to refer to the matzah eaten on Passover, which is a symbol of freedom, enslavement, and the humility of a person not puffed up with egotism.

L'shanah ha-ba'ah b'yerushalayim Lit. "Next year in Jerusalem" (Hebrew). The closing words of the seder, in which the participants express the hope that next year will bring the messianic redemption and the return of the Jewish people to Jerusalem.

ma'ariv Lit. "bringing of evening" (Hebrew). The evening service, consisting of the *shema* and its blessings, and the *amidah*.

maggid Lit. "one who tells" (Hebrew). The fifth and longest of the fourteen parts of the seder, consisting of the retelling of the Exodus narrative. The *maggid* includes the *mah nishtanah,* the four children, the Ten Plagues, *Dayeinu,* and the second cup of wine.

Makat bechorot Lit. "striking of the firstborns" (Hebrew). The tenth plague with which God struck Egypt, in which God killed all the firstborn Egyptians at midnight on the eve of the Exodus.

manna Lit. "portion" (Hebrew). The food miraculously given to the Israelites on their journey in the wilderness.

mar Lit. "bitter" (Hebrew). Term used in the haggadah to describe the embittered lives of the Israelite slaves under Egyptian domination.

maror Bitter herbs (Hebrew). The bitter horseradish eaten during the seder to remind Jews of the bitter enslavement of the Israelites in Egypt. The eating of the *maror* constitutes the eighth of the fourteen steps of the seder.

matzah Unleavened bread (Hebrew). Flat bread made of flour and water, eaten on Passover in memory of the unleavened bread prepared by the Israelites during their hasty flight from Egypt, when they did not have time to wait for their bread to rise.

mechitzah Lit. "partition" (Hebrew). The wall or curtain separating men and women in Orthodox religious prayer services.

melammed Lit. "teacher" (Hebrew). An elementary school teacher in *cheder,* the one-room schoolhouse in which most Jewish boys were educated in the villages of Eastern Europe in the eighteenth and nineteenth centuries.

mi shebeirach Lit. "the one who blessed" (Hebrew). A prayer for an individual's well-being, read following the blessing after the reading of the Torah in synagogue.

midrash From the Hebrew *darash,* "to inquire." 1. The commentary and expository literature developed in classical Judaism to interpret the Bible differently from its literal meaning. 2. The method of interpreting the Bible this way.

mikveh Lit. "gathering" (Hebrew). A ritual bath formed from a pool of "living water" collected from rain or from a spring, and used for spiritual purification. The *mikveh* is used primarily in conversion rituals and after a woman's menstrual cycles.

mincha Lit. "offering" (Hebrew). The afternoon prayer, consisting of the *amidah*, selected psalms, and short prayers, based on the offerings brought to the Temple before evening.

minhag Custom (Hebrew). A practice that, though not based on biblical or rabbinic law, has become accepted and binding through a long tradition of observance. Customs have historically played an important role in the development of Jewish law.

minyan Lit. "number" (Hebrew). A quorum of ten Jews over the age of thirteen, required for communal prayer services.

mishkan Tabernacle (Hebrew). The portable sanctuary that accompanied the Jews during their forty years of wandering in the desert; it was eventually replaced by the Temple in Jerusalem.

Mishnah Lit. "teaching" (Hebrew). The rabbinic interpretation of biblical law edited and compiled by Judah Ha-Nasi in the early third century C.E. The Mishnah is divided into six sections, or orders, concerned with all aspects of Jewish law.

mitzrayim Lit "narrow place" (Hebrew). Biblical name for Egypt, the kingdom that, under the rule of the Pharaohs, enslaved the Israelites until God led them to freedom.

mitzvah Lit. "commandment." *Mitzvah* refers to the 613 commandments given to Jews in the Torah. Commonly used to denote any Jewish religious obligation or good deed. Plural: *mitzvot*.

Nisan Seventh month of the Jewish civil calendar and first month of the Jewish religious year. Passover begins on the fourteenth day of Nisan.

parsha(t) Lit. "section" (Hebrew). One of the fifty-four sections of the Torah read in synagogue liturgy on an annual cycle.

Pesach Passover (Hebrew). One of the three pilgrimage or harvest festivals enumerated in the Bible; a celebration of the Israelites' liberation from Egyptian bondage. The name of the holiday originates in the last of the Ten Plagues, when God "passed over" the houses of the Israelites and spared their firstborns. The term "Pesach" also refers to the paschal sacrifice commanded by God on the eve of the Exodus.

Pharaoh Name of the kings of Egypt in biblical times; particularly used to refer to the Egyptian ruler during the enslavement and Exodus of the Israelites.

Purim (from the Persian for "casting of lots"). Festival on the fourteenth of Adar celebrating the deliverance of the Jews of Persia, as recounted in the Book of Esther.

Rebbe Rabbi (Yiddish). The title of the spiritual leader of the Chasidim.

Rosh Chodesh Lit. "head of the month" (Hebrew). The new moon festival celebrated at the beginning of each lunar month in the Jewish calendar, when the Hallel psalms and a *musaf* (additional) service are added to the regular liturgy. In recent years, Jewish feminists have reclaimed the holiday and observed it as a day of special significance for Jewish women.

Rosh Hashanah Lit. "head of the year" (Hebrew). The Jewish New Year, Rosh Hashanah occurs on the first and second days of the month of Tishrei, the seventh month of the Jewish year. One of the holiest days of the Jewish year, Rosh Hashanah is referred to in the Bible as *Yom Ha-Zikkaron* (the day of remembrance) or *Yom Teruah* (the day of the sounding of the shofar).

seder Lit. "order" (Hebrew). The festive ritual meal eaten in the home on the first night of Passover (on the first two nights in the diaspora). The seder is divided into fourteen steps and includes the retelling of the story of the Exodus from a haggadah text.

Sephardi Lit. "Spaniards" (Hebrew). Term used to designate Jews of Spanish and Portuguese descent whose ancestors spread throughout Africa, the Ottoman Empire, part of South America, Italy, and Holland following the expulsion of 1492. Plural: Sephardim.

Shabbat Sabbath (Hebrew). The Jewish Sabbath, lasting from sundown Friday night to sundown Saturday night. According to the Bible (Genesis 2:1–4), God rested from creation on the seventh day, so Jews are commanded to rest on this day.

shalom Peace (Hebrew). Also, a term of greeting and farewell.

shalom bayit Lit. "peace of the house" (Hebrew). Domestic tranquility; peace between husband and wife, held to be a very important ideal in Judaism.

Shavuot Lit. "weeks" (Hebrew). One of the three pilgrimage or harvest festivals enumerated in the Bible, celebrating the revelation of the Torah at Sinai. The holiday falls on the sixth (and, in the diaspora, seventh) of Sivan (May/June), exactly seven weeks after the second day of Passover.

Shechin Boils; the sixth plague with which God struck Egypt (Exodus 9:8–12).

shehecheyanu Lit. "who has sustained us" (Hebrew). Blessing recited for any special, long-awaited occasion, such as the celebration of a holiday or bar mitzvah ceremony. The blessing is included in the kiddush recited at the seder.

shefoch chamatcha Lit. "pour out your wrath" (Hebrew). Passage in the haggadah in which Jews ask God to pour out anger on those nations who do not worship God. This section, which consists of three verses from Psalms (79:6–7, 69:25) and one from Lamentations (3:66), is recited as the door is opened for Elijah.

Shekhinah Lit. "indwelling" (Hebrew). The Divine presence; in Kabbalah, the *Shekhinah* was associated with the feminine aspect of God.

shemonah esrai Lit. "eighteen blessings" (Hebrew). The central prayer of Jewish worship, originally consisting of a series of eighteen blessings. Also known as the *amidah*.

sheol Place where the dead go according to the Bible and some ancient Israeli sources. Discussions of sheol make no mention of reward and punishment.

shira Lit. "song" or "poem" (Hebrew). The feminine form of the Hebrew word for "song" or "poem." Used in the Bible to refer to a long poem of praise extolling God.

Shirat Hayam Lit. "song of the sea" (Hebrew). Long poem praising God, sung by Moses and the Israelites following the parting of the Reed Sea (Exodus 15). God is celebrated as a terrifying warrior-king who hurled the Egyptians and their chariots into the sea.

shmatte A rag or sullied garment; often derogatory (Yiddish).

shtetl A small Eastern European village of Jews; shtetls were the main demographic center of Ashkenazim in the eighteenth and nineteenth centuries (Yiddish).

Simchat Torah Lit. "rejoicing of the Torah" (Hebrew). A festival celebrating the conclusion of the annual reading cycle of the Torah, celebrated during the month of Tishrei (September/October).

sukkah Lit. "tabernacle" (Hebrew). A temporary, makeshift booth with a roof of branches or vegetation, in which Jews traditionally live during the holiday of Sukkot.

Sukkot Lit. "tabernacles" (Hebrew). One of three pilgrimage or harvest festivals commemorating the booths in which the Israelites lived in the wilderness following the Exodus from Egypt. Sukkot begins on the fifteenth of Tishrei (September/October) and lasts seven days (eight days in the diaspora).

tefillah Prayer (Hebrew).

tefillat haderech Lit. "prayer of the way" (Hebrew). Prayer recited before going on a long journey, which includes the request that God will lead the traveler in peace and shield him or her from all harm.

tikkun olam Lit. "fixing the world" (Hebrew). The Jewish obligation to repair the world through acts of social justice.

tishpishti Cake made with almonds and honey.

tof Drum or tambourine (Hebrew).

tzafun Lit. "hidden" (Hebrew). The eleventh step of the seder, consisting of the eating of the *afikomen*. After this step, no more food may be eaten at the seder.

yeshiva Lit. "sitting" (Hebrew). A Jewish rabbinic academy of higher learning, in which learning is undertaken for its own sake as a religious duty.

yetzer harah and *yetzer hatov* The evil and good instincts (Hebrew). According to Jewish tradition, people have free will to choose between good and evil.

yetziat mitzrayim Lit. "the Exodus from Egypt" (Hebrew), commemorated and celebrated on Passover.

Yom Kippur The Day of Atonement, the most holy day of the Jewish year.

zayde Grandfather (Yiddish).

zefardeya Frog (Hebrew); the second plague with which God struck Egypt (Exodus 7:26–8:11).

ziman cheruteinu Lit. "time of our freedom." One of the many names for Passover, emphasizing the liberation of the Israelites from Egyptian bondage.

Zohar Lit. "splendor" (Hebrew). Chief literary work of the kabbalists, written as an Aramaic midrash on the Bible. The *Zohar* is traditionally attributed to the followers of Simon Bar Yochai in the second century, though modern scholars accept that most of the book was written by Moses de Leon, a twelfth-century Spanish rabbi.

Bibliography

Sources on Passover and Holding a Seder

Bokser, Baruch. *Origins of the Seder*. Berkeley: University of California Press, 1984.

Dishon, David, and Noam Zion. *Leader's Guide to the Family Participation Haggadah: A Different Night*. Jerusalem: Shalom Hartman Institute, 1997.

Elias, Rabbi Joseph. *The Artscroll Haggadah*. Brooklyn, N.Y.: Artscroll Mesorah Publications, Ltd., 1999.

Fredman, Ruth Gruber. *The Passover Seder: Afikomen in Exile*. Philadelphia: University of Pennsylvania Press, 1981.

Steingroot, Ira. *Keeping Passover: Everything You Need to Know to Bring the Ancient Tradition to Life and Create Your Own Passover Celebration*. San Francisco: HarperSanFrancisco, 1995.

Wolfson, Ron. *Passover, 2nd Edition: The Family Guide to Spiritual Celebration*. Art of Jewish Living series. Woodstock, Vt.: Jewish Lights Publishing, 2003.

———. *Passover Seder Workbook*. Woodstock, Vt.: Jewish Lights Publishing, 1988.

———. *Passover Blessings*. Audiocassette. Woodstock, Vt.: Jewish Lights Publishing, 1988.

Yerushalmi, Yosef Hayim. *Haggadah and History*. Philadelphia: Jewish Publication Society, 1976.

Jewish Feminist Literature and Resources for Passover

Adelman, Penina V. *Miriam's Well: Rituals for Jewish Women Around the Year*. New York: Biblio Press, 1990.

Adler, Rachel. *Engendering Judaism: An Inclusive Theology and Ethics*. Boston: Beacon Press, 1999.

Agosin, Marjorie, and Roberta Gordenstein. *Miriam's Daughters: Jewish Latin American Women Poets*. Santa Fe: Sherman Asher Publishing, 2001.

Alpert, Rebecca. *Like Bread on the Seder Plate*. New York: Columbia University Press, 1998.

Ashton, Dianne, and Ellen M. Umansky, eds. *Four Centuries of Jewish Women's Spirituality: A Sourcebook*. Boston: Beacon Press, 1992.

Baskin, Judith, ed. *Jewish Women in Historical Perspective*. Detroit: Wayne State University Press, 1992.

Beck, Evelyn Torton, ed. *Nice Jewish Girls: A Lesbian Anthology*. Revised edition. Boston: Beacon Press, 1999.

Broner, E. M. *The Telling: A Group of Extraordinary Jewish Women Journey to Spirituality Through Community and Ceremony*. San Francisco: HarperSanFrancisco, 1993.

Cantor, Aviva. *Jewish Women/Jewish Men: The Legacy of Patriarchy in Jewish Life*. San Francisco: HarperSanFrancisco, 1995.

Chesler, Phyllis, and Rivka Haut. *Women of the Wall: Claiming Sacred Ground at Judaism's Holy Site*. Woodstock, Vt.: Jewish Lights Publishing, 2003.

Cohen, Debra Nussbaum. *Celebrating Your New Jewish Daughter: Creating Jewish Ways to Welcome Baby Girls into the Covenant*. Woodstock, Vt.: Jewish Lights Publishing, 2001.

Diament, Carol, Ph.D., ed. *Moonbeams: A Hadassah Rosh Hodesh Guide*. Woodstock, Vt.: Jewish Lights Publishing, 2000.

Falk, Marcia. *The Book of Blessings: New Jewish Prayers for Daily Life, the Sabbath, and the New Moon Festival*. Boston: Beacon Press, 1999.

Falk, Marcia. *The Song of Songs: A New Translation and Interpretation*. San Francisco: HarperSanFrancisco, 1993.

Frankel, Ellen. *The Five Books of Miriam: A Woman's Commentary on the Torah*. San Francisco: HarperSanFrancisco, 1998.

Goldstein, Elyse. *Revisions: Seeing Torah through a Feminist Lens*. Woodstock, Vt.: Jewish Lights Publishing, 2001.

Goldstein, Elyse. *The Women's Torah Commentary: New Insights from Women Rabbis on the 54 Weekly Torah Portions*. Woodstock, Vt.: Jewish Lights Publishing, 2000.

Gottlieb, Lynn. *She Who Dwells Within: A Feminist Vision of a Renewed Judaism*. San Francisco: HarperSanFrancisco, 1995.

Greenberg, Blu. *On Women and Judaism: A View from Tradition*. Philadelphia: Jewish Publication Society, 1981.

Harlow, Jules. *Pray Tell: A Hadassah Guide to Jewish Prayer*. Woodstock, Vt.: Jewish Lights Publishing, 2003.

Hendler, Lee Meyerhoff. *The Year Mom Got Religion: One Woman's Midlife Journey into Judaism.* Woodstock, Vt.: Jewish Lights Publishing, 1999.

Heschel, Susannah. *On Being a Jewish Feminist.* New York: Schocken, 1983.

Hyman, Paula. *Jewish Women in America: An Historical Perspective.* New York: Routledge, 1997.

Kaye/Kantrowitz, Melanie, and Irena Klepfisz, eds. *The Tribe of Dina: A Jewish Women's Anthology.* Boston: Beacon Press, 1989.

Ochs, Vanessa L. *Words on Fire: One Woman's Journey into the Sacred.* New York: Harcourt Brace Jovanovich, 1990.

Orenstein, Debra. *Lifecycles Volume 1: Jewish Women on Life Passages and Personal Milestones.* Woodstock, Vt.: Jewish Lights Publishing, 1994.

Orenstein, Debra, and Jane Rachel Litman. *Lifecycles Volume 2: Jewish Women on Biblical Themes in Contemporary Life.* Woodstock, Vt.: Jewish Lights Publishing, 1997.

Ostriker, Alicia Suskin. *The Nakedness of the Fathers: Biblical Visions and Revisions.* New Brunswick, N.J.: Rutgers University Press, 1997.

Plaskow, Judith. *Standing Again at Sinai: Judaism from a Feminist Perspective.* San Francisco: Harper & Row, 1990.

Pogrebin, Letty Cottin. *Deborah, Golda, and Me: Being Female and Jewish in America.* New York: Crown Publishing Group, 1991.

Ruttenberg, Danya, ed. *Yentl's Revenge: The Next Wave of Jewish Feminism.* Seattle: Seal Press Feminist Publishing, 2001.

Spiegel, Marcia Cohn, and Deborah Lipton Kremsdorf, eds. *Women Speak to God: The Poems and Prayers of Jewish Women.* San Diego: Woman's Institute for Continuing Jewish Education, 1987.

Weissler, Chava. *Voices of the Matriarchs: Listening to the Prayers of Early Modern Jewish Women.* Boston: Beacon Press, 1998.

Zornberg, Avivah Gottlieb. *The Particulars of Rapture: Reflections on Exodus.* New York: Doubleday, 2001.

Index

297

Notes

Notes

Notes

Notes

Notes

About JEWISH LIGHTS Publishing

People of all faiths and backgrounds yearn for books that attract, engage, educate, and spiritually inspire.

Our principal goal is to stimulate thought and help all people learn about who the Jewish People are, where they come from, and what the future can be made to hold. While people of our diverse Jewish heritage are the primary audience, our books speak to people in the Christian world as well and will broaden their understanding of Judaism and the roots of their own faith.

We bring to you authors who are at the forefront of spiritual thought and experience. While each has something different to say, they all say it in a voice that you can hear.

Our books are designed to welcome you and then to engage, stimulate, and inspire. We judge our success not only by whether or not our books are beautiful and commercially successful, but by whether or not they make a difference in your life.

We at Jewish Lights take great care to produce beautiful books that present meaningful spiritual content in a form that reflects the art of making high quality books. Therefore, we want to acknowledge those who contributed to the production of this book.

Stuart M. Matlins, Publisher

PRODUCTION
Sara Dismukes, Tim Holtz,
Martha McKinney & Bridgett Taylor

EDITORIAL
Rebecca Castellano, Amanda Dupuis, Polly Short Mahoney,
Lauren Seidman & Emily Wichland

JACKET DESIGN
Bridgett Taylor

TYPESETTING
Chelsea Cloeter, Tucson, Arizona

JACKET / TEXT PRINTING & BINDING
Lake Book, Melrose Park, Illinois

Spirituality

The Dance of the Dolphin
Finding Prayer, Perspective and Meaning in the Stories of Our Lives
by *Karyn D. Kedar*

Helps you decode the three "languages" we all must learn—prayer, perspective, meaning—to weave the seemingly ordinary and extraordinary together.
6 x 9, 176 pp, HC, ISBN 1-58023-154-3 **$19.95**

Does the Soul Survive?
A Jewish Journey to Belief in Afterlife, Past Lives & Living with Purpose
by *Rabbi Elie Kaplan Spitz;* Foreword by *Brian L. Weiss, M.D.*

Spitz relates his own experiences and those shared with him by people he has worked with as a rabbi, and shows us that belief in afterlife and past lives, so often approached with reluctance, is in fact true to Jewish tradition.
6 x 9, 288 pp, Quality PB, ISBN 1-58023-165-9 **$16.95**; HC, ISBN 1-58023-094-6 **$21.95**

The Gift of Kabbalah
Discovering the Secrets of Heaven, Renewing Your Life on Earth
by *Tamar Frankiel, Ph.D.*

Makes accessible the mysteries of Kabbalah. Traces Kabbalah's evolution in Judaism and shows us its most important gift: a way of revealing the connection between our "everyday" life and the spiritual oneness of the universe. 6 x 9, 256 pp, HC, ISBN 1-58023-108-X **$21.95**

God Whispers: *Stories of the Soul, Lessons of the Heart*
by Karyn D. Kedar 6 x 9, 176 pp, Quality PB, ISBN 1-58023-088-1 **$15.95**

Bringing the Psalms to Life: *How to Understand and Use the Book of Psalms*
by Rabbi Daniel F. Polish
6 x 9, 208 pp, Quality PB, ISBN 1-58023-157-8 **$16.95**; HC, ISBN 1-58023-077-6 **$21.95**

The Empty Chair: *Finding Hope and Joy—*
Timeless Wisdom from a Hasidic Master, Rebbe Nachman of Breslov **AWARD WINNER!**
4 x 6, 128 pp, Deluxe PB, 2-color text, ISBN 1-879045-67-2 **$9.95**

The Gentle Weapon: *Prayers for Everyday and Not-So-Everyday Moments*
Adapted from the Wisdom of Rebbe Nachman of Breslov
4 x 6, 144 pp, Deluxe PB, 2-color text, ISBN 1-58023-022-9 **$9.95**

Or phone, fax, mail or e-mail to: **JEWISH LIGHTS** Publishing
Sunset Farm Offices, Route 4 • P.O. Box 237 • Woodstock, Vermont 05091
Tel: (802) 457-4000 • Fax: (802) 457-4004 • www.jewishlights.com
Credit card orders: (800) 962-4544 (8:30AM–5:30PM ET Monday–Friday)
Generous discounts on quantity orders. SATISFACTION GUARANTEED. Prices subject to change.

Spirituality—The Kushner Series
Books by Lawrence Kushner

The Way Into Jewish Mystical Tradition
Explains the principles of Jewish mystical thinking, their religious and spiritual significance, and how they relate to our lives. A book that allows us to experience and understand the Jewish mystical approach to our place in the world.
6 x 9, 224 pp, HC, ISBN 1-58023-029-6 **$21.95**

Jewish Spirituality: *A Brief Introduction for Christians*
Addresses Christian's questions, revealing the essence of Judaism in a way that people whose own tradition traces its roots to Judaism can understand and appreciate.
5½ x 8½, 112 pp, Quality PB, ISBN 1-58023-150-0 **$12.95**

Eyes Remade for Wonder: *The Way of Jewish Mysticism and Sacred Living*
A Lawrence Kushner Reader Intro. by *Thomas Moore*
Whether you are new to Kushner or a devoted fan, you'll find inspiration here. With samplings from each of Kushner's works, and a generous amount of new material, this book is to be read and reread, each time discovering deeper layers of meaning in our lives.
6 x 9, 240 pp, Quality PB, ISBN 1-58023-042-3 **$18.95**; HC, ISBN 1-58023-014-8 **$23.95**

Invisible Lines of Connection: *Sacred Stories of the Ordinary* AWARD WINNER!
5½ x 8½, 160 pp, Quality PB, ISBN 1-879045-98-2 **$15.95**

Honey from the Rock: *An Introduction to Jewish Mysticism* SPECIAL ANNIVERSARY EDITION
6 x 9, 176 pp, Quality PB, ISBN 1-58023-073-3 **$15.95**

The Book of Letters: *A Mystical Hebrew Alphabet* AWARD WINNER!
Popular HC Edition, 6 x 9, 80 pp, 2-color text, ISBN 1-879045-00-1 **$24.95**; *Deluxe Gift Edition*, 9 x 12, 80 pp, HC, 4-color text, ornamentation, slipcase, ISBN 1-879045-01-X **$79.95**; *Collector's Limited Edition*, 9 x 12, 80 pp, HC, gold-embossed pages, hand-assembled slipcase. With silkscreened print. Limited to 500 signed and numbered copies, ISBN 1-879045-04-4 **$349.00**

The Book of Words: *Talking Spiritual Life, Living Spiritual Talk* AWARD WINNER!
6 x 9, 160 pp, Quality PB, 2-color text, ISBN 1-58023-020-2 **$16.95**; HC, ISBN 1-879045-35-4 **$21.95**

God Was in This Place & I, i Did Not Know: *Finding Self, Spirituality and Ultimate Meaning*
6 x 9, 192 pp, Quality PB, ISBN 1-879045-33-8 **$16.95**

The River of Light: *Jewish Mystical Awareness* SPECIAL ANNIVERSARY EDITION
6 x 9, 192 pp, Quality PB, ISBN 1-58023-096-2 **$16.95**

Because Nothing Looks Like God
by Lawrence and Karen Kushner; Full-color illus. by Dawn W. Majewski
11 x 8½, 32 pp, HC, Full-color illus., ISBN 1-58023-092-X **$16.95** For ages 4 & up

The Way Into... Series

A major multi-volume series to be completed over the next several years, **The Way Into... provides an accessible and usable "guided tour" of the Jewish faith, its people, its history and beliefs—in total, an introduction to Judaism for adults that will enable them to understand and interact with sacred texts.**

Each volume is written by a major modern scholar and teacher, and is organized around an important concept of Judaism.

The Way Into... will enable all readers to achieve a real sense of Jewish cultural literacy through guided study. Available volumes:

   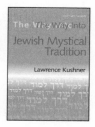

The Way Into Torah
by *Dr. Norman J. Cohen*

What is "Torah"? What are the different approaches to studying Torah? What are the different levels of understanding Torah? For whom is study intended? Explores the origins and development of Torah, why it should be studied and how to do it. An easy-to-use, easy-to-understand introduction to an ancient subject.
6 x 9, 176 pp, HC, ISBN 1-58023-028-8 **$21.95**

The Way Into Jewish Prayer
by *Dr. Lawrence A. Hoffman*

Explores the reasons for and the ways of Jewish prayer. Opens the door to 3,000 years of the Jewish way to God by making available all you need to feel at home in Jewish worship. Provides basic definitions of the terms you need to know as well as thoughtful analysis of the depth that lies beneath Jewish prayer.
6 x 9, 224 pp, HC, ISBN 1-58023-027-X **$21.95**

The Way Into Encountering God in Judaism
by *Dr. Neil Gillman*

Explains how Jews have encountered God throughout history—and today—by exploring the many metaphors for God in Jewish tradition. Explores the Jewish tradition's passionate but also conflicting ways of relating to God as Creator, relational partner, and a force in history and nature.
6 x 9, 240 pp, HC, ISBN 1-58023-025-3 **$21.95**

The Way Into Jewish Mystical Tradition
by *Rabbi Lawrence Kushner*

Explains the principles of Jewish mystical thinking, their religious and spiritual significance, and how they relate to our lives. A book that allows us to experience and understand the Jewish mystical approach to our place in the world.
6 x 9, 224 pp, HC, ISBN 1-58023-029-6 **$21.95**

Jewish Meditation

Aleph-Bet Yoga
Embodying the Hebrew Letters for Physical and Spiritual Well-Being
by *Steven A. Rapp;* Foreword by *Tamar Frankiel* & *Judy Greenfeld;* Preface by *Hart Lazer*
Blends aspects of hatha yoga and the shapes of the Hebrew letters. Connects yoga practice with Jewish spiritual life. Easy-to-follow instructions, b/w photos.
7 x 10, 128 pp, Quality PB, b/w photos, ISBN 1-58023-162-4 **$16.95**

The Rituals & Practices of a Jewish Life
A Handbook for Personal Spiritual Renewal
by *Rabbi Kerry M. Olitzky* and *Rabbi Daniel Judson;* Foreword by *Vanessa L. Ochs;* Illustrated by *Joel Moskowitz*
This easy-to-use handbook explains the why, what, and how of ten specific areas of Jewish ritual and practice: morning and evening blessings, covering the head, blessings throughout the day, daily prayer, tefillin, tallit and *tallit katan,* Torah study, kashrut, *mikvah,* and entering Shabbat. 6 x 9, 272 pp, Quality PB, Illus., ISBN 1-58023-169-1 **$18.95**

Discovering Jewish Meditation: *Instruction & Guidance for Learning an Ancient Spiritual Practice* by Nan Fink Gefen 6 x 9, 208 pp, Quality PB, ISBN 1-58023-067-9 **$16.95**

The Handbook of Jewish Meditation Practices: *A Guide for Enriching the Sabbath and Other Days of Your Life* by Rabbi David A. Cooper
6 x 9, 208 pp, Quality PB, ISBN 1-58023-102-0 **$16.95**

Meditation from the Heart of Judaism: *Today's Teachers Share Their Practices, Techniques, and Faith* Ed. by Avram Davis 6 x 9, 256 pp, Quality PB, ISBN 1-58023-049-0 **$16.95**

The Way of Flame: *A Guide to the Forgotten Mystical Tradition of Jewish Meditation* by Avram Davis 4½ x 8, 176 pp, Quality PB, ISBN 1-58023-060-1 **$15.95**

Minding the Temple of the Soul: *Balancing Body, Mind, and Spirit through Traditional Jewish Prayer, Movement, and Meditation* by Tamar Frankiel and Judy Greenfeld
7 x 10, 184 pp, Quality PB, Illus., ISBN 1-879045-64-8 **$16.95**

Entering the Temple of Dreams: *Jewish Prayers, Movements, and Meditations for the End of the Day* by Tamar Frankiel and Judy Greenfeld
7 x 10, 192 pp, Illus., Quality PB, ISBN 1-58023-079-2 **$16.95**

Ecology

Torah of the Earth: *Exploring 4,000 Years of Ecology in Jewish Thought*
In 2 Volumes Ed. by *Rabbi Arthur Waskow*
An invaluable key to understanding the intersection of ecology and Judaism. Leading scholars provide a guided tour of Jewish ecological thought.
Vol. 1: *Biblical Israel & Rabbinic Judaism,* 6 x 9, 272 pp, Quality PB, ISBN 1-58023-086-5 **$19.95**
Vol. 2: *Zionism & Eco-Judaism,* 6 x 9, 336 pp, Quality PB, ISBN 1-58023-087-3 **$19.95**

Ecology & the Jewish Spirit: *Where Nature & the Sacred Meet* Ed. and with Intros.
by Ellen Bernstein 6 x 9, 288 pp, Quality PB, ISBN 1-58023-082-2 **$16.95**

Theology/Philosophy

Love and Terror in the God Encounter
The Theological Legacy of Rabbi Joseph B. Soloveitchik
by *Dr. David Hartman*

Renowned scholar David Hartman explores the sometimes surprising intersection of Soloveitchik's rootedness in halakhic tradition with his genuine responsiveness to modern Western theology. An engaging look at one of the most important Jewish thinkers of the twentieth century.
6 x 9, 240 pp, HC, ISBN 1-58023-112-8 **$25.00**

These Are the Words: *A Vocabulary of Jewish Spiritual Life*
by *Arthur Green*

What are the most essential ideas, concepts and terms that an educated person needs to know about Judaism? From *Adonai* (My Lord) to *zekhut* (merit), this enlightening and entertaining journey through Judaism teaches us the 149 core Hebrew words that constitute the basic vocabulary of Jewish spiritual life. 6 x 9, 304 pp, Quality PB, ISBN 1-58023-107-1 **$18.95**

Broken Tablets: *Restoring the Ten Commandments and Ourselves*
Ed. by *Rabbi Rachel S. Mikva*; Intro. by *Rabbi Lawrence Kushner* AWARD WINNER!

Twelve outstanding spiritual leaders each share profound and personal thoughts about these biblical commands and why they have such a special hold on us.
6 x 9, 192 pp, Quality PB, ISBN 1-58023-158-6 **$16.95**; HC, ISBN 1-58023-066-0 **$21.95**

A Heart of Many Rooms: *Celebrating the Many Voices within Judaism* AWARD WINNER!
by Dr. David Hartman 6 x 9, 352 pp, Quality PB, ISBN 1-58023-156-X **$19.95**;
HC, ISBN 1-58023-048-2 **$24.95**

A Living Covenant: *The Innovative Spirit in Traditional Judaism* AWARD WINNER!
by Dr. David Hartman 6 x 9, 368 pp, Quality PB, ISBN 1-58023-011-3 **$18.95**

Evolving Halakhah: *A Progressive Approach to Traditional Jewish Law*
by Rabbi Dr. Moshe Zemer 6 x 9, 480 pp, HC, ISBN 1-58023-002-4 **$40.00**

The Death of Death: *Resurrection and Immortality in Jewish Thought* AWARD WINNER!
by Dr. Neil Gillman 6 x 9, 336 pp, Quality PB, ISBN 1-58023-081-4 **$18.95**

The Last Trial: *On the Legends and Lore of the Command to Abraham to Offer Isaac as a Sacrifice* by Shalom Spiegel 6 x 9, 208 pp, Quality PB, ISBN 1-879045-29-X **$17.95**

Tormented Master: *The Life and Spiritual Quest of Rabbi Nahman of Bratslav*
by Dr. Arthur Green 6 x 9, 416 pp, Quality PB, ISBN 1-879045-11-7 **$18.95**

The Earth Is the Lord's: *The Inner World of the Jew in Eastern Europe*
by Abraham Joshua Heschel 5½ x 8, 128 pp, Quality PB, ISBN 1-879045-42-7 **$14.95**

A Passion for Truth: *Despair and Hope in Hasidism* by Abraham Joshua Heschel
5½ x 8, 352 pp, Quality PB, ISBN 1-879045-41-9 **$18.95**

Your Word Is Fire: *The Hasidic Masters on Contemplative Prayer* Ed. by Dr. Arthur Green and Dr. Barry W. Holtz 6 x 9, 160 pp, Quality PB, ISBN 1-879045-25-7 **$15.95**

Life Cycle/Grief/Divorce

Divorce Is a Mitzvah: *A Practical Guide to Finding Wholeness and Holiness When Your Marriage Dies*
by *Rabbi Perry Netter;*
Afterword—"Afterwards: New Jewish Divorce Rituals"—by *Rabbi Laura Geller*
What does Judaism tell you about divorce? This first-of-its-kind handbook provides practical wisdom from biblical and rabbinic teachings and modern psychological research, as well as information and strength from a Jewish perspective for those experiencing the challenging life-transition of divorce. 6 x 9, 224 pp, Quality PB, ISBN 1-58023-172-1 **$16.95**

Against the Dying of the Light
A Parent's Story of Love, Loss and Hope
by *Leonard Fein*
The sudden death of a child. A personal tragedy beyond description. Rage and despair deeper than sorrow. What can come from it? Raw wisdom and defiant hope. In this unusual exploration of heartbreak and healing, Fein chronicles the sudden death of his 30-year-old daughter and reveals what the progression of grief can teach each one of us.
5½ x 8½, 176 pp, HC, ISBN 1-58023-110-1 **$19.95**

Mourning & Mitzvah, 2nd Ed.: *A Guided Journal for Walking the Mourner's Path through Grief to Healing* with *Over 60 Guided Exercises*
by *Anne Brener, L.C.S.W.*
For those who mourn a death, for those who would help them, for those who face a loss of any kind, Brener teaches us the power and strength available to us in the fully experienced mourning process. Revised and expanded. 7½ x 9, 304 pp, Quality PB, ISBN 1-58023-113-6 **$19.95**

Grief in Our Seasons: *A Mourner's Kaddish Companion*
by *Rabbi Kerry M. Olitzky*
A wise and inspiring selection of sacred Jewish writings and a simple, powerful ancient ritual for mourners to read each day, to help hold the memory of their loved ones in their hearts. Offers a comforting, step-by-step daily link to saying Kaddish.
4½ x 6½, 448 pp, Quality PB, ISBN 1-879045-55-9 **$15.95**

Tears of Sorrow, Seeds of Hope
A Jewish Spiritual Companion for Infertility and Pregnancy Loss
by Rabbi Nina Beth Cardin   6 x 9, 192 pp, HC, ISBN 1-58023-017-2 **$19.95**

A Time to Mourn, A Time to Comfort
A Guide to Jewish Bereavement and Comfort
by Dr. Ron Wolfson 7 x 9, 336 pp, Quality PB, ISBN 1-879045-96-6 **$18.95**

When a Grandparent Dies
A Kid's Own Remembering Workbook for Dealing with Shiva and the Year Beyond
by Nechama Liss-Levinson, Ph.D.
8 x 10, 48 pp, HC, Illus., 2-color text, ISBN 1-879045-44-3 **$15.95**   **For ages 7–13**

Healing/Wellness/Recovery

Jewish Paths toward Healing and Wholeness
A Personal Guide to Dealing with Suffering
by *Rabbi Kerry M. Olitzky;* Foreword by *Debbie Friedman*

Why me? Why do we suffer? How can we heal? Grounded in personal experience with illness and Jewish spiritual traditions, this book provides healing rituals, psalms and prayers that help readers initiate a dialogue with God, to guide them along the complicated path of healing and wholeness. 6 x 9, 192 pp, Quality PB, ISBN 1-58023-068-7 **$15.95**

Healing of Soul, Healing of Body
Spiritual Leaders Unfold the Strength & Solace in Psalms
Ed. by *Rabbi Simkha Y. Weintraub, CSW,* for The National Center for Jewish Healing

For those who are facing illness and those who care for them. Inspiring commentaries on ten psalms for healing by eminent spiritual leaders reflecting all Jewish movements make the power of the psalms accessible to all.
6 x 9, 128 pp, Quality PB, Illus., 2-color text, ISBN 1-879045-31-1 **$14.95**

Jewish Pastoral Care
A Practical Handbook from Traditional and Contemporary Sources
Ed. by *Rabbi Dayle A. Friedman*

Gives today's Jewish pastoral counselors practical guidelines based in the Jewish tradition.
6 x 9, 464 pp, HC, ISBN 1-58023-078-4 **$35.00**

Twelve Jewish Steps to Recovery: *A Personal Guide to Turning from Alcoholism & Other Addictions—Drugs, Food, Gambling, Sex . . .* by Rabbi Kerry M. Olitzky & Stuart A. Copans, M.D. Preface by Abraham J. Twerski, M.D.; "Getting Help" by JACS Foundation 6 x 9, 144 pp, Quality PB, ISBN 1-879045-09-5 **$14.95**

One Hundred Blessings Every Day: *Daily Twelve Step Recovery Affirmations, Exercises for Personal Growth & Renewal Reflecting Seasons of the Jewish Year* by Rabbi Kerry M. Olitzky 4½ x 6½, 432 pp, Quality PB, ISBN 1-879045-30-3 **$14.95**

Recovery from Codependence: *A Jewish Twelve Steps Guide to Healing Your Soul* by Rabbi Kerry M. Olitzky 6 x 9, 160 pp, Quality PB, ISBN 1-879045-32-X **$13.95**

Renewed Each Day: *Daily Twelve Step Recovery Meditations Based on the Bible* by Rabbi Kerry M. Olitzky & Aaron Z. Vol. I: *Genesis & Exodus;* Vol. II: *Leviticus, Numbers and Deuteronomy*
Vol. I: 6 x 9, 224 pp, Quality PB, ISBN 1-879045-12-5 **$14.95**
Vol. II: 6 x 9, 280 pp, Quality PB, ISBN 1-879045-13-3 **$14.95**

Life Cycle & Holidays

The Jewish Family Fun Book: *Holiday Projects, Everyday Activities, and Travel Ideas with Jewish Themes*
by *Danielle Dardashti* & *Roni Sarig*; Illustrated by *Avi Katz*

With almost 100 easy-to-do activities to re-invigorate age-old Jewish customs and make them fun for the whole family, this complete sourcebook details activities for fun at home and away from home, including meaningful everyday and holiday crafts, recipes, travel guides, enriching entertainment and much, much more. Illustrated.
6 x 9, 288 pp, Quality PB, Illus., ISBN 1-58023-171-3 **$18.95**

The Book of Jewish Sacred Practices
CLAL's Guide to Everyday & Holiday Rituals & Blessings
Ed. by *Rabbi Irwin Kula* & *Vanessa L. Ochs, Ph.D.*

A meditation, blessing, profound Jewish teaching, and ritual for more than one hundred everyday events and holidays. 6 x 9, 368 pp, Quality PB, ISBN 1-58023-152-7 **$18.95**

Celebrating Your New Jewish Daughter: *Creating Jewish Ways to Welcome Baby Girls into the Covenant—New and Traditional Ceremonies*
by Debra Nussbaum Cohen; Foreword by Rabbi Sandy Eisenberg Sasso
6 x 9, 272 pp, Quality PB, ISBN 1-58023-090-3 **$18.95**

The New Jewish Baby Book AWARD WINNER!
Names, Ceremonies & Customs—A Guide for Today's Families
by Anita Diamant 6 x 9, 336 pp, Quality PB, ISBN 1-879045-28-1 **$18.95**

Parenting As a Spiritual Journey
Deepening Ordinary & Extraordinary Events into Sacred Occasions
by Rabbi Nancy Fuchs-Kreimer 6 x 9, 224 pp, Quality PB, ISBN 1-58023-016-4 **$16.95**

Putting God on the Guest List, 2nd Ed. AWARD WINNER!
How to Reclaim the Spiritual Meaning of Your Child's Bar or Bat Mitzvah
by Rabbi Jeffrey K. Salkin 6 x 9, 224 pp, Quality PB, ISBN 1-879045-59-1 **$16.95**

The Bar/Bat Mitzvah Memory Book: *An Album for Treasuring the Spiritual Celebration* by Rabbi Jeffrey K. Salkin and Nina Salkin
8 x 10, 48 pp, Deluxe HC, 2-color text, ribbon marker, ISBN 1-58023-111-X **$19.95**

For Kids—Putting God on Your Guest List
How to Claim the Spiritual Meaning of Your Bar or Bat Mitzvah
by Rabbi Jeffrey K. Salkin 6 x 9, 144 pp, Quality PB, ISBN 1-58023-015-6 **$14.95**

Bar/Bat Mitzvah Basics, 2nd Ed.: *A Practical Family Guide to Coming of Age Together*
Ed. by Cantor Helen Leneman 6 x 9, 240 pp, Quality PB, ISBN 1-58023-151-9 **$18.95**

Hanukkah, 2nd Ed.: *The Family Guide to Spiritual Celebration*—The Art of Jewish Living
by Dr. Ron Wolfson 7 x 9, 240 pp, Quality PB, Illus., ISBN 1-58023-122-5 **$18.95**

Shabbat, 2nd Ed.: *Preparing for and Celebrating the Sabbath*—The Art of Jewish Living
by Dr. Ron Wolfson 7 x 9, 320 pp, Quality PB, Illus., ISBN 1-58023-164-0 **$19.95**

Passover, 2nd Ed.: *The Family Guide to Spiritual Celebration*—The Art of Jewish Living
by Dr. Ron Wolfson 7 x 9, 352 pp, Quality PB, ISBN 1-58023-174-8 **$19.95**

Children's Spirituality

Cain & Abel AWARD WINNER!
Finding the Fruits of Peace
by *Sandy Eisenberg Sasso*
Full-color illus. by *Joani Keller Rothenberg*

For ages 5 & up

A sensitive recasting of the ancient tale shows we have the power to deal with anger in positive ways. Provides questions for kids and adults to explore together. "Editor's Choice"—American Library Association's *Booklist*

9 x 12, 32 pp, HC, Full-color illus., ISBN 1-58023-123-3 **$16.95**

For Heaven's Sake AWARD WINNER!
by *Sandy Eisenberg Sasso*; Full-color illus. by *Kathryn Kunz Finney*

For ages 4 & up

Everyone talked about heaven, but no one would say what heaven was or how to find it. So Isaiah decides to find out. 9 x 12, 32 pp, HC, Full-color illus., ISBN 1-58023-054-7 **$16.95**

God Said Amen AWARD WINNER!
by *Sandy Eisenberg Sasso*; Full-color illus. by *Avi Katz*

For ages 4 & up

Inspiring tale of two kingdoms: one overflowing with water but without oil to light its lamps; the other blessed with oil but no water to grow its gardens. The kingdoms' rulers ask God for help but are too stubborn to ask each other. Shows that we need only reach out to each other to find God's answer to our prayers. 9 x 12, 32 pp, HC, Full-color illus., ISBN 1-58023-080-6 **$16.95**

God in Between AWARD WINNER!
by *Sandy Eisenberg Sasso*; Full-color illus. by *Sally Sweetland*

For ages 4 & up

If you wanted to find God, where would you look? This magical, mythical tale teaches that God can be found where we are: within all of us and the relationships between us.
9 x 12, 32 pp, HC, Full-color illus., ISBN 1-879045-86-9 **$16.95**

Noah's Wife: *The Story of Naamah*
by *Sandy Eisenberg Sasso*; Full-color illus. by *Bethanne Andersen* AWARD WINNER!

For ages 4 & up

Opens religious imaginations to new ideas about the story of the Flood. When God tells Noah to bring the animals onto the ark, God also calls on Naamah, Noah's wife, to save each plant on Earth. 9 x 12, 32 pp, HC, Full-color illus., ISBN 1-58023-134-9 **$16.95**

But God Remembered AWARD WINNER!
Stories of Women from Creation to the Promised Land
by *Sandy Eisenberg Sasso*; Full-color illus. by *Bethanne Andersen*

For ages 8 & up

Vibrantly brings to life four stories of courageous and strong women from ancient tradition; all teach important values through their actions and faith.
9 x 12, 32 pp, HC, Full-color illus., ISBN 1-879045-43-5 **$16.95**

Children's Spirituality

In Our Image
God's First Creatures   AWARD WINNER!
by *Nancy Sohn Swartz*
Full-color illus. by *Melanie Hall*

For ages
4 & up

A playful new twist on the Creation story—from the perspective of the animals. Celebrates the interconnectedness of nature and the harmony of all living things. "The vibrantly colored illustrations nearly leap off the page in this delightful interpretation." —*School Library Journal*
9 x 12, 32 pp, HC, Full-color illus., ISBN 1-879045-99-0 **$16.95**

 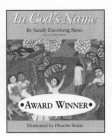 

God's Paintbrush   AWARD WINNER!
by *Sandy Eisenberg Sasso;* Full-color illus. by *Annette Compton*

For ages
4 & up

Invites children of all faiths and backgrounds to encounter God openly in their own lives. Wonderfully interactive; provides questions adult and child can explore together at the end of each episode. 11 x 8½, 32 pp, HC, Full-color illus., ISBN 1-879045-22-2 **$16.95**

Also available: A Teacher's Guide: **A Guide for Jewish & Christian Educators and Parents**
8½ x 11, 32 pp, PB, ISBN 1-879045-57-5 **$8.95**

God's Paintbrush Celebration Kit 9½ x 12, HC, Includes 5 sessions/40 full-color Activity Sheets and Teacher Folder with complete instructions, ISBN 1-58023-050-4 **$21.95**

In God's Name   AWARD WINNER!
by *Sandy Eisenberg Sasso;* Full-color illus. by *Phoebe Stone*

For ages
4 & up

Like an ancient myth in its poetic text and vibrant illustrations, this award-winning modern fable about the search for God's name celebrates the diversity and, at the same time, the unity of all people. 9 x 12, 32 pp, HC, Full-color illus., ISBN 1-879045-26-5 **$16.95**

What Is God's Name? (A Board Book)

For ages
0–4

An abridged board book version of award-winning *In God's Name.*
5 x 5, 24 pp, Board, Full-color illus., ISBN 1-893361-10-1 **$7.95** A SKYLIGHT PATHS Book

The 11th Commandment: *Wisdom from Our Children*
by *The Children of America*   AWARD WINNER!

For
all ages

"If there were an Eleventh Commandment, what would it be?" Children of many religious denominations across America answer this question—in their own drawings and words. "A rare book of spiritual celebration for all people, of all ages, for all time."—*Bookviews*
8 x 10, 48 pp, HC, Full-color illus., ISBN 1-879045-46-X **$16.95**

Children's Spirituality

Because Nothing Looks Like God

by *Lawrence and Karen Kushner*
Full-color illus. by *Dawn W. Majewski*

For ages 4 & up

MULTICULTURAL, NONDENOMINATIONAL, NONSECTARIAN

What is God like? The first collaborative work by husband-and-wife team Lawrence and Karen Kushner introduces children to the possibilities of spiritual life. Real-life examples of happiness and sadness—from goodnight stories, to the hope and fear felt the first time at bat, to the closing moments of life—invite us to explore, together with our children, the questions we all have about God, no matter what our age.

11 x 8½, 32 pp, HC, Full-color illus., ISBN 1-58023-092-X **$16.95**

*Also available: **Teacher's Guide,*** 8½ x 11, 22 pp, PB, ISBN 1-58023-140-3 **$6.95** For ages 5–8

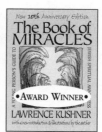

Where Is God?
What Does God Look Like?
How Does God Make Things Happen? (Board Books)

For ages 0–4

by *Lawrence and Karen Kushner*; Full-color illus. by *Dawn W. Majewski*

Gently invites children to become aware of God's presence all around them. Three board books abridged from *Because Nothing Looks Like God* by Lawrence and Karen Kushner.
Each 5 x 5, 24 pp, Board, Full-color illus. **$7.95** SKYLIGHT PATHS Books

Sharing Blessings
Children's Stories for Exploring the Spirit of the Jewish Holidays

For ages 6 & up

by *Rahel Musleah* and *Rabbi Michael Klayman*; Full-color illus.

What is the spiritual message of each of the Jewish holidays? How do we teach it to our children? Through stories about one family's life, *Sharing Blessings* explores ways to get into the *spirit* of thirteen different holidays.
8½ x 11, 64 pp, HC, Full-color illus., ISBN 1-879045-71-0 **$18.95**

The Book of Miracles   AWARD WINNER!
A Young Person's Guide to Jewish Spiritual Awareness

For ages 9 & up

by *Lawrence Kushner*

Introduces kids to a way of everyday spiritual thinking to last a lifetime. Kushner, whose award-winning books have brought spirituality to life for countless adults, now shows young people how to use Judaism as a foundation on which to build their lives.
6 x 9, 96 pp, HC, 2-color illus., ISBN 1-879045-78-8 **$16.95**

Spirituality

My People's Prayer Book: *Traditional Prayers, Modern Commentaries*
Ed. by *Dr. Lawrence A. Hoffman*

Provides a diverse and exciting commentary to the traditional liturgy, helping modern men and women find new wisdom in Jewish prayer, and bring liturgy into their lives. Each book includes Hebrew text, modern translation, and commentaries *from all perspectives* of the Jewish world.

Vol. 1—*The Sh'ma and Its Blessings*, 7 x 10, 168 pp, HC, ISBN 1-879045-79-6 **$23.95**
Vol. 2—*The Amidah*, 7 x 10, 240 pp, HC, ISBN 1-879045-80-X **$23.95**
Vol. 3—*P'sukei D'zimrah* (Morning Psalms), 7 x 10, 240 pp, HC, ISBN 1-879045-81-8 **$24.95**
Vol. 4—*Seder K'riat Hatorah* (The Torah Service), 7 x 10, 264 pp, HC, ISBN 1-879045-82-6 **$23.95**
Vol. 5—*Birkhot Hashachar* (Morning Blessings), 7 x 10, 240 pp, HC, ISBN 1-879045-83-4 **$24.95**
Vol. 6—*Tachanun and Concluding Prayers*, 7 x 10, 240 pp, HC, ISBN 1-879045-84-2 **$24.95**

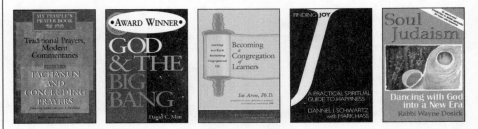

Six Jewish Spiritual Paths: *A Rationalist Looks at Spirituality*
by Rabbi Rifat Sonsino
6 x 9, 208 pp, Quality PB, ISBN 1-58023-167-5 **$16.95**; HC, ISBN 1-58023-095-4 **$21.95**

Becoming a Congregation of Learners
Learning as a Key to Revitalizing Congregational Life by Isa Aron, Ph.D.;
Foreword by Rabbi Lawrence A. Hoffman, Co-Developer, Synagogue 2000
6 x 9, 304 pp, Quality PB, ISBN 1-58023-089-X **$19.95**

Self, Struggle & Change
Family Conflict Stories in Genesis and Their Healing Insights for Our Lives
by Dr. Norman J. Cohen 6 x 9, 224 pp, Quality PB, ISBN 1-879045-66-4 **$16.95**

Voices from Genesis: *Guiding Us through the Stages of Life*
by Dr. Norman J. Cohen 6 x 9, 192 pp, Quality PB, ISBN 1-58023-118-7 **$16.95**

Ancient Secrets: *Using the Stories of the Bible to Improve Our Everyday Lives*
by Rabbi Levi Meier, Ph.D. 5½ x 8½, 288 pp, Quality PB, ISBN 1-58023-064-4 **$16.95**

The Business Bible: *10 New Commandments for Bringing Spirituality & Ethical Values into the Workplace*
by Rabbi Wayne Dosick 5½ x 8½, 208 pp, Quality PB, ISBN 1-58023-101-2 **$14.95**

Being God's Partner: *How to Find the Hidden Link Between Spirituality and Your Work*
by Rabbi Jeffrey K. Salkin; Intro. by Norman Lear AWARD WINNER!
6 x 9, 192 pp, Quality PB, ISBN 1-879045-65-6 **$16.95**; HC, ISBN 1-879045-37-0 **$19.95**

God & the Big Bang
Discovering Harmony Between Science & Spirituality AWARD WINNER!
by Daniel C. Matt 6 x 9, 224 pp, Quality PB, ISBN 1-879045-89-3 **$16.95**

Soul Judaism: *Dancing with God into a New Era*
by Rabbi Wayne Dosick 5½ x 8½, 304 pp, Quality PB, ISBN 1-58023-053-9 **$16.95**

Finding Joy: *A Practical Spiritual Guide to Happiness* AWARD WINNER!
by Rabbi Dannel I. Schwartz with Mark Hass
6 x 9, 192 pp, Quality PB, ISBN 1-58023-009-1 **$14.95**; HC, ISBN 1-879045-53-2 **$19.95**

Spirituality & More

The Jewish Lights Spirituality Handbook
A Guide to Understanding, Exploring & Living a Spiritual Life
Ed. by *Stuart M. Matlins, Editor in Chief, Jewish Lights Publishing*

Rich, creative material from over fifty spiritual leaders on every aspect of Jewish spirituality today: prayer, meditation, mysticism, study, rituals, special days, the everyday, and more.
6 x 9, 456 pp, Quality PB, ISBN 1-58023-093-8 **$18.95**; HC, ISBN 1-58023-100-4 **$24.95**

The Story of the Jews: *A 4,000-Year Adventure—A Graphic History Book*
Written and illustrated by *Stan Mack*

Through witty cartoons and accurate narrative, illustrates the major characters and events that have shaped the Jewish people and culture. For all ages.
6 x 9, 304 pp, Quality PB, Illus., ISBN 1-58023-155-1 **$16.95**

The Jewish Prophet: *Visionary Words from Moses and Miriam to Henrietta Szold and A. J. Heschel*
by *Rabbi Dr. Michael J. Shire*

This beautifully illustrated collection of Jewish prophecy features the lives and teachings of thirty men and women, from biblical times to modern day. Provides an inspiring and informative description of the role each played in their own time, and an explanation of why we should know about them in our time. Illustrated with illuminations from medieval Hebrew manuscripts.
6½ x 8½, 128 pp, HC, 123 full-color illus., ISBN 1-58023-168-3 **$25.00**

The Enneagram and Kabbalah: *Reading Your Soul*
by Rabbi Howard A. Addison 6 x 9, 176 pp, Quality PB, ISBN 1-58023-001-6 **$15.95**

Cast in God's Image: *Discover Your Personality Type Using the Enneagram and Kabbalah*
by Rabbi Howard A. Addison 7 x 9, 176 pp, Quality PB, ISBN 1-58023-124-1 **$16.95**

Mystery Midrash: *An Anthology of Jewish Mystery & Detective Fiction* AWARD WINNER!
Ed. by Lawrence W. Raphael 6 x 9, 304 pp, Quality PB, ISBN 1-58023-055-5 **$16.95**

Criminal Kabbalah: *An Intriguing Anthology of Jewish Mystery & Detective Fiction*
Ed. by Lawrence W. Raphael; Foreword by Laurie R. King
6 x 9, 256 pp, Quality PB, ISBN 1-58023-109-8 **$16.95**

Sacred Intentions: *Daily Inspiration to Strengthen the Spirit, Based on Jewish Wisdom*
by Rabbi Kerry M. Olitzky & Rabbi Lori Forman
4½ x 6½, 448 pp, Quality PB, ISBN 1-58023-061-X **$15.95**

Restful Reflections: *Nighttime Inspiration to Calm the Soul, Based on Jewish Wisdom*
by Rabbi Kerry M. Olitzky & Rabbi Lori Forman
4½ x 6½, 448 pp, Quality PB, ISBN 1-58023-091-1 **$15.95**

Embracing the Covenant: *Converts to Judaism Talk About Why & How* Ed. by Rabbi Allan Berkowitz & Patti Moskovitz 6 x 9, 192 pp, Quality PB, ISBN 1-879045-50-8 **$16.95**

Wandering Stars: *An Anthology of Jewish Fantasy & Science Fiction* Ed. by Jack Dann; Intro. by Isaac Asimov 6 x 9, 272 pp, Quality PB, ISBN 1-58023-005-9 **$16.95**

Israel—A Spiritual Travel Guide: *A Companion for the Modern Jewish Pilgrim* AWARD WINNER!
by Rabbi Lawrence A. Hoffman 4¾ x 10, 256 pp, Quality PB, ISBN 1-879045-56-7 **$18.95**